FINANCING RECURRENT EDUCATION

The Institute for Research on Educational Finance and Governance (IFG) was established with a five-year commitment from the National Institute of Education in 1979 and is administered through the School of Education at Stanford University. IFG is devoted to a program of policy-oriented research, dissemination and training on educational finance and economics, educational politics, educational organizations, and law and education.

Current research programs at IFG include the following:

- A Comparative Study of Private and Public Schooling Organizations
- Legalization, Regulation, and the New Federalism
- Cost and Cost Effectiveness of Educational Interventions
- Postsecondary Education and the Labor Market
- Planning Models for Local District Decision Making
- Intergovernmental Issues in Education

The Organization for Economic Cooperation and Development (OECD) was set up under a convention signed in Paris on December 14, 1960, that provides that the OECD shall promote policies designed

- to achieve the highest sustainable economic growth and employment and a rising standard of living in member countries, while maintaining financial stability, and thus to contribute to the development of the world economy;
- to contribute to sound economic expansion in member as well as nonmember countries in the process of economic development;
- to contribute to the expansion of world trade on a multilateral, nondiscriminatory basis in accordance with international obligations.

The members of OECD are Australia, Austria, Belgium, Canada, Denmark, Finland, France, the Federal Republic of Germany, Greece, Iceland, Ireland, Italy, Japan, Luxembourg, the Netherlands, New Zealand, Norway, Portugal, Spain, Sweden, Switzerland, Turkey, the United Kingdom, and the United States.

FINANCING RECURRENT EDUCATION

Strategies for Increasing Employment, Job Opportunities, and Productivity

edited by
HENRY M. LEVIN
and
HANS G. SCHÜTZE

Published in cooperation with the Institute for Research on Educational Finance and Governance, Stanford University, and the Organization for Economic Cooperation and Development

SAGE PUBLICATIONS
Beverly Hills / London / New Delhi

Portions of this book were previously published in *Education and Urban Society,* Volume 14, Number 3, May 1982.

For information address:

SAGE Publications, Inc.
275 South Beverly Drive
Beverly Hills, California 90212

SAGE Publications India Pvt. Ltd.
C-236 Defence Colony
New Delhi 110 024, India

SAGE Publications Ltd
28 Banner Street
London EC1Y 8QE, England

Printed in the United States of America

Library of Congress Cataloging in Publication Data

Main entry under title:

Financing recurrent education.

Papers originally presented at conference sponsored by the Institute for Research on Educational Finance and Governance, and the Center for Educational Research and Innovation.

Bibliography: p.

1. Continuing education—United States—Finance—Congresses. 2. Occupational training—United States—Finance—Congresses. 3. Educational leave—Europe—Finance—Congresses. I. Levin, Henry M. II. Schütze, Hans Georg. III. Institute for Research on Educational Finance and Governance (U.S.) IV. Centre for Educational Research and Innovation.

LC5225.F56F56 379.1′215′0973 83-11214
ISBN 0-8039-2068-7

CONTENTS

PREFACE

This volume had its origins in a conference on the costs and financing of recurrent education that was held at the Institute for Research on Educational Finance and Governance (IFG), Stanford University, in July 1980. That conference was cosponsored with the Center for Educational Research and Innovation (CERI) of the Organization for Economic Cooperation and Development (OECD) in Paris. Both the IFG and the OECD have devoted considerable resources to studying new approaches to financing postsecondary education generally, and recurrent education specifically. The outcome of the conference and a subsequent one in Bremen, West Germany, in October 1980 was *The Costs and Financing of Continuing Education and Training*—a volume on one of the most neglected aspects of recurrent education: its financing.

For reasons that are made explicit in the introductory chapter, we believe that recurrent education—a comprehensive strategy for distributing education and trainng over the life span of the individual in a recurrent manner with work and leisure—will become an important vehicle for addressing problems of employment, social mobility, and productivity. Yet, we are only in the early stages of discussing methods for financing recurrent education that are efficient, equitable, flexible, and comprehensive. The chapters in this volume draw upon a variety of ideas and experiences in the industrialized countries to provide alternatives for constructing such a framework. In this respect we are hopeful that the book makes an important contribution in advancing the necessary discourse.

We wish to thank both the OECD and the National Institute of Education for support of the intellectual activities and papers that led to this publication. We are also grateful to the German Marshall Fund of the United States for providing travel grants that enabled these scholars to attend the conferences at which their papers were first discussed. We are especially indebted to David Istance, Susan Peters, and Katherine Tobin for the many hours of capable devotion that they provided in helping to edit this volume. Of course, the views expressed in this book are those of the coeditors and authors, and not those of OECD, IFG, or any other institutions with which the authors are affiliated.

January 1983

Henry M. Levin
Hans G. Schütze

1

ECONOMIC AND POLITICAL DIMENSIONS OF RECURRENT EDUCATION

HENRY M. LEVIN
HANS G. SCHÜTZE

In the latter part of the twentieth century, the industrialized countries of the world will be facing a major educational and training challenge as labor force growth slows and technological change accelerates. There will be a rapid transformation of industries and occupations as economic shifts among nations and the introduction and application of new technologies create vast changes in the workplace. At the same time the growth of the labor force and particularly the entry of newly educated workers will fall to unprecedentedly low levels. Thus the newly trained labor market entrants can not be relied upon to sustain the changes that lie ahead. Without question the United States, Western Europe, and the other industrialized nations will have to pursue new educational and training strategies to prepare their existing labor forces for the new occupational demands. The purpose of this book is to address both methods and issues for financing a system of recurrent education that can accommodate the educational and training challenges that lie ahead.

> In its broadest definition, recurrent education can be defined as follows: a comprehensive educational strategy for all post-compulsory or post-basic education, the essential characteristic of which is the distribution of education over the total life span of the individual in a recurring way, i.e., the alternation with other activities such as work, but also with leisure and retirement [OECD, 1973: 24].

This definition of recurrent education contains two essential elements: First, it offers an alternative educational strategy to the conventional concentration of all formal and full-time education in youth. It proposes to spread postcompulsory education over the full life span of the individual, and thus accepts the principle of lifelong learning.

Second, it proposes a framework within which lifelong learning will be organized, this being the alternation and effective interaction between education (as a structural learning situation) and other social activities during which learning occurs. This general definition of recurrent education contains two properties. It refers to educational offerings that are flexible in structure and content, and it refers to educational experiences that will be available over the life cycle of an individual.

Under present conventions, formal education and training for most individuals takes place prior to entering the labor force or in the first few years of work experience. During the remainder of the life cycle, further education and training constitute an exception for all but a few persons in relatively high-level occupations. For males the work career is often uninterrupted in the absence of unemployment or occupational change. For females, voluntary interruptions are more likely to address child rearing and family; there is surprisingly little pursuit of further education and training as a basis for labor market reentry. That is, present education and training practices tend to be relatively rigid, without accommodating the need to retrain for new careers or to adapt to technological change.

A system of recurrent education would alter this traditional pattern by providing opportunities for education and training throughout the life cycle. Typically, individuals would intersperse periods of work and education to meet both personal needs and those of employers. A system of alternative educational and training opportunities would be constructed that would incorporate existing offerings such as apprenticeships, extension courses, on-the-job training, college and university courses of study, correspondence courses, and technical schools, as well as new offerings and approaches that address previously unattended needs. Such educational and training experiences should be provided both inside and outside the workplace as well as through educational television and computer-assisted instruction. Availability of these offerings must be highly flexible, and opportunities must be provided on weekends and evenings as well as during regular work hours.

Many aspects of recurrent education already exist, but the present oportunities fall considerably short of an integrated system in two major ways. First, the present approach is highly fragmented: It is more a motley collection of confusing and uncoordinated educational possibilities than a systematic approach to recurrent education. Although a recurrent educational approach might surely incorporate all or more of the existing opportunities, they would become part of a more purposive and systematized approach to the overall educational and training strategies of societies. In this respect, availability, access, and comprehensiveness become of far greater concern than they presently are. Second, a system of recurrent education can provide a more systematic approach to the financing of recurrent educational opportunities and the provision of sufficient time away from the workplace to pursue them. Indeed, a major purpose of this volume is to consider alternative ways of providing a comprehensive system of financing recurrent education that will provide equity in access, flexibility and adaptability in responding to needs, and efficiency in the use of private and social resources.[1]

In summary, a recurrent educational approach would go beyond the existing offerings to provide a systematic approach regarding such matters as finance, information, coordination, educational leave for workers, and certification of training experiences. Heavy emphasis would be placed on a total system of opportunities for individuals, small groups, and employers in creating a menu of offerings suited to their needs and demands.

CONSTRUCTING A SYSTEM OF RECURRENT EDUCATION

Major components of recurrent education have been around for some time in the form of on-the-job training, adult education, correspondence courses, continuing education, extension courses, and the movement towards lifelong learning (Mushkin, 1974; Peterson, 1979). Certainly since the early seventies there has been a worldwide movement to improve the efficiency, equity, and flexibility of education through greater attention to lifelong learning (Faure, 1973; Emmerij, 1974). A crucial question that must surely be raised is why these movements have not been welded together into a system of recurrent education.

This question can best be answered by reference to the different concepts and notions of recurrent education. Although the terms "recurrent" and "lifelong" education have been used to refer to education and training over the life span, the generalization in terminology tends to gloss over the great diversity in underlying approaches as well as social and educational concerns. Table 1.1

TABLE 1.1 Different Versions of Recurrent Education

Motive	*Rationale*	*Principal Clientele*	*Principal Forms*
Increasing Productive Efficiency	Increase worker productivity and adaptation to technical change	Workers and persons reentering labor market	Job-oriented education and training
Reducing Unemployment	Use of recurrent education to share existing jobs	Labor Force	Educational leave and sabbaticals to rotate existing jobs
Reducing Overeducation and Underemployment	Providing educational opportunities throughout working life to reduce demand for tertiary education before entering workplace	Workers	Diversity of educational and training opportunities as needed over working life
Worker Participation	Improve conditions of work and worker participation	Workers	Training in skills and knowledge necessary for worker participation in decisions
Improving Quality of Leisure	Improve ability to use leisure hours productively	All adults	Emphasis on music, poetry, art and other forms of intellectual, cultural, and recreational development

Reducing Inequalities of Disadvantaged	Compensating for inequalities of worker social backgrounds and previous educational experiences to increase their mobility	Unemployed and unskilled workers	Basic academic skills and further job training
Improving Social Participation	Providing knowledge for greater social and political participation to improve their conditions	Nonprofessional and nonmanagerial workforce, housewives, and senior citizens	Political and family education as well as arts and human needs
Rescuing Educational Institution	New clientele and functions for postsecondary institutions faced with falling enrollments	Adults	Courses and degrees according to demand
Deschooling Society	Reducing coercion of mandatory schooling and bureaucracy of traditional educational institutions for greater individual freedom and choice by creating more flexible and responsive offerings	All persons beyond primary age	Whatever is demanded in the educational marketplace

provides a summary of nine relatively distinct motives that seem to be behind the arguments for recurrent education. Each of these tends to suggest a specific target clientele and set of offerings, and in many cases the overlap among clientele and offerings is minimal.

INCREASING PRODUCTIVE EFFICIENCY

The view that recurrent education can improve productive efficiency proceeds largely from the assumption that worker skills have a tendency to become obsolete under conditions of rapid technological change. As the nature of jobs evolves with new capital investment, workers will need to learn new skills or refresh old ones to adapt to new technologies. From this perspective, recurrent education provides the flexibility for retraining workers as skill rejuvenation is needed. Such an approach can improve worker productivity and earnings as well as increase the productivity of the firm and its profitability. Or, in time of rapid technical progress and change, recurrent education might be needed to maintain worker productivity which would otherwise decline. There is a particular incentive for employers to promote this approach, especially to the extent that recurrent education can reduce costs of training through economies of scale and can shift a portion of training costs from the private to the public sector.

The target clientele for this version of recurrent education is both the existing workforce and persons who are planning to reenter the workforce after periods of absence. (Housewives who have left employment to raise children are a good example of the latter.) Specifically vocational experiences would be offered to train persons for changing work roles and job requirements. The principal argument for public support of recurrent education that increases productive efficiency is that it would increase national productivity and economic growth while reducing inflation (through providing productivity gains commensurate with rising wages) and making products more competitive in world markets.

REDUCING EMPLOYMENT

A related motive for providing recurrent education is the role that it might play in reducing unemployment. However, what is referred to here is the use of recurrent education to rotate workers between periods of employment and periods of training, enabling a larger portion of the labor force to experience regular employment. By providing recurrent education for experienced workers at any point in time, job openings are provided for new members. Of course, to the degree that it improved the productivity of the labor force and made a country's goods more competitive in world markets, it might also contribute to job expansion.

The audience for such an approach is that of the labor force, but recurrent educational offerings can take several forms. Of most importance is the emphasis on recurrent education as an "active labor market policy" (Meidner and Anderson, 1973) as advocated in the chapters by Rehn and Emmerij in this volume. This approach must include provisions for inducing persons to leave the workforce to obtain further training or other types of education. One possible version is to create incentives for persons to take such leave when there is high unemployment in their industries or when retraining is needed in response to technical change. Other versions would make all workers eligible for such sabbaticals, with the expectation that they might be pursued most frequently when workers have incentives for retraining or switching careers to more prosperous sectors of the economy. While there is some overlap with the productive efficiency motive for recurrent education, the emphasis on the direct reduction of unemployment is grounds for viewing this approach as distinct.

REDUCING OVEREDUCATION AND UNDEREMPLOYMENT

In a very different sense, recurrent education may be used to reduce the number of overeducated members of the workforce —a considerable problem in many societies. Although there may be a growing shortage of certain skills in their economies as industrial reorganization and technical change accelerate, there is presently a surplus of persons with postsecondary education in virtually all of the Western industrialized countries. The phenomenon of overeducation or underutilization of educated labor is a waste of resources. Many people are trained who will not be able to obtain appropriate jobs in the careers for which they are trained (Freeman, 1976; Rumberger, 1981). At the same time it can represent a major source of social and political ferment as the job expectations of university and other postsecondary graduates are not fulfilled (Levin, 1976). The increasing costs of postsecondary education at a time of national fiscal crises in conjunction with an inability to employ graduates at appropriate job levels has stimulated a search for ways to reduce the demands by students and their families for traditional forms of higher education. However, given that education has been perceived as the main channel for upward mobility by the vast majority of the population, the demand for university participation will not be significantly reduced unless there are alternative channels of mobility.

In this respect, the provision of ample recurrent educational opportunities can be seen as a way of assuring secondary graduates that they need not undertake all of their educational experiences prior to entering the labor market. Presumably, under a system of recurrent education, employers would be expected to hire more secondary graduates and encourage them to seek out recurrent educational offerings that enable them to meet both their own needs and those of their employers. If such a shift from traditional timing and forms of postsecondary education to recurrent education were successful, it might reduce the perceived need for university training and thus reduce the number of overeducated persons. That is, recurrent education would be used to "cool off" the high demand for participation in traditional postsecondary education.

The main clientele would be secondary graduates who would enter the labor market at relatively lower levels and seek mobility through recurrent educational participation. The principal forms of recurrent education would be those that were highly related to job and career needs. The major obstacles to realizing this type of shift are that even fewer job opportunities are available for secondary graduates than for university graduates, and employers tend to use credentials at the point of labor market entry for assigning workers to occupational strata. Unless jobs become more plentiful at the secondary level and career mobility becomes closely linked with recurrent educational experiences rather than initial credentials, it is unlikely that there will be a profound shift in educational patterns.

WORKER PARTICIPATION

A rationale for recurrent education that is especially strong in Western Europe is its use in improving the quality of working life through worker participation. An underlying assumption is that working life is oppressive because of the high degree of division of labor and systems of managerial control that alienate workers from both the work process and their fellow workers. The response has been to develop a variety of ways in which workers can participate either directly or through representation in making decisions that affect the overall organization and functioning of the workplace as well as daily work operations.

Broadly speaking, this movement has come to be called "industrial democracy" or "workplace democracy." In part, employers have tried to increase the intrinsic attractiveness of the workplace through greater worker participation in order to reduce high levels of worker turnover and absenteeism and to raise productivity. In part, it has resulted from laws and collective bargaining agreements supported by labor that have mandated worker participation in the operations of the firm. For example, the codetermination laws of West Germany require that there be worker members on the boards of directors of large firms as well as worker councils for joint determination of employment and work operations (Furstenburg, 1977). Sweden has a national law requiring worker participation on all major decisions regarding employment and the nature and distribution of work (Ministry of Labor, Sweden, 1975). Other nations have also experienced increasing worker participation in their enterprises and government sponsorship of initiatives in this direction.

The need for recurrent education under such circumstances is to educate workers about their responsibilities and functions in a participative organization; to provide them with the knowledge that they will need to make good decisions; and to enable them to develop their other skills more fully for both occupational advancement and human development (Schuller, 1981; Turner and Count, 1981). Specific forms of recurrent education include the availability of educational and training sabbaticals, worker circles for discussion of all pertinent issues relative to the role of workers in such organization, and the availability of courses for workers on the basis of sufficient worker demand. Clearly the audience for this form of recurrent education is that of the present workforce.

IMPROVING QUALITY OF LEISURE

Advocates of recurrent education as a means of improving the quality of leisure often assume that a high standard of living in the industrialized countries requires a minute division of labor where most jobs have little skill content and are highly routinized. Therefore, they see little hope of transforming work into a more humane activity without a large sacrifice in living standards. But, they would argue that the redemption of this approach is that an "inhuman" technology has tended to shorten the work week and increase the amount of leisure that workers can enjoy.

Therefore, if the price of such affluence has been the destruction of the human spirit in the workplace—as Terkel (1974) has emphasized—the response must be to resurrect it outside of the workplace by bringing music, poetry, art, and other forms of cultural development into the lives of workers through recurrent or lifelong education. The clientele for recurrent education would include virtually all adults, and the opportunities would be scheduled during evenings, weekends, vacations, and other heavy concentrations of leisure hours. A major audience would be that of senior citizens who have retired from the workplace. Presumably, the alienation of the workplace or the home in the case of housewives would be compensated for in intellectual stimulation, spirituality, social interchange, knowledge, and human development provided by recurrent educational activities outside of work.

REDUCING INEQUALITIES OF THE DISADVANTAGED

Much discussion of recurrent education has viewed it as a way of redressing inequalities that emanate from the social origins of workers and their previous education (Levin, 1978). Because it has been evident that previous levels of educational attainment and their occupational rewards are heavily conditioned by the social origins of workers, recurrent education is seen as an opportunity for providing further educational opportunities for those workers who are least advantaged in labor markets. In particular, workers who are most susceptible to unemployment or underemployment by virtue of their previous educational experiences would represent the primary target for eligibility and financing of recurrent education. The expectation is that by using recurrent education to compensate this group for their labor market disadvantages, it will be possible to increase their occupational and earnings mobility. Indeed, this is largely the premise behind the various publicly supported training programs for the disadvantaged found in the United States (Mirengoff and Rindler, 1976) and Western Europe.

This approach to recurrent education focuses primarily on persons who are susceptible to unemployment and who are relatively unskilled. Recurrent education strategies include an attempt to provide basic academic skills where these were lacking as well as specific job training. A broader version of using recurrent education for reducing inequality would integrate a "prodisadvantaged" approach into a national system of recurrent education. The disadvantaged would be given greater financial assistance and a wider range of choices to meet their special needs. In this way, the concern for equalization could be integrated into comprehensive approaches to recurrent education for the entire population.

IMPROVING SOCIAL PARTICIPATION

A related perspective on recurrent education sees it as a means of increasing social participation in political, economic, and cultural life. In this framework, recurrent education is viewed as a way of increasing the democratization of political, economic, social, and cultural participation by providing educational experiences that enhance the ability of those who are least likely and least able to participate in these spheres of life. For example, persons from less advantaged educational and work backgrounds tend to participate less in the political process and tend to have greater difficulty in understanding complex political issues. Recurrent educational strategies could focus on increasing political participation by involving such persons in political discussions and enabling them to be more conversant with the important issues.

The attempt to increase social participation in all spheres of life by those who are most disenfranchised could extend to literacy, family planning, consumer knowledge, health and hygiene, and utilization of the political process to attain objectives. For example, senior citizens could be provided with instruction and other forms of experience that would increase their ability to organize collectively to meet their needs. Recurrent educational opportunities could also focus on greater involvement in the performing and fine arts and voluntary community services, as well as provide them with knowledge on nutrition and health care unique to their situations.

Clientele would be drawn largely from those groups who have the lowest levels of social participation and the fewest resources to improve their circumstances. These groups might include lower-level workers, housewives, the handicapped, senior citizens, and poverty populations. Essentially, recurrent education would be used as a way to provide the knowledge needed to increase participation and create social progress for those groups who are least able to provide such results on their own behalf. This approach to recurrent education is profoundly and overtly political, and it is inherently more controversial than the political motives of most other approaches.

RESCUING EDUCATIONAL INSTITUTIONS

At odds with the motive for using recurrent education to reduce overeducation is that of using it to rescue educational institutions that are losing enrollments because of reductions in the population of youth. Virtually all of the highly industrialized countries are experiencing historically low birthrates that have resulted in demographic shifts in the population (Acsadi and Johnson-Acsadi, 1980). As the population grows older, there are fewer persons in the age groups that in the past have pursued traditional forms of postsecondary education, so colleges and universities are facing declines in enrollments. Particularly affected are those institutions that proliferated and expanded to meet the demographic bulges of the "baby boom" period. A major strategy for maintaining enrollment levels has been for institutions to seek new clientele and educational directions.

Clearly, a major source of such clientele are those persons who are in the workplace or home and are beyond the normal age for postsecondary participation. By providing recurrent educational opportunities to these persons, it is hoped that empty classrooms and deficit budgets can be avoided. Indeed, the principal motive of many postsecondary institutions in promoting recurrent education is that of institutional survival. Many strategies have developed to support this quest: Such institutions have started satellite campuses in local communities and in corporate and government workplaces to attract students; have granted credits for "life" experiences to increase the attractiveness of further study towards a degree; have promoted more flexible degree requirements in terms of both scheduling and rigor with evening and weekend offerings and minimal library demands on students; and have expanded the range of offerings in both programs providing credit towards degrees and those that do not. Although many of these strategies have tended to compromise the quality of educational offerings, a deterioration of quality should not be considered intrinsic to the expansion of recurrent education.

"DESCHOOLING" THE POSTCOMPULSORY SYSTEM

A final motive for expanding recurrent education is to replace the highly institutionalized forms of traditional schooling. It is argued that mandatory schooling is coercive and that even traditional postsecondary education has become mandatory for those who seek to achieve placement in higher occupations. By making the routes for both training and occupational achievement more flexible and subject to individual demand and choice, much unnecessary schooling will be eliminated and coercion will be reduced. Since this view is often held by those who wish to see a "deschooling of society" (for example, Illich, 1971), it can be characterized under that rubric. The expectation is that such a system would be more flexible and efficient in the use of resources in addition to being more humane.

All persons beyond compulsory school age would constitute the clientele for such an approach, and the educational offerings would simply depend on what was demanded in the educational marketplace. Illich (1971) has suggested that every community could have documentation centers using the latest technology that would make information on any subject available through printed and electronic media. Individuals would learn how to use such centers to instruct themselves on topics that arose in their daily work lives, politics, or social relations, or on which they were curious. Issues of social priorities in what would be offered or who would be served would not be of importance under such an arrangement—it would be designed to minimize government regulations and other institutional encumbrances. However, it is conceivable that a regulated market approach might be developed with government-funded entitlements that could be used to pay for educational offerings that met certain stipulated criteria. Recurrent educational approaches responding to the deschooling motive could range from unregulated ones with little government support to highly regulated situations with continuing government funding and involvement.

POLITICAL AND ECONOMIC CHALLENGES

Thus far we have presented nine different motives for advocating the systematic expansion of recurrent education. For many observers at least some of them will represent persuasive arguments for recurrent education. Taken together, one might think that the political and economic support for recurrent education would be substantial. Yet, paradoxically, the very diversity of approaches may be the greatest political obstacle to adoption and implementation.

The political challenges can be seen most clearly if one looks at the different versions of recurrent education in terms of their rationales, clientele, and principal applications. Even a cursory comparison would suggest considerable differences among them that may inhibit the formation of political constituencies. Before reviewing these areas of potential discord, it is important to note that virtually all of the approaches can be viewed under three themes: those contributing to improvements in the functioning of labor markets and productivity; those contributing to improved social participation and equity; and those that are designed to achieve major institutional change.

Labor Market and Productivity Strategies
- **Increasing Productive Efficiency**
- **Reducing Unemployment**
- **Reducing Overeducation and Underemployment**

Social Participation and Equity
- **Worker Participation**
- **Improving Quality of Leisure**
- **Reducing Inequalities of Disadvantaged**
- **Improving Social Participation**

Institutional Change
- **Rescuing Educational Institutions**
- **Deschooling of the Postcompulsory System**

Even among these three major areas there are substantial differences in goals and constituencies. For example, the enhancement of social participation and equity may be important goals on their own merits, but they are not designed to contribute to institutional change or increase productivity. To some degree the various approaches are in conflict; at the very least, resources that are committed to one version may not be available for the pursuit of other approaches.

However, incompatability between the nine specific approaches (see Table 1.1) is even more acute. Even within major categories such as institutional change, the strategies differ immensely in objectives and clientele. For example, using recurrent education to broaden the mission of postsecondary educational institutions that are losing enrollments represents an attempt to strengthen existing institutional forms—a goal that is sharply in contrast with the motive of deschooling postcompulsory education. Using recurrent education to reduce overeducation or the underutilization of educated labor is also incompatible with using it to rescue traditional postsecondary educational institutions. As these conflicts are also evident in comparisons of many other categories, it is difficult to see how a single, comprehensive plan for recurrent education could encompass all of the various approaches.

Indeed, this situation has seemed to be a major political weakness of recurrent education in the past, especially in the United States. A single rubric has been used to refer to what are essentially a variety of competing and conflicting versions of lifelong education. By bringing them under a single descriptive term—recurrent education—it has been possible to get a large and diverse coalition to support the concept in the abstract. However, any implementation of recurrent education would obviously require that specific forms be adopted and financed that would either neglect or be incompatible with other forms. That is, once the broad notion of recurrent education is translated into particular strategies with particular goals, it becomes a narrower concept which may support the objectives of one constituency at the expense of another. In the United States there has been an indeterminacy in forging a politically acceptable strategy for implementation. This political challenge must be overcome in the future.

The economic obstacles are inherent in the present disincentives for individuals to undertake the recurrent education route in place of the traditional one. In order to make recurrent education vocationally relevant, a number of conditions must be met: (1) Employment opportunities must be readily available for persons who have completed high school and have not continued into postsecondary education; (2) career ladders and training options must be provided in conjunction with such jobs; and (3) later participation in and completion of educational programs on a recurrent basis must provide occupational advancement and income that are commensurate with the cost of those training programs and their value when they have been completed prior to entering the labor force.

The availability of employment is an obvious and important requirement for individuals seeking to take jobs prior to completing their formal education and training and then to pursue subsequent recurrent educational strategies. Presumably, individuals could begin their careers at entry levels and undertake additional education and training as needed. To do this, numerous work opportunities would have to be available for high school graduates. Unfortunately, unemployment rates for young high school graduates are substantial and considerably higher than for college graduates. For example, in March 1979 the U.S. unemployment rate for high school graduates 16-17 years of age was about 24% and for 18-19 years olds was almost 12% although the overall unemployment rate for all groups was about 6% (U.S. Department of Labor, 1981: A-22). Thus, high school graduates who were under 20 years of age had unemployment rates that were two to four times the national average. Since that time unemployment rates have risen in all categories, and the relatively poor position of young high school graduates has deteriorated further. The data suggest that many individuals will have difficulty in finding the employment necessary to pursue a recurrent educational strategy, and the incentives may encourage improving employment possibilities through taking a college degree prior to entering the labor market in spite of the problems faced by those with college degrees (Freeman, 1976; Rumberger, 1981).

This disincentive is reinforced by the nature of entry-level positions. To a large degree these positions are not the first steps on a career ladder, but are "dead-end" positions that lead nowhere (Brown, 1982). Examples include one of the primary sectors for employment of untrained youth—fast-food restaurants. This industry is predicated upon operations that are largely determined by the machines and technology employed, and as a result the simple labor operations can be learned quickly and few skills are learned on the job. Further, there are few positions above this entry-level since relatively small numbers of supervisors can monitor very large numbers of workers in jobs that are so highly routinized. Although fast-food preparation in the past meant that individuals might develop skills as short-order cooks that could be transferred to more advanced kitchen and restaurant positions, this is not likely today.

Such jobs do not lend themselves to a demand for recurrent education and training for skill development because of the lack of career ladders in such employments. Rather, they reinforce the view that these are dead-end jobs, and the only way to improve one's employment is to get more advanced credentials that will provide employment opportunities in better occupations. Thus, both the relative dearth of jobs and the lack of career ladders for those jobs that are available tend to discourage individuals from considering recurrent educational strategies.

Beyond these disincentives to pursuing recurrent education in place of more traditional educational patterns, there is the related issue of the availability of training opportunities within firms. Unfortunately, many entry-level positions neither lead to career opportunities that require additional skills nor provide opportunities to learn new skills on the job. The most extensive training programs are generally provided for persons who have already acquired considerable formal education, generally at least at the level of a university degree. This also leads to incentives to complete postsecondary education prior to joining the labor force.

Finally, the issue arises as to whether individuals acquiring training and education in the recurrent fashion will do as well in the job market as persons who have acquired formal educational credentials prior to entering careers. For example, assume that a high school graduate decides to take a position as a clerical or assembly worker while pursuing a B.A. degree simultaneously on a part-time basis. The question is how that person will be viewed on the labor market when he or she completes the B.A. degree and applies for a management training position. One might think that a person with other work experience at lower levels would be even a more attractive candidate for a management trainee position than an inexperienced graduate with the same level of formal education.

However, it is not clear that firms behave in that way. An assembly worker or clerical worker with a new B.A. degree obtained on a part-time basis is more likely to be treated as an assembly worker or clerical worker who has overachieved, while the inexperienced worker with the newly acquired B.A. that was earned on a full-time basis is considered to be the more appropriate candidate for management training. In the United States one finds few recipients of law degrees or M.B.A. degrees who have studied on a part-time basis, being considered for the most prestigious positions that require these credentials. That is, firms do not seem to attach the same weight to part-time study as to equivalent full-time study in hiring and promotion decisions.

In summary, the logic of recurrent education for improving the efficiency and equity of utilization and training of human resources is not matched by appropriate incentives to individuals to forego traditional educational patterns for those of recurrent education. From all of the information available it seems reasonable to conclude that higher employment rates, better jobs and career mobility ladders, greater access to on-the-job training, and greater success in obtaining access to prestigious positions are available to those who enter the labor market with at the least the completion of a university degree. Finally, it is important to note that financial aid is rarely available for the part-time student, creating an additional disincentive to undertake a more flexible approach to post-secondary education and training. This situation does not serve to promote the more flexible work and study patterns associated with recurrent education. Yet, the near future appears to be a time when these challenges will be overcome and recurrent education will become more fully recognized as a force for improving training, employment, and productivity.

RECURRENT EDUCATION AS A RISING STAR

In the last two decades of the twentieth century, two phenomena will make recurrent education a vital strategy for promoting workplace productivity, employment, and occupational mobility. The first is the fact that enormous shifts in occupational skills will take place as old industries subside and new ones take their place. At the same time there will no longer be massive inflows of new workers with the latest training, so adaptation and retraining will necessarily need to focus largely on the existing workforce. Second, while relative expansion of high technology jobs will be substantial, such expansion will account for only a small proportion of new job positions. Since most of the expansion of employment will be in relatively low-skill areas that require modest initial educational qualifications, there will be a need for further education and training to create mobility and avoid a caste-like segmentation of large numbers of workers in low-skill jobs. Let us consider each of these in turn.

It is widely accepted that as the United States and Western Europe recover from the serious economic situation of the 1970s and early 1980s, the composition of industries and employment will change drastically. The production of steel, automobiles, and heavy machinery will have shifted substantially and will continue to shift to such Third World countries as Brazil, South Korea, and Taiwan—often under the aegis of multinational corporations that are headquartered in the industrial countries. At the same time, new industries will be rising and experiencing rapid growth in microelectronics, microcomputers, computer applications and software, robotics, and biotechnology. Beyond the rise and expansion of these industries themselves, their products will have profound effects on the nature of the work process and production in existing workplaces. The use of robotics and microprocessors to execute and control production will alter the characteristics of the workplace and the skills and training required of workers; biotechnology should have profound effects on the production of chemicals and pharmaceuticals.

Although the transformation of industry and the workplace has certainly been a constant feature of the nineteenth and twentieth centuries, the pace of change is accelerating because of rapid technological developments, information advances that permit extremely rapid diffusion of technology, and a desperate search for higher profits at a time of poor economic performance.

At the same time there will be a drastic decline in the inflow of newly trained workers: Falling birthrates in the industrialized countries have reduced the number and proportion of young persons. In the recent past, the need for workers with advanced skills was largely met through the introduction of newly educated workers into the labor force. This fact is reflected dramatically in estimates of the U.S. Department of Labor: While the labor force grew at an annual rate of about 2.2% between 1965-1975 and 2.7% in 1975-1979, the rate of increase will fall to 1.9% in 1979-1985, 1.3% in 1985-1990 and less than 1% in 1990-1995 (Fullerton, 1982: 49). Although there was a net addition of over 10 million workers to the labor force from 1975 to 1979, the net addition projected for the five-year period between 1990 and 1995 is less than 6 million (Fullerston, 1982: 51).

This means that to a sharply increased extent, the development of new skills to match the jobs generated by both industrial shifts and new technologies will have to be met through training and retraining of the existing labor force. It is difficult to see how this massive task can be accomplished efficiently without the initiation of a comprehensive system of recurrent education. Such a system must be organized to provide a level of comprehensiveness and adaptability that will accommodate the inevitable demands for workers that are qualified to meet the requirements of the new technologies and work tasks. If such a system is not forthcoming, it is conceivable that severe bottlenecks in production and costly inefficiencies in retraining will arise since the present approach to continuing education and employer training is probably not adequate to anticipate and accommodate the enormous changes that lie ahead. For this reason, concerns for future employment and productivity will be powerful stimuli for the development by both states and the national government of a systematic and responsive approach to the promotion and provision of recurrent education.

The second important reason that recurrent education is likely to become a more important factor on the political and educational agenda is the urgency of avoiding a permanent under-class of unskilled and low-paid workers. So-called high technology jobs will be expanding at a faster rate than many of the more traditional ones, but they will represent only a very small portion of the total number of new jobs that will be created in the next two decades. For example, although the number of positions for such jobs as computer operators is expected to double in the 1978-1990 period, this will amount to the net creation of only about 160,000 new jobs in that area (Carey, 1982: 42). However, during the same period, the number of new jobs for janitors and sextons is expected to approach almost 700,000; nurses' aides and orderlies—594,000; sales clerks—591,000; cashiers—546,000; waiters and waitresses—532,000; general office clerks—530,000; and food preparation and service workers in fast-food restaurants—492,000 (Carey, 1982: 40). In fact, among the 20 occupations that are expected to generate the most new jobs, there are no high-technology occupations represented, and no more than 4 seem to require any postsecondary education; professional nurses, elementary school teachers, accountants and auditors, and licensed practical nurses (if we assume that office skills can be acquired in secondary school). Even more important is the dearth of possibilities for career mobility, for in most of these cases there are no evident career ladders. That is, under normal circumstances, one does not move from the job of janitor to that of a skilled worker, and in many cases there are simply few higher-level positions of any sort in the firms that will hire this labor. Thus, we are facing an expansion of unskilled jobs that will typically lack opportunities for advancement in the absence of further training.

To a large degree, the sole hope for occupational mobility for vast segments of the labor force will lie in the establishment of a system of recurrent education that will prepare persons entering these jobs for the relatively smaller number of jobs in the economy that will require higher skills. That is, although large numbers of persons will enter jobs requiring little preparation and training, they will be able to advance to more demanding and remunerative work only if the opportunities to acquire appropriate training are available. By having such opportunities, incentives to take lower-level jobs and to perform well will be enhanced by the promise of more advanced training and opportunities. In this way, firms will be able to fill jobs at the lower levels, while workers who take those jobs can have access to the training required for upward mobility. At the present time, the very high turnover of workers in such positions is largely attributable to the routine nature and dead end careers associated with such jobs combined with a lack of access to further career training opportunities.

It may even be appropriate to tie eligibility for subsidized recurrent education opportunities to employment tenure so that individuals who spend a year or more in one of these ubiquitous low-skill areas will be rewarded with an expanded list of training options for higher-level employment. It is important to point out that much of such training must necessarily be made available outside of the place of employment, since many employers of low-skill workers will not have the resources or higher-skill positions to train workers for.

In summary, both the need to adapt an existing labor force to industrial shifts and changes in technology as well as the need to provide mobility routes for large numbers of workers who will be forced to accept employment in unskilled occupations that lack career ladders will necessitate consideration of a new system for the training and retraining of the work force. It is exactly these needs that are addressed most fully by a comprehensive system of recurrent education, and pressures from both directions will contribute to the formation of such a system.

FINANCING RECURRENT EDUCATION

As we stated at the outset, the goal of recurrent education is to create mechanisms that will promote alternative education and work patterns that can draw upon existing resources while providing incentives for new ones to emerge in a systematic way. Such a system would improve education, training, employment, and productivity by making access to a comprehensive system of recurrent education a universal option for individuals and firms, and would utilize educational resources more effectively than does the traditional pattern which places great urgency on completing one's formal education and training before seeking regular employment.

The focus of this volume is not to design a single approach to financing recurrent education as much as it is to set out alternatives for doing so. Depending on the goals of recurrent education and the existence of supportive resources, there are many different approaches that can be pursued. The following chapters provide a provocative discussion of these alternatives that enables one to evaluate them according to their strengths and weaknesses. This evaluation can be used as a basis for further discussion, planning, and action. The first part of the book addresses the complex issues surrounding overall models for financing recurrent education. The second part examines the financing of recurrent educational programs in the United States. Finally, the third part explores the financing of paid educational leave, using four case studies from Western Europe.

COMPREHENSIVE MODELS FOR FINANCING RECURRENT EDUCATION

The purpose of this section of the book is to set out several models for financing education that might be evaluated with regard to such criteria as equity, flexibility, comprehensiveness, efficiency, cost, and distribution of the cost burden. Three different financing approaches are presented, and they are assessed along with other financing possibilities in a common framework.

The chapter by Henry M. Levin on "Individual Entitlements" for recurrent education constructs the case for financing recurrent education through vouchers or entitlements that are issued to individuals when their compulsory education requirements are completed. The entitlements could be used for a wide variety of education and training opportunities including colleges and universities, employer- or union-sponsored training programs, correspondence courses, apprenticeships, and so on. Entitlements would be based upon both loans and grants, with the composition between the two dependent upon family resources. The ingredients of a system of finance, regulation, and information are discussed, and the GI Bill (by which educational entitlements were provided to military veterans) is used to evaluate the efficiency, equity, and responsiveness of the entitlement approach.

In contrast, Gösta Rehn proposes a different approach in the chapter entitled "Individual Drawing Rights." Each person would be able to use a portion of his social security account to take educational leave from work for retraining or preparing for other careers. The goal of this approach would be to maximize the ability of individuals to allocate their time among work, study, and leisure over the life span. These choices would be integrated into an active labor market policy that would create incentives for individuals to use their drawing rights for recurrent education when job prospects in their industries were declining and jobs were expanding in other industries. The plan might also augment drawing rights for the poor and handicapped in order to provide greater social equity. A major advantage is that existing social security accounts could be used as a basis for expanding individual choice and to support a diverse set of possibilities for participating in recurrent education.

A third approach is presented by Werner Clement in "Intermediate 'Parafiscal' Financing Schemes." In this approach, the focus for financing recurrent education would be on such intermediate entities as trade unions, employer associations, professional organizations, and other voluntary groups. The government would enable any such group to levy taxes on its members to support a program of recurrent education that would address its specific needs. Under such an arrangement, Clement suggests that people would be able to express their preferences for recurrent education through groups of a convenient size with common goals, and that costs would be reduced while participation would be encouraged.

In the final chapter in this section, Dieter Timmermann attempts to evaluate these three plans and others in "Financing Mechanisms: Their Impact on Postcompulsory Education." A number of criteria are established, and a self-financing or market model, a single-employer financing model, and a state financing model are assessed in addition to the use of entitlements, drawing rights, and intermediate institutions. Timmermann concludes that a mixed model incorporating aspects of each individual model might be most appropriate.

FINANCING RECURRENT EDUCATION IN THE UNITED STATES

Such traditional activities as adult education, university and college extension courses, on-the-job training, military training, other government training programs, and trade union educational and apprenticeship programs can all be incorporated into a comprehensive approach to recurrent education. But, since these educational and training programs are funded and sponsored by a wide range of state, local, and federal government agencies as well as private benefactors, it is difficult to know the extent of such programs, their sources of support, and the magnitude of participation and funding. This section of the volume represents a selective survey of recurrent education activities and their funding in the United States.

Alan P. Wagner attempts to piece together the myriad of existing programs in "An Inventory of Programs and Sources of Support." On the basis of his detective work, he concludes that in 1980 about 50 million individuals in the United States participated in at least one type of organized learning activity within the recurrent educational rubric, and the estimated costs were in the neighborhood of $55 billion. Wagner attempts to review the types and magnitudes of each type of program and the costs and sources of funding. Finally, he provides information on the characteristics of participants by sex, age, race, and employment status. Thus this chapter serves as a useful background for understanding the scope of present approaches to financing recurrent education in the United States.

Although employer-sponsored education is acknowledged widely as a substantial part of the existing system of recurrent education, surprisingly little systematic analysis of this mode has been carried out. This is the subject of Gregory B. Smith's chapter on "Employer-Sponsored Programs." Smith focuses on the purposes, forms, effects, and magnitude of training programs that are financed by employers. After this general survey, he addresses one of the most prevalent forms of employer-sponsored programs in recurrent education: tuition-assistance programs. Most of these programs suffer from low rates of employee participation, so Smith has chosen to review three relatively effective cases to ascertain what can be learned about making such programs more attractive and useful.

Clearly, unions also have an important stake in the recurrent education of their members. Only recently have there been concerted efforts to understand the extent of union involvement in recurrent education in general, and specifically the degree to which such provisions are financed by collective bargaining agreements. In "Unions and Postsecondary Education," Nevzer Stacey and Ivan Charner examine the role of unions. Specific types of programs and subsidies for recurrent educational activities are examined, and illustrative programs are indicated. The authors also reflect on emerging factors that may make such educational and training programs more important in the future, and they suggest that unions would be wise to consider these issues in their future policies.

Just as the recurrent education phenomenon began to become more fully articulated, a movement with important implications for public funding of programs gained momentum: the tax and expenditure limitation movement. In states such as California with Proposition 13 and Massachusetts with its Proposition 2½, state initiatives limited tax revenues from the property tax. Other states have passed expenditure limitation measures, and the substantial tax and expenditure cuts of the Reagan administration indicate that the thrust of federal policy is also in this direction.

In "Tax Limitation Measures: Their Impact in California," Harold E. Geiogue examines the impact of the $7 billion reduction in property taxes generated by the passage of California's Proposition 13 in 1978. Because of its weaker political constituency relative to that of the more entrenched forms of education, Geiogue found that recurrent educational offerings seem to have experienced greater funding reductions than did more traditional forms of postsecondary education. He concludes with an analysis and interpretation of this phenomenon—a view that is not optimistic with respect to the future of recurrent education under conditions of budgetary stress.

In the United States, much of the overall discussion of recurrent education has been situated at the federal level. In the autumn of 1980, the Education Amendments signed by President Carter provided an expansion of educational opportunity for adults and a commitment to recurrent education. In "An Opportunity Deferred: Lifelong Learning in the United States," Pamela H. Christoffel reviews the history of recurrent education at the federal level with major attention to the background and details of the 1980 amendments. Unfortunately, the exciting and productive changes that would have provided a federal stimulus to recurrent education did not receive funding appropriations at a time of severe budgetary distress. Nevertheless, they represent a background at the federal level for what might follow as the economy improves and job retraining becomes more pressing.

Overall, then, the rather rapid developments that took place in the United States in recurrent education have experienced setbacks in recent years, largely because of a poor economy and government fiscal stringencies. As we have argued above, we view this situation as a temporary one, for the realities of a slowdown in labor force growth and drastic changes in the structure of industries and occupations will create renewed pressures for more comprehensive ways of providing and funding recurrent education. An important aspect of that development might certainly be the provision of educational leave policies.

FINANCING PAID EDUCATIONAL LEAVE

Working individuals need more than just access to recurrent educational opportunities for pursuing further education and training over their working lives: They also need the time to dedicate themselves to further study. While in some cases this study can take place outside of working hours, for example during weekends and evenings, in other cases the intensity and depth of recurrent education and training will require a period of study that is unfettered by work obligations. In 1974, the International Labor Organization (ILO) Convention expressed a commitment to the granting of paid educational leave for training at any level. Many countries in Western Europe have moved in this direction by providing educational leave of absence provisions for workers. Since these may have profound consequences for future U.S. policies, this final section of the volume reviews four rather different approaches to financing educational leave.

It is generally recognized that Sweden has gone farther than virtually all of the Western European countries in providing training and educational opportunities for adults. In "The Swedish Model," Kjell Rubenson reviews the background and overall approach for financing recurrent educational opportunities in Sweden. Of particular importance is the integration of financial support for recurrent education that includes both the direct costs of the education and training as well as a stipend for covering the living costs of the participants. These programs are part of the overall labor market policies in Sweden, and they are designed to contribute to maintaining high levels of employment and productivity growth.

One of the earliest national laws regarding paid educational and training leave is the French Act of 1971. In 1979 almost 3 million French workers took part in training activities at a cost of almost $3 billion. In "French Law on Continuing Vocational Training," Pierre Caspar reviews the French experience as well as the patterns of financing and participation. Caspar suggests that there are a number of lessons to be learned from the French case, especially the need to avoid overregulation and the proliferation of detailed legal statutes on permissible program activities. He also suggests that many workers fear that if they take paid educational leave, their jobs may evaporate during their absence.

In contrast with France and its national laws, provisions for paid educational leave in West Germany are provided primarily at the state level. In his chapter on "The Federal Republic of Germany," Hans G. Schütze examines the provisions and experiences of the five states that have adopted extensive leave policies. Important comparisons are made of both the laws of the different states and their patterns of participation. Interestingly, although both the national setting and level of government sponsorship differ between the French and German cases, the Schütze chapter reports many parallels with respect to patterns of participation. The state-oriented nature of the Western German approach is likely to be of particular interest in the United States where much of the responsibility for education is concentrated at the state level.

The final chapter, "Paid Educational Leave: A Proposal Based on the Dutch Case" by Louis Emmerij, reviews the Dutch situation and makes a novel proposal: Emmerij suggests that the payments that are presently used for public assistance and unemployment compensation for unemployed workers be used to provide paid educational leave. Not only does he argue that such a policy would use more efficiently the funds that are already being spent on the unemployed by retraining them and increasing their marketable skills, he suggests also that systematic participation of employed workers in recurrent educational programs would open up considerable job opportunities for new workers. That is, the openings created by the constant movement of the experienced workforce into recurrent educational and training programs would serve to introduce new workers to those jobs and provide job mobility for workers at lower levels.

Thus, the variety of schemes for paid educational leave in Western Europe serves as a provocative set of experiences for U.S. consideration of such policies. The French and Swedish cases provide insights into national financing provisions and costs, and the West German case demonstrates how states might adopt and implement paid educational leave policies. As the Emmerij chapter suggests, such a policy can reduce unemployment and can be funded substantially from the various forms of public assistance and unemployment compensation that are presently used to support the unemployed. By implication, a U.S. policy might incorporate the participation of both states and the federal government, while integrating paid educational leave into overall policies for reducing unemployment and increasing productivity.

NOTE

1. For an earlier attempt at addressing these issues, see Benson and Hodgkinson (1974) and OECD (1975).

REFERENCES

ACSADI, G. T. and G. JOHNSON-ACSADI (1980) "Recent trends and determinants of fertility in developed countries," in A. A. Campbell (ed.) Social, Economic, and Health Aspects of Low Fertility. U.S. Department of Health, Education, and Welfare, Public Health Service, NIH Publication 80-100. Washington, DC: U.S. Government Printing Office.

BENSON, C. and H. L. HODGKINSON (1974) Implementing the Learning Society. San Francisco: Jossey-Bass.

BROWN, C. (1982) "Dead-end jobs and youth unemployment," in R. Freeman and D. Wise (eds.) Youth Unemployment. Chicago: Univ. of Chicago Press.

CAREY, M. L. (1982) "Occupational employment growth through 1990," pp. 34-47 in Economic Projections to 1990. U.S. Department of Labor, Bureau of Labor Statistics Bulletin 2121. Washington, DC: U.S. Government Printing Office.

EMMERIJ, L. (1974) Can the School Build a New Social Order? New York: Elsevier.

FAURE, E. et al. (1973) Learning to Be. Unesco, Paris. Toronto: Ontario Institute for Studies in Education.

FREEMAN, R. B. (1976) The Over-Educated American. New York: Academic Press.

FULLERTON, H. N., Jr. (1982) "The 1995 labor force: a first look," pp. 48-58 in Economic Projections to 1990. U.S. Department of Labor, Bureau of Statistics Bulletin 2121. Washington, DC: U.S. Government Printing Office.

FURSTENBERG, F. (1977) "West German experience with industrial democracy." Annals, 431 (May): 44-53.

ILLICH, I. (1971) Deschooling Society. New York: Harper & Row.

KUHLENKAMP, D. and H. G. SCHÜTZE [eds.] (1982) Kosten und finanzierung der beruflichen und nichtberuflichen Weiterbildung. Frankfurt am Main: Verlag Moritz Diesterweg GmbH & Co.

LEVIN, H. M. (1976) "Educational opportunity and social inequality in Western Europe." Social Problems 24 (December) 2: 148-172.

——— (1978) "Financing higher education and social equity: implications for lifelong learning." Social Rev. 86 (May) 3: 327-347.

MEIDNER, R. and R. ANDERSON (1973) "The overall impact of an active labor market policy in Sweden," in L. Ulman (ed.) Manpower Programs in the Policy Mix. Baltimore: Johns Hopkins Univ. Press.

Ministry of Labor, Sweden (1975) Proposals for an Industrial Democracy Act: A Summary of the Proposals of the Labour Legislation Committee. Vallingby, Sweden: Ministry of Labor.

MIRENGOFF, W. and L. RINDLER (1976) The Comprehensive Employment and Training Act: Impact on People, Places, Programs—An Interim Report. Washington, DC: National Academy of Sciences.

MUSHKIN, S. J. [ed.] (1974) Recurrent Education. U.S. Department of Health, Education, and Welfare, National Institute of Education. Washington, DC: U.S. Government Printing Office.

Organization for Economic Cooperation and Development [OECD] (1975) Recurrent Education: Trends and Issues. Paris: Author.

——— (1973) Recurrent Education: A Strategy for Lifelong Learning. Paris: Author.

PETERSON, R. E. et al. (1979) Lifelong Learning in America. San Francisco: Jossey-Bass.

RUMBERGER, R. W. (1981) Overeducation in the U.S. Labor Market. New York: Praeger.

SCHULLER, T. (1981) "Common discourse? the language of industrial democracy." Econ. and Industrial Democracy 3 (May) 2: 261-291.

TERKEL, S. (1974) Working. New York: Pantheon.

TURNER, R. and R. COUNT (1981) "Education for industrial democracy: an evaluation of the experimental trade union studies project." Econ. and Industrial Democracy 2 (August) 3: 371-394.

U.S. Department of Labor, Bureau of Labor Statistics (1981) Educational Attainment of Workers, March 1979. Special Labor Force Report 240. Washington, DC: U.S. Government Printing Office.

I

COMPREHENSIVE MODELS FOR FINANCING RECURRENT EDUCATION

2

INDIVIDUAL ENTITLEMENTS

HENRY M. LEVIN

Recurrent education is a theme that has come into widespread use throughout the Western industrialized countries. In general, this term refers to the broadening of both the scope and timing of educational and training activities in order to make such opportunities available over the entire lifespan and to encompass a spectrum of endeavors from traditional university instruction and apprenticeships to retraining programs and cultural enrichment (OECD, 1975, 1978; Stalford, 1978; Peterson, 1979). Under more conventional arrangements, education and training are typically limited to that period in one's life prior to entering the labor force and during the first few years of work. Under a program of recurrent education, the timing and nature of educational and training activities would reflect the specific needs of the individual to meet his or her occupational or nonoccupational goals as they arise over the lifecycle. While this definition represents only a general vision of the concept of recurrent education rather than a concrete description, its actual translation into specific forms is currently a subject for policy debate in the United States, Japan, Australia, and most of the countries of Western Europe.

The advantage of the recurrent education approach is its purported ability to meet specific individual needs for training and education as they arise as well as to incorporate a wider range of possible alternatives into the education and training system. Under the present educational and training approaches, the heavy emphasis on youth tends to neglect the periodic retraining, revitalization, and education necessary for the career mobility of adults. These needs are especially likely to be concentrated within the experienced workforce and among mothers who wish to enter or reenter the labor market after raising young children. The purpose of this chapter is to explore the use of a system of individual educational entitlements for financing recurrent education.

SOCIOECONOMIC CONTEXT OF EDUCATION AND TRAINING

Before describing a plan of individual entitlements for financing recurrent education, it is important to establish the terms of reference that will be assumed in the discussion. The most important of these refer to the socioeconomic context of education and training in the Western industrialized countries.

(1) With only a few exceptions, these countries are capitalist societies that are characterized by: (a) relatively few firms dominating most sectors of the economies; (b) distribution of income in which the top 5-10% of income recipients have a greater share of national income than do the poorest 40-50% of the population; (c) relatively low levels of economic growth for the foreseeable future; (d) relatively high levels of unemployment in comparison with the levels of 1945-1970; and (e) increasing pressures for expansion of social services to alleviate inequalities and hardships on the populations created by the "harsh edges" of monopoly capitalism.[1].

Taken together, these conditions suggest initial inequalities among individuals and families associated with the existing economic and social systems, increasing intervention by the states to cushion the inequalities and maintain the conditions of social reproduction, and a diminishing ability to provide the social resources to provide such services because of a falling rate of economic growth.

(2) These inequalities are reflected within the Western industrialized countries in the educational attainments of their populations (Levin, 1976, 1978a). The amount and quality of education received is largely a function of the social class origins, sex, and geographical location of the individual. Youngsters from families of modest income and occupational attainments, females, and persons from rural origins are likely to receive less schooling and schooling of a lower quality than males and persons from higher socioeconomic origins and from urban areas. Further, at the same level of educational attainment, persons from higher socioeconomic backgrounds have access to better jobs, occupational attainments, and incomes. In addition, there is considerable unemployment and underemployment at all educational levels, including that of university completion. The labor markets of these countries have shown an inability to absorb the large increases in recent years of university-educated young adults.

(3) During the compulsory period of schooling at the elementary and secondary levels, almost all schooling will take place in public institu-

tions. While inequalities by social class, sex, and geographic location still persist in these institutions, those inequalities have been diminishing over time. Moreover, there will continue to be substantial increases in the proportion of the young that complete secondary school, and especially those that obtain the qualifications for obtaining admissions to postsecondary educational institutions.

(4) The present system of providing postcompulsory education and training tends to provide the greatest public support for students from the most advantaged families, and the least public subsidies for persons from the least advantaged backgrounds (Levin, 1976, 1978b). This pattern is established by the fact that youngsters from lower-income families are least likely to complete secondary training, and therefore they are less likely to be eligible for postsecondary educational opportunities. Further, the most advantaged students will complete an academic course of study at the secondary level, so they will be eligible to attend the most highly subsidized part of the postsecondary educational system: the university. Students from lower socioeconomic backgrounds will be more likely to take postsecondary training—if they participate at all at that level—in community college, technical institutes, and short-course institutes. Programs associated with these alternatives tend to be of much shorter duration than university degree programs, and they also entail smaller resource requirements and public subsidies. Therefore, the present systems of postsecondary education and training tend to be inegalitarian with respect to their distributional implications.

(5) The present approaches to postsecondary education and training also introduce various distortions into both the educational choices of young people and the economic opportunities that will be afforded them later. First, public subsidies are not provided for all types of postsecondary educational and training experiences, but only certain types of orthodox educational alternatives such as the university and various other institutional training programs. While some countries provide training subsidies as part of their active labor market policies, even these are restricted to selected areas (see Lenhardt, 1978). The high level subsidization for some educational and training alternatives inevitably creates a bias in favor of choosing them in preference to those that are not subsidized.

Second, to the degree that the state assists the young in obtaining economic opportunities by providing such subsidies, it creates a bias towards overinvestment in "human capital" as opposed to physical capital. To a large degree these subsidies tend to stimulate the expansion of the supply of educated labor to corporate and government bureaucracies while reducing the training costs of these entities. Since most of the young who are fortunate enough to obtain postsecondary education and training do not have access to capital for creating self-employment, they must depend on the existing firms for jobs. These firms are able to take advantage of an expanding supply of trained labor with concommitant downward pressure on wages. Thus, indirectly the subsidies for postsecondary education and training represent a subsidy to existing owners of capital by reducing the wage costs of trained workers and by limiting the vast majority of the population to publicly subsidized investments in their training rather than providing assistance in obtaining ownership of capital.

IMPLICATIONS FOR FINANCING RECURRENT EDUCATION

What are some of the implications of this socioeconomic context for financing recurrent education? First, it would seem that *any system of financing recurrent education would necessarily have to be integrated with existing forms of postcompulsory education and training*. That is, it would seem that the design and finance of a system of postcompulsory education would include all education and training beyond the compulsory schooling period. This distinction between compulsory versus voluntary education and training represents the major distinction that characterizes adult recurrent education. That is, following the compulsory schooling period, one can choose the amount, type, and timing of further education and training. Thus, the existing set of postcompulsory opportunities must be integrated into the overall recurrent educational system, since all are voluntary options that are made *after* completion of compulsory schooling. Accordingly, a comprehensive approach to recurrent education must encompass all traditional forms of postsecondary education and training along with any new forms that may emerge.

A second implication is that no approach to recurrent education in and of itself will solve problems of inequalities that emanate from the nature of the economic and social systems of the Western industrialized countries (Levin, 1976, 1978a). The fact that the young will enter the postcompulsory period with different socioeconomic advantages and educational attainments is reason in itself to be wary of claims that adult recurrent education will resolve these inequalities that have not been resolved earlier. However, these inequalities should not be used as a basis for further unequal treatment in favor of advantaged populations. To the contrary, *the organization and financing of national systems of recurrent education ought to be distinctly equalizing in both intent and outcome.* As we will note below, this can be better achieved by providing entitlements with larger potential subsidies for further education and training to those populations that are the least advantaged.

A third implication is that *any system for financing recurrent education should be flexible enough to support a large number of nonorthodox educational and training alternatives as well as to provide a diversity of patterns of utilization.* That is, if only the traditional forms of postsecondary instruction are eligible for support, the ability to create diversity in types of educational training experiences as well as flexibility in their utilization will be seriously compromised. A system of recurrent education should be designed in such a way that various options that are presently unavailable or even beyond our existing imagination might emerge and be compatible with the overall system of finance.

A final implication is that even with future reductions in the number of youth who will be entering labor markets, problems of unemployment and underemployment are likely to continue into the future. *Accordingly, the organization and financing of recurrent education ought to promote increases in employment opportunities as well as the expansion of trained labor.* Vehicles for doing this will be discussed below.

THE NATURE OF INDIVIDUAL ENTITLEMENTS

Given this socioeconomic context and its implications, it is possible to present a plan for financing recurrent education through a plan of postcompulsory entitlements for individuals.[2] An entitlement approach refers to the provision of a guaranteed amount that would be provided by the government for each eligible person to obtain education and training in the postcompulsory education period. The entitlements could be used for a wide variety of educational and training experiences including universities, teacher-training colleges, short-cycle vocational programs, apprenticeships, on-the-job training, retraining programs, and both vocational and nonvocational adult education courses.

Essentially, the plan would work as follows. Each person would become eligible for an entitlement for further training and education at age 16 or the age at which the compulsory schooling period terminates. These entitlements could be used to obtain further education and training in any program that meets the requirements set out by the government for program eligibility. Such programs could be sponsored by governments, nonprofit agencies such as trade unions and religious institutions, or profitseeking institutions. They could include virtually all of the existing postsecondary institutions such as colleges, universities, and training programs, as well as apprenticeship and on-the-job training programs. The exact nature of eligibility would be determined by the goals of the recurrent education approach. Program eligibility to receive and redeem entitlements from students would be based on standards set out by the government such as financial accountability, educational and training content, procedures for handling complaints from participants, and the provision of sufficient and accurate information on programs.

Such entitlements could be composed of both loans and grants. The total amount and composition of the entitlement would depend upon the family resources and other background characteristics of the student. For example, one might expect that the lower the income of the student and his or her family, the larger the entitlement amount and specifically the grant portion would be. In addition, the entitlement might vary according to the student's choice of training or education, with more support being provided for study in those fields that are considered to have a high social priority and unusually high costs.

Perhaps the most important aspect of the entitlement approach is that individuals could use it for any combination of eligible training or education programs up to the maximum amount of the entitlement. Moreover, the entitlement could be drawn upon over a considerable period of time both prior to entering the workforce and during the working period. In fact, it might be reasonable to permit entitlement accounts to accumulate interest as an incentive for the participant to consider carefully the recurrent and continuing education and training possibilities that will exist over the life cycle. Programs would compete for students and their entitlements, and new offerings would arise in response to emerging training needs.

A public information system would be developed that would make entitlement recipients aware of particular education and training programs as well as the opportunities that are available in different occupational fields. This systematic provision of information would also keep potential providers of programs informed about which areas showed high student or trainee demand and which ones were less attractive. Government support of postcompulsory education and training would be vested predominantly in the form of entitlements to individuals rather than of grants to support institutions directly, and these entitlements would create financial support for institutions according to the choices of the student or trainee participants. Moreover, all of the existing sources of public funding would be coordinated into one overall system of financial support to replace the present confounding diversity of funding programs.

To summarize, a system of postcompulsory entitlements would have the following five general properties:

(1) Public support of postsecondary education and training would be channeled to the student in the form of a promissory note or entitlement.

(2) The entitlement would obligate the government to provide a specified amount of grants and loans that could be used for participating in education and training programs that had met eligibility requirements.

(3) The entitlement could be used over the lifetime of the student, and the unused portion would draw interest. The amount of the entitlement and its composition between grants and loans would be determined by the family resources of the student and other pertinent factors.

(4) Any education or training program approved as eligible by the government could accept students with entitlements and redeem these entitlements for cash from the government treasury. Such institutions would probably include most existing colleges, universities, training institutes and training programs of trade unions, government, and industry. New programs would also be eligible to participate by meeting the specified eligiblity requirements.

(5) Governments would sponsor an information and regulatory agency that would provide data for participants on training alternatives and their costs as well as program descriptions and job prospects among different occupations and training specializations. The agency would also set out the specific eligibility regulations to determine both the conditions of student and trainee participation on the one hand, and the requirements that must be satisfied for program eligibility on the other.

Within this framework there are a variety of plans that might be constructed, each responding to different objectives. It is not possible to analyze the consequences of a postcompulsory entitlement approach without discussing the main features that will determine its outcome.

The three major components of a postcompulsory entitlement plan are (1) the finance system, (2) the regulatory system, and (3) the information system.[3] The specific details of these three systems when taken together will determine the operation and outcome of the entitlement approach. The finance system refers to the determination of how much the entitlement will be and how it will vary according to the characteristics of the participants and the options that they choose. The finance component includes determination of how the entitlements will be composed—that is, the particular combination of loans and grants. The details of the loan and grant provisions, the method by which the government will obtain revenues for supporting the entitlement system, and the estimate of the total support requirements for the entitlement plan must also be determined through the finance system.

The regulatory system embraces the rules, regulations, and conditions under which the system will operate. These aspects include the definition of who is eligible to receive an entitlement, the amount of the entitlement as set out by the finance system and the conditions under which the entitlement could be used, the requirements of eligibility to redeem vouchers among providers of educational and training services, and the nature and responsibilities of the regulatory agency as it served to monitor the postcompulsory entitlement approach.

Since an entitlement approach places a heavy emphasis on alternatives and choice, an information system must be constructed to provide useful and accessible information on these choices for both the individual participants and for the institutions and enterprises that wish to offer education and training to entitlement recipients. Examples of information that might be needed by the individual participants include program descriptions, personnel qualifications, curriculum, costs, enrollments, facilities, placement services, experiences of graduates, and the proportions of students completing training. Information for potential providers of services might include the distributions and levels of enrollments by types of education and training, costs, geographical distribution, and changes in the patterns of these indicators from year to year that might reflect trends. Of course, data on occupational trends would be useful also. Finally, the regulatory agency would require data to evaluate the success of the existing provisions, and it would also need an efficient system for disseminating the information to the appropriate clientele.

Obviously the finance, regulatory, and information systems are not strictly independent of each other. For example, the definitions of eligibility for both individual participants and providers of training and educational services will have an important impact on the financial requirements of the entitlement plan. Likewise, the degree of equity that is desired will have implications for both the regulatory mechanism and the finance system in that requirements will be set out with respect to how the entitlement might vary with the financial resources of the family of the recipient. These regulations will affect the method by which entitlements are allotted as well as the distribution and level of financial support for postcompulsory education and training across the population. Thus, while each of the three component systems might be addressed separately for purposes of constructing a postcompulsory entitlement plan, their interdependence should also be recognized.

Before reviewing these three components more specifically with respect to their design and implementation, it is important to consider the potential of the individual entitlement approach for financing recurrent education and meeting the various criteria with respect to comprehensiveness, equity, flexibility, and the promotion of increases in employment that were set out in an earlier section.

COMPREHENSIVENESS

Individual entitlements enable a complete integration of existing forms of postcompulsory education and training as well as emerging ones, since the entitlement is neutral with respect to these alternatives. Under more conventional forms of financing postcompulsory education, educational and training institutions can only be established on the basis of a direct financing commitment from the government. This means that the provision of new opportunities must depend upon the acquisition of government support which creates cumbersome requirements for the initiation of new offerings as well as the loss of many potential training and educational programs that might be offered by private and nonprofit sponsors. In contrast, the entitlement approach enables adults to use their education and training subsidies directly, whether for traditional university education or any other eligible postcompulsory alternative. Indeed, the financing mechanism is neutral with respect to the type of education or training, so that new offerings can be considered on their own merits rather than on whether or not they fit a more traditional system of direct institutional subsidies. Individual entitlements enable a comprehensive approach to financing recurrent education that can not be found in the more "piece-meal" approaches that characterize the present system. And, they can easily encompass future alternatives that are not yet on the drawing board.

EQUITY

While no claim is made that the distribution of income or adult opportunities will become more equal under a plan of individual entitlements or any other system of financing recurrent education, there are strong reasons for believing that the distribution of educational and training opportunities can become more equal.[4] There are three bases for this: (1) By making each person aware of the existence of an entitlement for postcompulsory education and training, it is more likely that he or she will make use of it. Under the present approach, only those persons who are aware of available educational and training opportunities—generally the more advantaged members of society—will seek out those options.[5] (2) It is expected that under a system of postcompulsory entitlements, new education and training choices will arise that will be more accessible and attractive to the less advantaged members of society. That is, there will be an incentive by educational and training agencies to attract the "new clientele" who are not presently participating in postcompulsory education and training, but who will have the entitlements to do so under this new approach. (3) Under a system of postcompulsory entitlements, it is possible to tailor the size of the entitlement and the conditions of its use to favor persons from less advantaged backgrounds. In contrast, the present systems of financing postcompulsory education provide subsidies to institutions according to their educational and training costs rather than according to the socioeconomic backgrounds of their clientele. By providing larger entitlements to persons from lower-income families, such individuals will have a greater incentive to undertake postcompulsory education and training, and will have the ability to undertake a greater amount of such experience.

FLEXIBILITY

The individual entitlement approach maximizes the flexibility of the overall recurrent education approach, since the subsidy can be used for any combination of training and educational opportunities that are selected by the entitlement recipient. The entitlement can be partially utilized before entering the workforce and partially utilized during intermittent periods of training during the individual's career. Or, the individual can apply the entitlement to a university education immediately following his graduation from school. Alternatively, the use of the entitlement can be deferred for several years beyond the time of leaving school, until after the recipient establishes his career. All of these patterns can be accommodated without the need for special arrangements.

Further, the entitlement can be utilized for any combination of accredited educational or training activities. The government need only set out the various eligibility criteria with respect to the organizational requirements and types of education and training that will be eligible to be funded by entitlements. Both the state and private sector can offer education and training experiences, and there will be a strong incentive to meet the requirements and needs of students and trainees in order to attract adequate enrollments. Rather than the government facing the difficult challenge of setting out financing arrangements for large numbers of possible recurrent educational and training activities, the activities can be initiated with the knowledge that if they are attractive they will receive funding from the entitlements of their enrollees.

Finally, there is great flexibility in this funding mechanism, since particular policy goals with respect to equity or special educational needs can also be targeted in an effective manner. For example, larger entitlements can be given to persons from underdeveloped areas or persons who will study in fields of high national priority. As we stated previously, the entitlement can be "pro-poor" in providing more resources to those who have the least ability to finance preparation for their own careers and who lack other advantages that enhance adult opportunities.

INCREASING EMPLOYMENT

The mechanism of individual entitlements can also be used to increase employment for both individuals and groups of workers. The problem of both youth and adult unemployment is a very serious one, and the slow rates of expected economic growth as well as the rapid technological change (e.g., the revolution in minicomputers) may make the existing job situation even more dismal. Postcompulsory investments in education and training operate only on the supply of human skills and capabilities, not on the demand for them. Accordingly, policies for increasing jobs must accompany policies for expanding training and educational opportunities.

At the very least, active labor market policies must be pursued to provide appropriate employment for educated and trained labor, and these policies should be coordinated with any policy of recurrent education.[6] However, the individual entitlement approach has some attractive features for addressing both the retention of existing jobs and the creation of new ones. In at least three ways the entitlements can be used to create jobs for trained labor as an overall part of the recurrent education strategy.

First, many of the industrialized countries are experiencing plant closures by multinational corporations as these firms shift their activities to Third World countries that promise greater profitability because of low wages and state repression of trade unions. In many of these cases the activities that are being transferred are still economically viable, but not as profitable as in countries where the permissable degree of labor exploitation is considerably higher. In such cases, the closure of the firm creates unemployment and great public expense in the form of redundancy or unemployment payments and public assistance.

If the firm can be shown to be viable, the workers can be offered the use of their unemployment pay to purchase it with the assistance of government loans, and their remaining educational and training entitlements can be used to assist them in acquiring the training to undertake the management and operations of the plant. In this way, the state could assist the employees by training them at the employment site to operate their own firm as a producer cooperative or another form of self-managed enterprise. It would seem that entitlements might be part of an effective strategy to retain jobs under the aegis of worker-owned firms in such circumstances.

Second, the entitlements might also be used to create jobs through permitting groups of adults to combine their entitlements to prepare them for starting collective enterprises that might be owned and managed as cooperatives. For example, if a group of persons proposed the creation of a small enterprise to the government, the appropriate government agency might investigate the potential viability of such a firm. If the basic plan seemed sound, the government might lend the group the necessary capital while using the firm's assets as collateral for the loan.[7] But, one of the crucial determinants for successful operation would be the proficiencies of the labor force for operating the business in a viable manner. It is here that postcompulsory educational entitlements can be combined to cover a training program for the workforce. Such training might be provided by the government with funding from the entitlements, and the fact that it would be done collectively rather than individually would enable persons to be trained to work with a unique set of coworkers for the specific requirements of the firm that was being established.

A third area in which postcompulsory educational and training entitlements might be used for job creation would be to set out a policy in which a portion of the entitlement could be used to purchase tools and equipment that are required for self-employment. Many persons who receive training in particular careers lack the access to capital to be self-employed. Examples include the manual crafts such as carpentry, welding, painting, and so one as well as professional ones such as accounting, law, and architecture. Rather, persons with training in these areas must typically seek employment with existing firms.

An alternative arrangement would permit entitlement recipients to acquire education and training and to use the entitlements for those capital investments that are approved by the regulatory agency as being pursuant to their careers. In this way some persons could not only acquire relevant job skills, but they could create jobs for themselves by investing in the physical capital that is necessary for those careers.

The use of entitlements on both an individual and collective basis to provide training and the necessary physical capital could create additional jobs—especially in the service sector where large amounts of capital are not as necessary as they are in production. Such services include mechanics, carpenters, artists, bookkeepers and accountants, landscape architects, maintenance specialists, gardeners, and business consultants among others. While these uses of en entitlement approach would not address all of the employment problems of the industrialized countries, they could be part of a policy mix that combines education and training with a job creation and retention approach.

EVIDENCE ON THE POTENTIAL OF ENTITLEMENTS

Thus far we have asserted that individual entitlements represent a more comprehensive, equitable, and flexible approach to financing recurrent education, and we have suggested that they also have greater potential for combining education and training with job creation. Fortunately, there exists a substantial experience with individual entitlements in the United States, so it is possible to review the validity of some of these claims. Since 1944 the U.S. Government has provided educational benefits to military veterans under the GI Bill.[8] Eligible veterans are provided with monthly payments while they are enrolled in accredited education and training programs. In 1978, a single veteran who was studying on a full-time basis received $311 a month, and veterans with dependents received more. For example, a veteran with two dependents received $422 a month. Benefits could be used for up to 45 months of study. Thus, a single veteran was eligible for a total entitlement of about $14,000, and a married veteran with a child was eligible for an entitlement of about $19,000. An enormous variety of training and educational programs are accredited for GI Bill enrollees; an institution is required to meet educational, legal, financial, and reporting criteria for eligibility.[9]

Since 1944, more than 14 million veterans have received educational benefits under the three GI Bills that have been enacted during the last 35 years. In fiscal year 1976 about $6 billion was paid to veterans in educational benefits. This represented more than half of the expenditure on postsecondary education and training (O'Neill and Ross, 1976: 1). In sum, the GI Bill provides veterans with the equivalent of individual entitlements that can be used for a wide variety of educational and training options in both the public and private sectors. Further, it is a very substantial program with three decades of experience. Accordingly, it is interesting to observe the results of the GI Bill educational entitlements with respect to their comprehensiveness, equity, flexibility, and labor market effectiveness.

The comprehensiveness and flexibility aspects of the GI Bill can be reviewed together because of their obvious overlap. The comprehensiveness is evident in that the entitlements can be received for enrolling in a wide range of approved programs including most colleges and universities, training institutes, on-the-job training programs, correspondence schools, and so on. In the 1977 fiscal year, almost three-quarters of the GI Bill recipients chose to enroll in colleges and universities (Congressional Budget Office, 1978: 6). Of course, a substantial number of these were enrolled in the two-year community colleges in career training programs rather than in four-year academic courses of instruction. About one-tenth were studying in vocational and technical institutes, with almost an equal number engaged in on-the-job and farm training programs. The remainder were involved in correspondence schools, flight instruction, and high school completion. Among all veterans, almost 80% were in public institutions (Congressional Budget Office, 1978: 7).

Since the GI Bill permits veterans to utilize their educational benefits over the ten years following their military service, there is considerable time in which to choose and undertake educational experiences. Of course, even a decade is a limitation, so presumably participation would be higher over a longer permissable period. The use of the educational benefits can apply to part-time or full-time study, and they can also be used for correspondence school courses taken while one is fully employed. The benefits for anything less than full-time study are set at proportionately lower levels than for fulltime enrollees. The overall resut of this comprehensiveness and flexibility is a rather high rate of utilization of educational benefits, with the current estimate that significantly over three-fifths of recent veteran cohorts will use their educational benefits (O'Neill and Ross, 1976: 44). This proportion is considerably higher than the postsecondary participation of nonveterans, which is somewhere between 40-50%. Further, it has been concluded from statistical analysis of enrollments that about one-third of all veteran students would not have undertaken the education and training in the absence of the GI Bill benefits (Congressional Budget Office, 1978: 12-13).

Even more impressive are the equity implications of the enrollment patterns. Although in the general population the amount of postcompulsory enrollment of blacks is considerably lower than for whites, among veterans utilizing the educational benefits of the GI Bill the blacks showed slightly higher rates of participation (O'Neill and Ross, 1976: 53). After adjusting for test scores and prior educational attainments, the participation rate for blacks was found to be some nine percentage points higher than for equivalent whites (O'Neill and Ross, 1976: 58). Thus, the GI Bill entitlements seem to be considerably more effective in providing education and training to at least one major economically disadvantaged group than are the more traditional approaches.

But, of course, one question that might be raised is that of the quality of choices. That is, if the enrollees are simply using their entitlements in frivolous ways, the mere existence of a higher level and more equitable pattern of enrollments is not tantamount to a higher level of and more equitable educational benefits. Among a variety of sophisticated analyses comparing the earnings of veterans who had taken vocational training under the GI Bill and those who had not, it was found that earnings were about 10% higher per year among the GI Bill group.[10] This is about twice as great a gain as that associated with government-sponsored Manpower Development Training Act (MDTA) programs. For black veterans who used their GI Bill benefits, the gains were even greater—a differential of 15% higher earnings over comparable blacks with similar educational attainments and test scores but with no GI Bill training. Similar earnings gains were found for veterans who had used their entitlements for on-the-job training or college enrollments, although no racial comparisons were made.

In summary, extensive experience with the GI Bill has shown that a general system of individual entitlements can be more comprehensive, flexible, and equitable than the more conventional methods for financing postcompulsory education and training, and there is some evidence that it is more effective in imparting skills that are remunerated in labor markets. The fact that blacks participate more fully in postcompulsory education and training and receive relatively larger benefits than whites is also a rather remarkable finding. Indeed, the redistributive effect of the GI Bill entitlements is particularly surprising when one considers that no compensatory entitlements are provided on the basis of family background—blacks, whites, the rich, and the poor all receive the same entitlements. The experience of the GI Bill suggests that individual entitlements represent a forward-looking approach for constructing an overall method for financing recurrent education.

IMPLEMENTING A PLAN OF INDIVIDUAL ENTITLEMENTS

While the general description of a plausible entitlement plan can be described quite readily, the actual details require very careful formulation. At the end of the compulsory education period—for instance, at age 16—individuals would be registered with the national entitlement agency. Based upon the various criteria of eligibility, they would be informed of their "drawing rights" under the entitlement mechanism. Moreover, they would be assigned an identification number that would be used to keep records on their use of the entitlement so that one could ascertain quickly (through computerized access) the amount of entitlement that still remained and other pertinent information. In order to utilize the remaining value of the entitlement, the individual would apply to the entitlement agency to undertake additional study or training from an eligible provider. The agency would provide a draft or voucher that could be redeemed by the provider for cash by submitting it upon receipt to the government treasury.

All of the accounting and records would be maintained by the national entitlement agency, and an annual or periodic report would be issued to each registered individual regarding the drawing rights that where still credited to him. Possibly the unused balances would draw interest in order to compensate individuals who distribute their entitlement over longer periods. And, at retirement age it might be appropriate to refund to the individual any unexpended balance or it would be given to his estate in case of early death. In this way the entitlement recipients would not be pressed to utilize the entitlement in frivolous ways, and the returns to any use would be balanced against simply permitting the value to accumulate with interest until retirement. This would be an especially important provision for establishing equity for persons from less advantaged backgrounds, who historically have been less able and less likely to take advantage of postcompulsory schooling opportunities.[11]

FINANCE

A number of particular questions be resolved to construct the other financing details. These include (1) the source of revenues, (2) the size of entitlements, (3) the manner by which entitlements will vary according to the characteristics of the recipient and training choice, (4) composition of entitlements between grants and loans, and (5) total public support requirements. Each of these will be addressed briefly.

Source of Revenues

There is no single approach to the method of providing government revenues for postcompulsory entitlements. Different countries have different tax systems with respect to the degree that they rely upon value-added or turnover taxes, personal income taxes, excise taxes, and business taxes. But a strong case can be made for obtaining revenues from a broad-based tax rather than a payroll tax. That is, such a program should not be paid for by workers alone, but by all segments of the population.[12]

Unfortunately, much of the recent literature on the particular forms of recurrent education and training such as educational sabbaticals has focused on the use of a payroll tax that would provide a trust fund for such expenditures somewhat similar to the social security programs in the United States.[13] The principle underlying this view seems to be that educational leave and lifelong education are necessary ingredients for everyone—at least everyone in the labor force—and a provision should be made for this by imposing a mandatory tax on employers and employees that would be earmarked for such a function.

However, the use of a payroll tax for such purposes has a number of very serious deficiencies.[14] First, unlike the social insurance concept, the use of the entitlement is voluntary rather than based upon a certain event such as retirement or a contingency such as death or disability. Those persons who did not utilize their entitlements would nevertheless pay for them, and the historical record suggests that the least advantaged workers would be the least likely to utilize fully their entitlements (Rosenthal, 1976; Levin, 1976, 1978b; Cross, 1978; Harnqvist, 1978). Thus, a payroll tax on all workers would imply a subsidy of those who did use fully their entitlements by those that did not, a redistribution of wealth in favor of the more advantaged (unless unused entitlements were permitted to accumulate interest and revert to the worker at retirement or to his estate in case of premature death).

Moreover, payroll tax tends to be regressive. In fact, it has been found to be the most regressive major tax in the U.S. tax system (Pechman and Okner, 1974: 59). Since it is a tax on labor earnings rather than on sources of unearned income such as rents, dividends, profits, and interest), the very sources of income that characterize the rich are untouched while the working poor and middle classes are forced to support the entitlement system. That is, the one-third or so of national income that is derived from capital and that is concentrated among the wealthiest families in all societies would not contribute to the postcompulsory education and training system. If the tax is levied in a fashion similar to the present social security tax in the United States, it would apply as a constant tax rate up to a maximum level of earnings, and earnings beyond the maximum level would not be taxed. This too means that a higher proportion of a poor person's income will be taxed. Indeed, it was estimated for 1966 that the U.S.

payroll tax represented about twice as high a proportion of annual incomes for recipients under $15,000 as it did for those with incomes in the $30,000-50,000 range (Pechman and Okner, 1974: 59). Thus, the use of a payroll tax to support postcompulsory entitlements should be examined with great circumspection.

Size of Entitlements

The following factors would seem to be important in setting the size of the basic entitlements: the costs that the government presently incurs in subsidizing students in public institutions of higher education and public-supported training programs; the total direct cost of the various postcompulsory education and training programs; and the foregone earnings or the costs of maintenance for the normal living expenses of a student. The importance of the present government subsidy is that it gives a guideline for the level of support to postcompulsory education that the government has already shown a willingness to provide. The total cost of various types of training might be instructive for modifications of this amount. Finally, it is important to consider the other costs of obtaining postsecondary education and training that are reflected in the lost earnings of students or the costs of maintaining the student during his or her periods of study in order to ascertain whether these should be subsidized.

For example, the average subsidy per student in four-year public institutions in states such as California is about $2,500-3,000, suggesting that the state is willing to pay about $10,000-12,000 for the four-year course of studying leading to the B.A. degree. Of course, the state and federal governments provide other types of support for particularly needy or exceptional students as well as for those eligible to receive benefits under the programs for military veterans and social security. As a first approximation, it might be useful to think of this $10,000-12,000 as the basic entitlement that would be made available to all students, not just those who complete a four-year program at a public college or university.

But even this amount would not be adequate to cover the indirect costs of study reflected in foregone earnings and living expenses of students and trainees. Accordingly, it may be necessary to consider possible additions to the entitlements under some circumstances as well as the provision of loan programs for expenses beyond the entitlement. The composition of such loans and grants might vary according to the social-class background of the eligible individual and other factors.

Characteristics that Might Alter Basic Entitlements

While the setting of the basic entitlement is necessary for establishing a general baseline for the entitlement program, it is useful to consider the circumstances under which the entitlement might be varied because of the particular characteristics or educational choices of the recipient. For middle- and upper-income families an entitlement of $12,000 might be quite adequate for enabling their offspring to undertake postsecondary education and training. While $12,000 might not be enough to pay all of the direct costs and the living costs of the postcompulsory endeavor, such families have additional resources to provide such payments. Thus, a combination of family resources, students earnings from part-time summer employment, and loans could be used to supplement the entitlement.

But, persons from lower-income backgrounds are not in such an enviable position. Their families are less likely to provide either the additional direct costs of postsecondary education such as the balance of tuition or expenses for books and materials that might not be covered by entitlements. They are also less able to provide the living expenses and to forego the earnings that would be obtained from work. Finally, even their access to part-time work might be compromised relative to their more-advantaged counterparts because they lack the connections and information that often secure such jobs for middle and upper class youngsters.

Accordingly, it would seem that to obtain high levels of participation in postsecondary education and training among low-income populations it will be necessary to provide entitlements that would cover other educational expenses as well as the costs of maintaining the trainee or student. One important aspect of the finance system would be to design the entitlements to take account of differences in family backgrounds and resources.

A second situation in which entitlements might vary would be in the case of training programs that are of unusually long duration but have great social benefit. In those instances the amount of the entitlement might be increased to account for the relatively long training period and to encourage persons to enter those professions. Of course, this type of problem might also be solved by a liberal policy of loans that could be repaid from the future earnings of the recipients. Certainly, additional subsidies for the training of physicians will not in themselves expand the number of physicians who are trained, and such graduates can easily pay their loans out of the extraordinarily high incomes they receive during their professional lives (at least in countries like the United States and West Germany). Thus the adjustment of entitlements for long program duration and high program costs should be justified on the basis of associated social benefits; there should not simply be allocation of a larger entitlement for more expensive training.

Also, an entitlement might be increased in exceptionally meritorious cases in which it could be argued that the development of extremely scarce talent required the additional investment. For example, persons of exceedingly high scholarly, artistic, mechanical, or scientific merit might be chosen to receive highly specialized training beyond that which might be available for the average person. Again, the social benefits of developing such talent represent the basis for larger, special entitlements for talent that could be identified by some reasonable set of procedures. The social benefits of such a policy would be in the potential cultural, scientific, and technical discoveries, as well as in potential contributions to the artistic, cultural, and material well-being of the society.

Composition of Entitlements Between Loans and Grants

A very important issue that has arisen more generally in the debate over postcompulsory educational and training finance is the justification for providing loans rather than grants. According to some analysts the primary benefits from postsecondary investments are those received by the individual in the form of higher earnings. Accordingly, they recommend that assistance for such education and training take the form of income-contingent loans to be repaid out of the higher earnings received by those with the additional training.[15] An alternative argument is that the benefits of such educational and training endeavors are shared between society and the individual and some basis is supplied for providing a subsidy for postsecondary educational and training endeavors. These benefits include those of equalizing access to educational opportunities. Even in this case it is not argued that society should bear all of the costs of postcompulsory education, but only the portion that reflects the social benefits.

But, the territory between the social provision of complete grants for all postcompulsory training and education and that of just loans is vast, including all types of combinations of loan and grant plans. Thus, it is important to reflect on the composition of entitlements between loans and grants. We suggested at the outset of the entitlement design that one possibility would be to provide a $10,000-12,000 entitlement for everyone with some increase in entitlement for selected populations that are considered to be disadvantaged with respect to postsecondary education and training opportunities. We also suggested that a system of loans should be provided for persons who need more than the $10,000-12,000 or some other set amount.

But, there exist a number of other possibilities for combining grants and loans into "dual entitlements." For example, it may be more useful to think of every person as being eligible for a specified sum of grants and loans depending upon family background. In such an instance the person from a very wealthy background would only be eligible for a "loan" entitlement to be repaid out of his future income. The person from the most disadvantaged families would be eligible for a "grant" entitlement that would cover both the direct costs of education as well as living costs. Between these two extremes the plan would provide various combinations of loans and grants so that the person who came from the middle of the social-class distribution received the $10,000-12,000 grant entitlement and was also eligible for loans. An individual somewhat higher on the social-class scale would receive $8,000 in grants and loan eligibility.

Such an approach would have a number of advantages over the flat entitlement grant. First, individuals who came from families that had ample resources to pay for their postcompulsory training and educational experiences would not receive as large a subsidy as those from families who lacked such resources. Yet, even if the children in such families wished to establish independent status they would be eligible for loans so that they would not have to depend on their families' largesse. Since the loans would be repaid out of their future income and they would be likely to share in the financial resources of their families eventually, such an arrangement would provide flexibility, independence, and still a modicum of equity. Second, individuals from middle-income backgrounds would receive a dual entitlement of grants and loans that would provide an appropriate subsidy while accounting for their family resources. Again, a substantial amount of flexibility would be afforded the student and his family in choosing how much of the expense beyond the entitlement grant would be funded from savings and family contributions, part-time or full-time earnings during postcompulsory programs, and loans that would be repaid from future earnings.

Total Public Support Requirement

A final related issue on financing an entitlement plan is what it will cost government. The answer to this query depends on several factors: the size of entitlements and patterns of participation; the specific construction of the plan between loans and grants; and the degree to which public subsidies under existing grant programs to postcompulsory institutions, training programs, and individuals would be combined to underwrite an entitlement approach. The complicated nature of this problem is reflected by the fact that most direct support for postcompulsory education is provided to particular institutions with another portion going to students and trainees in the form of scholarships, fellowships, and maintenance grants or loans. These would have to be combined under an entitlement approach, and institutions would be required to obtain their support directly from student entitlements rather than from the government budgets.

Of course, it might be possible to provide direct support for institutions such as universities so that tenure obligations and budgetary planning could continue on the same basis as before while simply charging the student entitlement accounts for those persons attending the university. If student enrollments shrink below those that are adequate to provide entitlement support for university budgets, the government might require a long-run reduction of university resources for meeting student needs. However, this process would certainly cushion the short-run fluctuations that might disrupt the university planning processes if they were to depend for their income exclusively on the entitlements that they were able to obtain from one enrollment period to the next. Another alternative would be to require universities to obtain their support directly from the entitlements while permitting a substantial financial reserve to cushion short-run fluctuations from period to period.

For planning purposes it would be possible to estimate the approximate public expense for postcompulsory entitlements on the basis of a concrete determination of eligibility requirements for participants, size of entitlements, and fields in which entitlements could be used. This would be done by first ascertaining the number of eligible recipients and calculating the total amount of entitlements that they would receive in the forms of grants and loans. Next, we would need to assess the probable behavior of different subgroups with respect to the amount of their entitlement that they would utilize and the time pattern of utilization. This would yield an estimate of total annual entitlement costs for a particular cohort. For the United States, some data might be derived on these matters from the experience under the GI Bill.

REGULATION OF THE ENTITLEMENT SYSTEM

In addition to the financial arrangements for constructing a system of postcompulsory entitlements, it would be necessary to establish a regulatory system. In this section we review briefly the nature of this regulatory system and the types of decisions that must be made with respect to setting out regulations. A national entitlement agency would need to be established to administer the entitlements. This agency would have at least six major functions:

(1) The agency would process applications for entitlements, establishing the eligibility of the individual according to the law.

(2) The level and composition of each entitlement would have to be determined for each applicant on the basis of the appropriate criteria.

(3) Continuous and accurate records on the utilization of the entitlement and unexpended portions would be maintained for each individual.

(4) An information system would be designed and operated by the agency, and dissemination of accurate information to both individuals and institutions on educational and training alternatives would be provided.

(5) The regulatory agency would enforce eligibility standards for participating institutions and programs through initial screening of providers followed by periodic audits and reviews of complaints or violations.

(6) An adjudicatory mechanism would be maintained by the regulatory agency for settling disputes that might arise between program sponsors and enrollees.

In addition to establishing a regulatory agency to administer the entitlements for recurrent education, a number of laws and regulations would have to be created for the operation of the entitlement system. Among these are the following:

(1) Who is eligible to receive an entitlement?

(2) What are the characteristics that determine the size of the entitlement?

(3) What types of education and training experiences or other types of investments can the entitlement be used for?

(4) What are the eligibility requirements for accrediting educational and training institutions to receive entitlements?

(5) What kinds of information would the regulatory agency collect for purposes of dissemination on the characteristics and performance of the accredited educational and training institution?

The criteria for answering these questions and constructing an entitlement plan are reviewed at some length in a more extensive discussion on the subject (Levin, 1977b) so they will not be discussed in this chapter. However, the answers to these questions will depend clearly on national policy toward recurrent education as well as on other factors that are unique to each country.

SUMMARY

The whole notion of recurrent education is one that is characterized by diversity. Both the types of educational experiences and their timing over the lifespan would deviate from the predictable conventions of existing educational and training sytems. The very notion of recurrent education suggests that it cannot be codified easily according to existing educational and training institutions, experiences, or certificates. Rather, the offerings under such an approach are likely to evolve in directions that cannot be readily projected at the moment.

The individual entitlement approach represents a device for financing recurrent education that is perfectly compatible with both the diversity and uncertainty of future developments in this direction. Rather than proposing specific financing approaches for each type of recurrent education, individual entitlements enable a systematic solution to the financing issue. Further, we have asserted that the individual entitlement mechanism can provide a financing scheme that is more comprehensive, flexible, and equitable than present government educational and training programs. Finally, it offers greater possibilities for effectively integrating policies for job creation and retention with those for education and training.

One question that has not been addressed is the cost of individual entitlements in the aggregate. Obviously, it is impossible to provide any estimate of costs without a clear specification of a particular entitlement plan and the designation of a specific country. However, given some rudimentary notion of the particular arrangements for any society, it would be possible to provide an approximate picture of the costs. Of course, it should be borne in mind that not all of the costs associated with entitlements would be added ones. A very high proportion of them would be covered by funds that are already obligated for existing educational and training commitments since the proposed entitlements would largely replace the present system of postcompulsory education.

NOTES

1. Data on the income distributions are found in Jain, 1975. Economic growth prospects are summarized in the various issues of *Economic Outlook* issued regularly by OECD.

2. This presentation on individual entitlements builds on a number of previous papers written on the subject. See particularly Levin, 1977a and 1977b, and Kurland, 1977.

3. The detailed presentation and analysis of these three components are found in Levin, 1977b.

4. The distinction between the distribution of educational opportunites and outcomes, and adult opportunities and outcomes with respect to occupational attainments and income are addressed in Levin, 1978b.

5. In 1975 only about one-fifth of adult learners in the United States had not participated in education at the college level. That is, about four-fifths had undertaken at least some college training, and almost 60% had at least one college degree. See Cross, 1978: 9.

6. See the survey of these policies in Haveman and Christainsen, 1978, and Palmer, 1978. The origins of an active labor market policy are generally credited to G. Rehn. See Rehn and Lundberg, 1963, and Meidner and Anderson, 1973.

7. Government policies to promote employee ownership are discussed within a much wider framework in Meidner, 1978.

8. For recent evaluations and analyses of the GI Bill see Congressional Budget Office, 1978; O'Neill, 1977; and O'Neill and Ross, 1976.

9. These provisions are described in O'Neill and Ross, 1976: Appendix A.

10. All of the findings on earnings are in O'Neill and Ross, 1976: chap. 2.

11. See Harnqvist, 1978; Rosenthal, 1977; and Cross, 1978 for evidence on this contention, as well as Levin, 1976 and 1978b.

12. It may appear that because most payroll taxes require a mandatory contribution by the employer, that it is employers who are bearing at least that portion of the tax. However, it is generally agreed that in the long run such "employer" contributions are shifted to employees in the form of lower wages and salaries than would otherwise be received. See Brittain 1972: 60-81.

13. Suggestions in this direction are found in Kurland, 1974; Striner, 1972; U.S. Department of HEW, 1973: 126-134; and are reflected in actuality in the French Law of 1971 on educational leave for workers. See Levine, 1974.

14. See the useful discussion by Emmerij, 1979, especially with reference to the Dutch case regarding the use of social security funding.

15. A comprehensive treatment of student loan plans is Hartman, 1971.

REFERENCES

BRITTAIN, J. (1972) The Payroll Tax for Social Security. Washington, DC: Brookings Institution.

Congressional Budget Office (1978) Veterans' Educational Benefits: Issues Concerning the GI Bill. Washington, DC: U.S. Government Printing Office.

CROSS, K. P. (1978) "A critical review of state and national studies of the needs and interests of adult learners," pp. 7-19 in C. Stalford (ed.) Adult Learning Needs and the Demand for Lifelong Learning. Washington, DC: National Institute of Education.

EMMERIJ, L. (1979) "Paid educational leave with particular emphasis on its financial aspects." Prepared for the Project on Financing Recurrent Education, OECD, Paris.

HARNQVIST, K. (1978) Individual Demand for Education. Paris: OECD.

HARTMAN, R. W. (1971) Credit for College. New York: McGraw-Hill.

HAVEMAN, R. and G. CHRISTAINSEN (1978) "Public employment and wage subsidies in Western Europe and the U.S.: what we're doing and what we know." Discussion Paper 522-78, Institute for Research on Poverty, University of Wisconsin.

JAIN, S. (1975) Size Distribution of Income. Washington, DC: The World Bank.

KURLAND, N. [ed.] (1977) Entitlement Studies, NIE Papers in Education and Work 4. Washington, DC: National Institute of Education.

——— (1974) "Financing lifelong learning: proposal for an age-neutral educational entitlement program." New York State Educational Department, Albany. (mimeo)

LENHARDT, G. (1978) "Problems in reforming recurrent education for workers." Comparative Education Review 22 (October) 3: 452-463.

LEVIN, H. M. (1978a) "The dilemma of comprehensive secondary school reforms in Western Europe." Comparative Education Rev. 22 (October) 3: 434-451.

——— (1978b) "Financing higher education and social equity: implications for lifelong learning." School Rev. 86 (May) 3: 327-347.

——— (1977a) "Financing recurrent education with postcompulsory entitlements." Prepared for the meeting on Recurrent Education of the OECD, March 28-30. (To be published by OECD.)

——— (1977b) "Postsecondary entitlements: an exploration," chap. 1 in N. Kurland (ed.) Entitlement Studies, NIE Papers in Education and Work 4. Washington, DC: National Institute of Education.

——— (1976) "Educational opportunity and social inequality in Western Europe." Social Problems 24 (December) 2: 148-172.

LEVINE, H. A. (1974) "Strategies for the application of foreign legislation on paid educational leave to the United States." Prepared for the Career Education Program, National Institute of Education, NIE-C-74-0107.

MEIDNER, R. (1978) Employee Investment Funds. London: George Allen and Unwin.

——— and R. ANDERSON (1973) "The overall impact of an active labor market policy in Sweden," in L. Ulman (ed.) Manpower Programs in the Policy Mix. Baltimore: Johns Hopkins Univ. Press.

OECD, Centre for Educational Research and Innovation (1978) Alternation Between Work and Education. Paris: OECD.

——— (1975) Recurrent Education: Trends and Issues. Paris: OECD.

O'NEILL, D. M. (1977) "Voucher funding of training programs: evidence from the GI Bill." J. of Human Resources 12 (Fall) 4: 425-445.

——— and S. ROSS (1976) Voucher Funding of Training: A Study of the GI Bill, PRI 312-76. Arlington, VA: Public Research Institute.

PALMER, J. L. (1978) Creating Jobs. Washington, DC: Brookings Institution.

PECHMAN, J. A. and B. A. OKNER (1974) Who Bears the Tax Burden? Washington, DC: Brookings Institution.

PETERSON, R. E et al. (1979) Lifelong Learning in America. San Francisco, CA: Jossey-Bass.

REHN, G. and E. LUNDBERG (1963) "Employment and welfare: some Swedish issues." Industrial Relations 2 (February): 1-4.

ROSENTHAL, E. L. (1977) "Lifelong learning—for some of the people." Change (August): 44-45.

STALFORD, C. B. [ed.] (1978) Conference Report: Adult Learning Needs and the Demand for Lifelong Learning. Washington, DC: National Insititute of Education.

STRINER, H. E. (1972) Continuing Education as a National Capital Investment. Kalamazoo, MI: W.E. Upjohn Institute for Employment Research.

U.S. Department of Health, Education, and Welfare (1973) Work in America. Cambridge, MA: MIT Press.

U.S. Federal Trade Commission (1976) Proprietary Vocational and Home Study Schools. Bureau of Consumer Protection. Washington, DC: Government Printing Office.

3

INDIVIDUAL DRAWING RIGHTS

GÖSTA REHN

AIMING AT FREE CHOICE

This chapter is a plea for establishing a deliberate policy to promote diversification and flexibility in the regulation and allocation of time for work, study, and leisure (including retirement) allowing for the greatest possible freedom of individual choice (Rehn, 1974, 1977). While the arguments presented here range beyond recurrent education as such, an attempt is made to provide an important example of the application of such a system.

First, some of the general reasons why greater flexibility in working life is desirable in industrialized countries will be discussed. The basic starting point will be the value judgment that the desirability of individual freedom is indisputable in allocating one's time for different uses during a lifetime as well as during each year, week, or day. Second, the main features of a system of drawing rights will be presented—in essence, the right to utilize one's assets in a broadened social insurance system for income maintenance during nonwork periods with a greater degree of self-determination than traditionally is the case. A number of trends already observable in industrialized countries will be set forth that support the feasibility and desirability of such a scheme.

As a technical and administrative apparatus, the drawing rights model could be applied to achieve very different ends or meet a diverse set of priorities—for example, to influence the income distribution toward or away from equality. Because of the general nature of this system, its precise form and features must remain somewhat an open question, but in this chapter I express my personal inclinations towards specific goals and ensuing specifications.

In the last section of the chapter, more specific questions relating to recurrent education will be taken up and issues involved in furthering of adult studies by a drawing rights system will be discussed.

THE NEED FOR GREATER FLEXIBILITY

We have already stated the judgment that it is desirable for individuals to have greater flexibility throughout their lifetime as well as on an annual or weekly basis in allocating their working time. In reference to national or societal effects, we should also consider how a policy for influencing the allocation of time for work and nonwork could be integrated into labor market policies—policies for matching labor supply and demand, alleviating the unemployment-inflation dilemma, and promoting labor productivity. Freedom of choice in allocating periods of work, study, and leisure throughout the course of a lifetime presupposes the availability of a greater variety of work-time patterns and an apparatus for the transfer of liquidity (under risk-sharing insurance) between periods of directly productive work and other periods in each individual's life.

In an increasingly diversified and affluent society it is more effective to promote socially desirable behavior by economic incentives rather than by standardized rules. The question of economic incentives versus standardized rules straddles both individual and national perspectives. We will suggest a principle of individual self-determination combined with the offering of economic incentives designed to stimulate those who are willing and able to undertake adjustments in the labor market voluntarily (under partial utilization of their rights in the general insurance system) instead of making "social cases" of those who are most vulnerable to unemployment and least adaptable for new jobs by laying most of the burden of adjustment on the weaker groups.

A good deal of what we pay into the social insurance system is in reality a transfer of income between different parts of our own lives. These funds should therefore be regarded to a great extent as the individual's own property, the use of which could be substantially liberated from bureaucratic supervision. Instead, their use should be influenced by incentives that one may accept or reject according to one's own preferences. Furthermore, these funds can be used to rectify a number of inequities in some existing income transfer schemes for education and related purposes. The financing of university studies is a good example of such inequity: Everybody, including those in the lower-income brackets, has to pay taxes to provide advantages for the benefit of young people who can attend universities in order to enter the higher-income brackets. The suggested system of general income insurance and drawing rights would imply that those who were on the paying side in their young years would have at least some part of their payment as an account for use later in life for purposes of their own choice. Equity considerations can thus be included among the reasons for moving in the direction advocated here.

At the national level, there is a need for more rational policymaking that takes alternative allocations of working time into account. Decisions to reduce working time by lowering retirement age, prolonging vacations, lengthening young people's education, or shortening the work week have usually been evaluated separately; there has been little consideration of the extent to which the selection of one alternative inhibits the use of others, or of the actual preferences of particular groups or of the population as a whole. That is, there has been little explicit consideration of whether one sort of progress is preferred or quantifiably more valuable than the others.

Enhanced rationality would occur in two ways. First a new policy would streamline and coordinate what are, at present, quite separate funds and arrangements. Second, it should be possible to integrate its use into labor market policies. It ought to be possible to encourage workers' voluntary alternating between work and nonwork in such a way that the resulting changes in labor supply coincide with variations in the demand for labor. Periods of threatening unemployment could be changed into agreeable leisure or useful study. Clearly this has many implications for recurrent education and its economics. If abstention from directly productive work can ultimately improve one's future efficiency, the cost is obviously relatively low; if a period of destructive unemployment can be turned into one of agreeable or useful nonwork (leisure or training), the cost may even be converted into positive economic gain in addition to the social advantages involved.

The reforms envisaged here should also counteract the trend towards the limitation of individual freedom which is currently making itself felt in various ways in some countries (e.g., in the guise of guarantees of employment security and other incentives to work-force stabilization within the enterprise). As these protective rules reduce individual freedom by making a withdrawal from one's work place costly and risky (due to the ensuing loss of advantages built on length of service or enterprise-specific training), the need increases for counter-balancing arrangements that are designed to promote freedom without such loss. Inversely, the introduction of the latter types of security should reduce the need and demand for more rigid and counter-productive forms of protection that may function in some parts of the economy but not in all.

We should therefore promote this "security by wings" as opposed to "security under shells" to counteract the tendency towards a polarization of the labor force between those who can enjoy security and good incomes on condition that they stay where they once happened to settle, and those who are formally free from any ties but have to live in poverty and insecurity with only intermittent and marginal employment.

THE DRAWING RIGHTS SYSTEM: WHAT IT WOULD LOOK LIKE

What is therefore being recommended is a single comprehensive system for financing all periods of voluntary or age-determined nonwork that would replace the present systems for financing youth education, adult studies, vacations, old age retirement, and other leisure periods that need income maintenance (such as sabbaticals, long service leave and temporary retirement). Here every citizen would have his personal account (as already provided for in any retirement pension insurance system), registering year by year how much he or she is to be credited as contributions to the funds or streams of money going to those purposes. These contributions, however they may be gathered, would be counted as "points" with a constant value (i.e. indexed for inflation) which would represent the basis for the individual's right to receive benefits. The enjoyment of these benefits is now subject to strict rules such as age of retirement, level of pension, and number of vacation days to be taken every calendar year, with administratively determined conditions for receipt for subsistence money during studies. A certain part of the credits gathered under the consolidated system should be open to self-determination: a right to draw money on one's account at any time and for any purpose of one's own choosing. Obviously, this implies that money used for one purpose during one period will reduce the money that is available for another purpose or during another period.

The crediting of points may (as one possible alternative) function as do payroll taxes under present systems with due consideration of any change in the size of the benefits to be enjoyed. Self-employed persons would have to pay a similar proportion of their income according to their tax assessments.

It may be expected that the amount of normally enjoyed nonwork time will be further increased in the coming decades through laws or collective agreements regarding shorter working hours, prolonged vacations, increased access to education, lower age of retirement, and so on. It is mainly this increase in time for nonwork that could be presented as additionally accessible through income maintenance in the form of drawing rights for free use by the individual, but even part of current nonwork and income maintenance could be given this freer form.

The reduction of normal full-time work in a lifetime from the present average of about 80,000 hours to 70,000 hours in the space of one or two decades would imply a relative reduction of concomitant income. This would be counterbalanced by increased efficiency that could stem from reduced work fatigue and from improved skills conferred by more education, by the decline in unemployment that may be achieved through the reduction of working time if properly managed (see below), and by the increase in the activity rate induced by providing people who would otherwise be kept out of the labor market with greater access to part-time jobs and other flexible work opportunities. In any case, with the normal expected increases in incomes and salaries, we are actually considering a limited reduction in the rate of increase of income (in its distorted definition that fails to count voluntary leisure as part of the national or personal income).

The general and compulsory membership of all citizens in this financing system implies a guarantee that each individual will pay a certain amount to the general income insurance fund. This, in turn, makes one automatically credit worthy in relation to the system: He or she can be given the right to draw on his or her account even if in the beginning this implies an overdraft—something that is necessary in financing the studies of young people. The total amount of money to be made available to a person during a normal lifetime may be assumed to be equivalent to his or her contributions, with due actuarial allowance for risk-sharing and time-discounting. It would also be possible to use the system as an element of income redistribution. However, the drawing rights cannot be unlimited: The individual should not be able to empty his or her account to such an extent that nothing is left for old age pension, thus a considerable amount must be kept sacrosanct.

The introduction of such a general, integrated scheme would of course not mean that existing forms of insurance or income support would disappear. Disablement, sickness, and accident insurance would still function largely as at present. And individuals would always be free to keep to the ordinary unemployment insurance if they lost their job and did not wish to use up any part of their drawing rights in these circumstances.

Social and economic reasons have been emphasized for moving towards a general drawing rights sytem. It also needs to be noted that it would rationalize the jungle of existing forms of social insurance and reallocation of money between different parts of the individual's life. To keep track of one's rights to pensions, vacations, adult training, unemployment insurance benefits, redundancy payments, and so on is difficult, if not impossible, scattered as these are among the many different bookkeeping institutions. Therefore, while such rationalization would certainly assist one in using one's rights to study and leisure more freely and interchangeably, it would also be desirable in its own right.

The positive use of a flexible drawing rights system in labor market policies has been indicated in general already, but the possible uses of economic incentives to these ends still needs to be spelled out in a little more detail. Labor market authorities would be authorized to make an offer to workers in branches or areas with slackening demand for labor: Those in such branches who use their rights for recurrent education, their accumulated rights for intermittent long vacations, or for early, temporary, or partial retirement would not need to cover more than a part of their income maintenance during voluntary absence from work through drawing on their accounts because such voluntary absence would reduce the charge or the unemployment insurance system or other expenditure for helping the unemployed.

It must be expected that a number of workers in all categories would use these opportunities for leisure purposes, to study, or to train for jobs with a better future at less than normal cost. The system could be used equally to encourage temporary reductions of weekly working hours by providing income maintenance for the hours not worked and to stimulate use of those hours for vocational or theoretical studies through financial incentives. It could also be useful in situations of sectoral employment expansion by offering special stimuli to those who use their rights to train for occupations in growing demand to those on prolonged leave from one job who thus could be helped and encouraged to look for another job with better prospects in another geographical area. Determining the size of the financial incentives (i.e., the supplements to the drawing rights) needed to achieve the intended effects would have to be a matter for experimentation and experience.

FACTORS LEADING TO MORE FLEXIBILITY

In industrialized countries a number of trends can be noted that suggest that the demand for flexibility is growing and that the reduction of overall work time (which is assumed to be necessary in fully implementing these ideas) is already partially achieved.[1] While not all countries have shared equally in all trends and one can never be absolutely certain of the future, the trends lend support to the feasibility—apart from the desirability—of the arguments outlined above.

First, one can note certain trends in the duration of work time and out-of-work time. The progressive reduction of total hours worked in an average lifetime can be expected to continue along with an increase in the level of real income per hour. This will lead to greater variation and flexibility. Increases in the use of prolonged annual vacations lead one to question the principle that one's whole allotted vacation has to be used before a certain date (such as the end of the year). The reduction of weekly working hours increases the possibilities for deviations from "normal" patterns of work (such as flex-time and staggered schedules). As the age of retirement generally has been lowered and retirement pension provisions have been improved, arrangements around retirement age have become more flexible: There are now provisions for early or partial retirement, reduced work load through part-time work, and, conversely, the continuation of some form of work beyond the usual retirement age.

Two other factors can be mentioned in this context. One is the intergenerational inequality in educational experiences that resulted from the general postwar expansion of educational systems. This has been one of the principal factors behind the emerging demand for recurrent education. For this reason (and because there are those who may not wish to take up adult studies but who want some other form of advantage), the demand for greater interchangeability and flexibility will be all the more prominent. A second and different kind of factor is the increasing diversification of the economy and the increasing internationalization of production and trade. These changes frequently call for large-scale readjustments of the industrial structure and terms of the labor market which will be difficult to manage with just the traditional instruments of labor market policy.

FURTHER ASPECTS OF FINANCIAL EQUITY

In discussing any system of financing income maintenance, two aspects need to be distinguished. On the one hand, there is the question of how the money or revenue is to be raised in the form of social charges and other sorts of taxes. On the other hand, one must consider how the funds should be distributed to individuals and how these persons should be able to use their money for specific purposes (e.g., for recurrent education or for income maintenance in retirement).

With regard to the raising of revenues, in the field of recurrent education and training as well as other fields, there is a wide variety of schemes—both existing and suggested. They are intended to distribute the financial burden in precise ways between individuals and groups according to various notions of justice and equity. Moreover, these issues have been the source of considerable controversy in some countries. On closer examination, however, it becomes clear that there are only very limited possibilities to find out who *really* pays, no matter which system is in place.

An insurance fee or an indirect tax, formally paid by employers as a percentage of the wage bill or the sales volume, can be assumed to be borne largely by consumers through higher prices or by workers whose wages and salaries would be lower than what they otherwise would have been. Direct taxes that are levied progressively on income may have influenced these salaries upwards in a way that in turn affects the prices paid by consumers. Thus all tax systems that are based upon the registration of a money flow that is received by individuals from employers or other sources contain a large element of uncertainty and arbitrariness.

In order to keep the introductory presentation simple, the principle for raising revenues for the general income insurance and drawing rights system was assumed above to be a traditional payroll tax. We stress here, therefore, that it must be an open question what actually should be regarded and registered as the source of each individual's contributions—a part of income taxes, of payroll taxes, or a certain percentage of one's registered income, assumed to be paid via prices of consumer goods irrespective of the structure of the tax system. This structure should (under rational decision making) be formed in a way that promotes its equity and effectiveness regardless of what part of public revenues are formally earmarked as contributions by individuals to the general income insurance system.

When it then comes to the other side—the distribution of benefit rights to individuals—these rights may or may not be made equivalent to the (fictionally) calculated contributions. As in all social insurance systems, one can introduce modifications to that principle that can lead to greater or less equality or can stimulate desirable behavior by means of incentives. The main point is that everyone should constantly be able to see how he or she stands in relation to the system; that is, how great are the rights one has accumulated, what the consequences will be of using a certain amount immediately, and what temporary or permanent advantages society is offering in order to induce a desirable utilization of the drawing rights (e.g., extra advantages for sabbaticals during a slack period or for retraining towards jobs in growing demand).

One may perhaps ask why an individual should be compelled to pay taxes to a central fund and then give that person considerable freedom in its use? Why not let people save voluntarily for the various purposes of their choice? One reason is the general experience that adherence to private and voluntary insurance schemes is lowest and most difficult among those who need them the most for both themselves and their families. With compulsory membership and accounts supplemented by incentives, everyone can benefit roughly in proportion to what they are supposed to have contributed, with the additional possibility of modifications to favor the least privileged. It may also be true that having to abide by the same rules as everyone else can make the ensuring (relative) income reductions more acceptable and encourage a more careful use of these personal assets. However, at least as important is the fact that under this compulsory, general drawing rights system, the state can guarantee compensation for inflation better than smaller, private and segmented insurance institutions can, and that each individual is automatically credit worthy on reaching a certain age (the end of obligatory schooling being a possible starting point). This latter advantage of the system outlined here would mean that young people could finance part of their education out of their account in advance of actually accumulating their drawing rights through contributions. The availability of such drawing rights might well result in less advantaged young people increasing their participation in higher education.

A rather different advantage of the integrated system is that it is administratively cheap and simple. In this respect it can be contrasted with the current ideas and proposals in the debate on the "crisis of the welfare state" which suggest that more and more social needs should be covered by a highly segmented, differentiated insurance system, comprised of private agencies. This would, in fact, result in many additional costs, problems, and inequities. For example, each insurance company would have to engage in the expensive business of not only persuading people to take on that particular insurance in the first place but to do this with them rather than with a rival firm. It would also result in the mushrooming of contracts for old-age, sickness, and unemployment insurance between employers and trade unions, making for great complications for those who move between employers and insurance schemes. The experience of the United States in this respect is illuminating: It is a notorious feature of the American system that many people have great problems both in working out their rights and in ensuring that they receive what they are entitled to.

Indeed, it may be argued that an integrated system, despite the complications implied in the drawing rights, would cost less than the present maze of overlapping, inequitable, and often inadequate separate arrangements for income maintenance, which exist even in European countries despite their more centralized social insurance systems. Through a more integrated, general system, we could not only reduce the amount of involuntary unemployment and the amount of unpleasant and unproductive employment, we could also help the individual more efficiently and equitably to utilize the value of the productivity gains which accrue over his or her lifetime—namely, by facilitating the individual's adjustments to variations in economic structure.

THE USE OF DRAWING RIGHTS FOR RECURRENT EDUCATION

Recurrent education, as defined and discussed in various OECD publications and documents, is like the drawing rights model in that it is a general guiding concept which, if realized, would be shaped and molded by each country to its own traditions and institutions. And like the system of general drawing rights, it is envisaged that recurrent education would emerge through evolutionary reform rather than sudden, total change. Therefore, the question of how to apply drawing rights to recurrent education can only be treated in rather broad terms, short of developing very specific scenarios. It is assumed here, however, that the desirable development of recurrent education would mean that everyone would undertake some kind of postcompulsory study, and that menial jobs for which no particular qualifications are needed would be spread out more evenly and be regarded as a transition stage in the lives of most citizens.

One reasonable assumption is that it would not be economically possible to supply every citizen with drawing rights adequate to cover *all* education beyond compulsory schooling (i.e., equivalent to the customary two or three years of upper secondary school, four years of college or similar undergraduate studies, and additional years for postgraduate studies). In that case, much of the cost of postcompulsory education would still have to be paid with funds outside the drawing rights insurance system, including the traditional sources of student finance such as loans, stipends, parental or family support, and so on. Moreover, with all the different traditions for the financing of education in different countries, it would not be expected that a common or single pattern would apply universally to all the specific financing needed for recurrent education.

Nonetheless, whatever the tradition of educational finance in a given country, we suggest that the drawing rights system would make it possible for everyone to draw on their account to cover the cost of a certain amount of postcompulsory education. A feasible example would be that everyone would be offered three years of full-time postcompulsory study to be financed by drawing on their account. In theory, this would require roughly 10% of the average incomes of all taxpayers (three years being roughly 10% of the average number of working years per person). This would, however, not imply a concomitant increase in taxes as, at present, many people already receive income maintenance, tuition, or both through taxpayers' funds. The advantage of registering the equivalent amount of tax payments on each taxpayer's account is precisely the fact that the individual is thereby shown how much he or she is entitled to and can use this sum according to his or her own choice.

If the individual decides to use this opportunity for studies immediately after the completion of compulsory schooling, he or she would obviously have to go into overdraft. In this case, certain restrictions and controls would be necessary. For example, it might be stipulated that until age 30 using the drawing rights would only be possible for bona fide studies under similar regulations as those pertaining to traditional school and university stipends. It could also be stipulated that once the limit of the advance on the account was reached, a person would not be able to draw on the account for any further purpose until the overdraft had been compensated or paid back through one's automatic contributions. After age 30 the control would be relaxed and the individual could use his or her rights for education in the same way as for any other chosen purpose within the general regulations governing the drawing rights scheme. This is of course only one possible alternative.

Variations around the theme of developing recurrent education suggest a number of possibilities in these respects. Drawing rights for studies, for example, could be made available only at a later date than the completion of compulsory schooling, obliging the student who nonetheless wishes to continue his or her studies immediately to rely on the traditional sources of finance as at present. Or it would be possible to ensure that the number of points annually available for studies on each person's account would be relatively low during the first years after compulsory schooling, but would grow at more than the rate of interest up to a certain age (say, 30 years). This, too, would better meet the greater income requirements of adults compared with those of young people, most of whom have yet to acquire costly responsibilities. These different ways of discriminating in favor of older adults can be seen either as a way of discouraging the continuation of studies in the period immediately after compulsory schooling, or as a way of encouraging or compensating "second chance" entry into education.

It would, of course, be possible to modify the drawing rights system by introducing economic incentives that would make adult studies an attractive alternative. But if it is true that the marginal productivity of additionally expanding the education system or volume of studies is relatively limited, this too argues in favor of not restricting such incentives to education only.

A possible compromise between the interest of stimulating studies and the interest of economic equity among people with and without postcompulsory studies would be to provide all tuition free of charge (i.e., let taxpayers finance it irrespective of their own participation in such studies) but to let subsistence during studies be the individual's own responsibility. The need for liquidity would be met (beside by the traditional system of bursaries and easy loans) by access to drawing rights as described above.

CONCLUSION

A number of the possible ways in which a drawing rights system could be used for recurrent education have been discussed. It can be seen that the general features of the model, as outlined in the earlier parts of this chapter, would allow adults (and young people) to use their rights for educational purposes in a more flexible way than is possible in many countries at present. As envisaged here, the widespread use of economic incentives as a vehicle of labor market policy would to a great extent imply the promotion of education and training, thereby providing an important additional basis for the establishment of a more developed recurrent education system. On the whole, the drawing rights system would forcefully reduce the rigid compartmentalization of life in three distinct periods—study, work and retirement. Instead, it would promote freedom of choice, seen as both a social value and as a possibility for more rapid and humane forms of adjustment in the labor market—both of which are needed for full employment and improved rates of growth.

NOTE

1. In my earlier article (Rehn, 1972) and in later published versions the arguments for "flex-time" (free variations and timing of work *hours*) was an important element. As this can be implemented without income maintenance through drawing rights, this aspect is bypassed here.

REFERENCES

REHN, G. (1974) "Towards flexibility in working life," in S. Mushkin (ed.) Recurrent Education. Washington, DC: Institute of Education, Department of Health, Education, and Welfare.

——— (1972) Prospective Views on Patterns for Working Time. Paris: OECD.

WIATR, J. and R. ROSE [eds.] (1977) Comparing Public Policies. Wroclaw.

4

INTERMEDIATE ("PARAFISCAL") FINANCING SCHEMES

WERNER CLEMENT

In the decades ahead, postsecondary education will very likely be one of the fastest growing areas of the educational system. Demographic factors, a probable increase in individual propensity for further learning, as well as other reasons of educational, social, and economic policy will all contribute to this growth. The existing plans of provision and those for the future make it likely that the organization of this educational area will differ significantly from the traditional models. Whereas in Europe, for example, formal education tends to be dominated by the state, alternative arrangements that comply with the manifold forms and expressions of recurrent education are needed and are being sought after.

Of course, reasons and rationales can always be found for any arrangement of provision and finance for recurrent education—whether it be a central-collectivist one, or an individualistic organization operating in a market. This depends largely on the ideology behind each proposal. Thus a tightly centralized, state-financed system may be discussed alongside one that operates as a market where individuals use vouchers for education. The major claim of this chapter is that a number of social factors and a range of theoretical considerations support a system which is neither purely public nor private—rather, an "intermediate" scheme for the provision and finance of recurrent education.

Further education within a recurrent framework is a sector in which there are high risks; there are those attached to government control on the one hand, and to market failures on the other. Therefore, if this area of education and training is not be "nationalized" or organized subject

---

AUTHOR'S NOTE: *I acknowledge gratefully comments made by C. Badelt, D. Istance, H. M. Levin, H. G. Schütze, D. M. Windham, and several participants of the Stanford Conference.*

to the criteria of private optimization, then a social and economic terrain—the contours of which have begun to be mapped only recently—must be entered. Provisionally, we can call it the "intermediary" sector.

While the analysis of this intermediary sector in economic theory awaits a much fuller treatment, there are nonetheless existing branches and strands of economics that are closely related to this idea which together can provide the basis of a more complete consideration. The economic theories of politics (theories of group behavior, clubs and collective action, and bargaining theory) and public choice theory (the nature of goods, externalities, and theories of intermediate "parafiscal" finance) together provide much of the conceptual apparatus required. Additional relevant branches include the new "third-sector economics," the economics of grants and of the institutional arrangements of quasi-public agencies. Pluralism, as political theory and constitutional reality, can also provide political and normative support to the theoretical development of this intermediary sector.

It would be a formidable task to exploit all these approaches with a view of building a "pure" theoretical model of the provision and finance of recurrent education. But by examining even briefly what already exists in countries, one finds an array of highly interesting institutional settings for further education which lie somewhere in the zone between state and that which is purely private. Examples are the Industrial Training Boards in the United Kingdom, the autonomous agreements ("conventions") and funds financed by special contributions in France, and arrangements under the Labor Promotion Act and paid educational leave regulations in the Federal Republic of Germany as well as many other similar devices in other European countries. More traditional settings, such as workers' education by trade unions or management courses given by employer federations, are equally relevant.

Yet, to conduct a simple stocktaking of these examples through national studies would not be sufficient to clarify the issues involved, nor could it provide a systematic analysis of these intermediate schemes and arrangements for the provision and finance of recurrent education. Such a systematic approach to the problems should make use of both theories and actual experiences drawn from case studies. For this reason the chapter is divided in two sections: the first discusses the theoretical considerations necessary to formulate the foundations of an intermediate scheme. This section, which can be skipped by a reader less interested in theoretical foundations, is followed by an attempt to conceptualize a realistic framework for such an intermediate scheme. The simple logic runs in the following way: Recurrent education may safely be considered a mixed good (using the language of economic theory) that has both public and private characteristics. For mixed goods, there is strong theoretical support that these goods should be provided by groups (as suggested by the analysis of the logic of collective action or theory of clubs.) For such provisions, an adequate scheme of finance has to be found.

Special funds or, more generally, financing schemes covered by the concept of parafiscality seem to provide the most suitable solutions. It is important then, first of all, that systematic guidelines for such intermediate financing schemes be elaborated that are general enough to fit the peculiarities of different countries. Although such an intermediate sector cannot totally replace state and private provision of further education and training, it can certainly be argued that it could well form a major part of total provision.

COLLECTIVE PROVISION OF RECURRENT EDUCATION AS THE RATIONALE FOR INTERMEDIATE (PARAFISCAL) SCHEMES

THE OPTIMAL PROVISION OF A MIXED GOOD

Education is usually viewed as a merit good or mixed good because it has both public and private chararacteristics. On the one hand, some education and training would be produced in the absence of public support because of the private demand created by individuals and their families. On the other hand, the production of education is believed to produce social benefits that are external to the individuals receiving the education: a more effectively functioning democracy and system of production, greater technological and cultural progress, and a "better" society (Bowen, 1977; Haveman and Weisbrod, 1977; and Weisbrod, 1964). Accordingly, education is viewed as having social merit and thus as deserving of both public and private support as a mixed good. Since it seems reasonable to view recurrent education in this light, we will assume that it is a mixed good also. It is therefore possible to apply the theoretical discussion on the provision of this category of goods to recurrent education. Beginning with the work of Tiebout (1956) and

Buchanan (1964), this area is usually considered under the heading of the "economic theory of clubs" (Sandler and Tschirhart, 1980).

A good starting point is the presence of a partial rivalry in consumption which is typical of mixed goods. Additional users joining the group of people who consume a mixed good collectively (i.e., the club) can create additional benefits for the original consumers, but only if every consumer takes part in financing the mixed good. Excluding it from certain people—"nonmembers"—prevents people from benefiting at others' expense (free-riding). However, once a certain level or number of club members is attained, rivalry occurs so that a further enlargement of the group may lead to higher marginal costs than marginal benefits to the existing members. This is usually labelled the "crowding" effect in the consumption of mixed goods.

Generally speaking, this problem can be formulated as a functional relationship between the average costs (which result from the provision of a mixed good) and the number of persons being engaged in its production and consumption. This was the original problem raised by Buchanan (1964) which was further developed by Oakland (1972) emphasizing that the crowding function is strongly determined by the frequency with which the club members make use of the mixed good.

One of the principal aims of the economic theory of clubs is to determine optimal club size given a certain amount of the mixed good. Optimal conditions can be formulated where both the amount of the good and the number of club members are variable. The optimal club size is attained when the net benefits from membership for an entrant equal the crowding costs resulting from that person's entire utilization of the mixed good. The optimal amount of provision is found when the marginal benefits from crowding reduction as a result of increased provision equal the marginal costs of provision (Sandler and Tschirhart, 1980).

These theoretical considerations give, albeit in extremely abstract form, some guide to the orientation of policy. Their application in reality would demand, however, a vast amount of concrete specification and empirical research. In particular, since the optimal club size in the case of recurrent education is determined by the benefits and costs of its provision, a functional specification of these two terms would be necessary. Independent variables that could be used for the specification of these relationships are, for example, the number of group members, the frequency with which clients use the educational facilities, and desired ratios between teachers and the consumers of recurrent education.

THE INSTITUTIONAL DECISION: INTERMEDIATE BODIES AS PROVIDERS OF RECURRENT EDUCATION

These optimum conditions do not a priori determine the institutional form that the club should take. Buchanan, for example, stressed that a club requires the organization of some sort of cooperative, sharing arrangement, that needs to be not only for nonprofit organizations (such as intermediate bodies) but may cover public arrangements and even profit-making firms (Buchanan, 1965).

It is argued here, however, that because of the "mixed good" nature of recurrent education, it can easily be demonstrated that institutional arrangements in the form of intermediate bodies have particular advantages over the others. First, it must be mentioned that the totally private provision of recurrent education is neither very likely to occur—due to the limited opportunities for profit in this field—nor would be desirable politically. That is, the high prices resulting from full-cost pricing would exclude the majority of potential consumers from access to education facilities and thus would not be acceptable. Second, one of the principal messages of economic theories of the voluntary sector is that state provision of public (or mixed) goods can present considerable disadvantages. As Olson (1965) has argued, the attributes of collective goods suggest only that they should be provided as a result of a collective decision-making process, because decisions at an individual level would fail. But collective need not necessarily refer to the state: Olson argues that it is necessary to analyze how smaller collectivities such as intermediate bodies would make these decisions (Badelt, 1981).

Apart from Olson's conclusions (which apply mainly to large groups), many educational institutions reflect already the basic idea that common valuations and preferences for continuing education may bring individuals together into groups engaged in the provision of education. There is, of course, a variety of motivations for participation: for example, social commitment (particularly expressed by churches and voluntary organizations); the desire for improving professional career prospects; a group feeling emanating from a common regional, social-class, or ethnic background; the desire to foster through education the ideologies and values of an organization;

and more immediate and personal needs such as those met by family or leisure activities. One can hardly deny that such attitudes and motivations have exercised a strong positive influence on developments of vocational and nonvocational adult education institutions.

While these are examples rather than an attempt to generalize, it should be stressed that by its very nature, the concept of recurrent education is flexible enough to include different institutional settings in its provision. What will be advocated here is that collective organizations (groups) are especially well adapted for such provision. A number of reasons, supported by theories of public choice and the emerging theory of the voluntary sector, may be forwarded in support of this view. The three arguments below underline that the state alone is unable to provide and cater for a sufficient supply of recurrent education (Weisbrod, 1978):

- governmental decisions are oriented towards short-term political criteria (for example, immediate popularity) that reflect neither "true" preferences nor politically desirable preferences (in the case of a merit good, such as education).
- governmental decisions have to be more or less centralized—a fact which has serious consequences in areas such as the dissemination of information.
- the ratio of costs to benefits is often much higher compared with alternative sources of provision.

The first of these three is elaborated by Weisbrod (Weisbrod, 1977; Weisbrod et al., 1978). He assumes that public policy, in pursuing maximization of votes, is oriented towards the demand of the median voter. This results in an undersupply of many collective goods and, in consequence, dissatisfaction among certain groups of consumers. One of the possible results is then "that a class of voluntary organizations will come into existence as extragovernmental providers of collective-consumption goods" (Weisbrod, 1977). The relatively low response of the eligible population to an extensive provision of recurrent education (as, for example, with the law of 1971 in France) may help explain why many governments were somewhat reluctant to make recurrent education a central political issue. On the other hand, such reluctance may leave many sections of the population without adequate opportunities. Again, therefore, the provision of education tailored to the needs of specific groups is one possible and feasible way out of that dilemma.

The second of the three arguments asserts that state provision of recurrent education has to be organized in a far more centralized way than is necessary with other forms of provision. However, centralization leads to limited and frequently biased information for decision makers (Downs, 1966; Orzechowski, 1977). This is particularly problematic for mixed goods which, as mentioned above, can be characterized by joint public and private consumption. It is certainly questionable to assume that any governmental institution could acquire the relevant information to cluster people who have more or less homogenous preferences. Yet this is the precondition to the realization of an efficient provision of recurrent education in the sense of a club.

In theory, there is only one way around this problem: This can be called "voting with the feet." This way of monitoring or showing preferences would suggest that governmental decisions should be decentralized until groups with relatively homogenous preferences emerge (Tiebout, 1956). This would require high mobility of consumers who would continue to move until they settled in a community where the provision of public goods largely corresponded to their preferences (Mueller, 1979). Although this theoretical alternative hardly could become directly applicable in practice—and certainly not in Europe—it has, nevertheless, the heuristic purpose of indicating that the problem of information can be relieved through decentralization in the public sector. One form of decentralization is precisely the provision and financing of recurrent education by parafiscal institutions.

The third problem, that of disadvantageous costs to benefits, is closely linked with the centralization issue. Drawing again on the economic theory of clubs, it suggests that the collectivity represented by the government would normally be considerably larger than the optimal club size. Hence, a reduction in the size of the club would save more in marginal costs than it would cost in marginal benefits, resulting in a net gain in benefits. One reason why larger units produce at relatively high costs is the existence of various forms of transaction costs such as those of information or of control. These aspects have been debated thoroughly and widely, often under the heading of "the costs of bureaucracy" (Tullock, 1965; Borcherding, 1977; Habermann and Loser, 1980).

To summarize: Neither the private profit-making nor the traditional public sector are capable of meeting the (potential) demand for recurrent education completely. Beyond these technical and theoretical arguments, a number of normative judgments related to recurrent education as a politically shaped concept can be used to underline the advantages of the provision of recurrent education by an intermediary sector. Such additional criteria, which carry implications for the specific institutional forms the provision of recurrent education should take, can be derived from the OECD model of recurrent education (OECD/CERI, 1977). For example, there are the objectives of providing a wide choice of learning opportunities, of allowing a significant degree of self-determination or self-management of the learning, and of allowing and encouraging innovation. The argument here is that an intermediary sector is particularly well suited to realizing these objectives.

THEORETICAL FINANCING SCHEMES FOR GROUP PROVISION

GENERAL ASPECTS

The economic theory of clubs also contains a nucleus of considerations concerning the financing of a mixed good. This is included in what is called the "toll condition" for the optimal supply of a mixed good. The toll condition basically requires financing of the provision at an equal rate or toll for all members. However, since utilization can vary between individuals, the total payment by each member need not be the same. Several authors have shown that the sum of ("efficient") tolls paid by all members sufficies to finance marginal costs of provision.[1] Consequently, it fails to finance the mixed good completely whenever average costs exceed marginal costs (i.e., when increasing returns to scale are present). In this case, optimal financing of recurrent education—a mixed good—requires a two-part tariff: To avoid deficits, a fixed membership charge *and* a utilization fee are necessary. This is the basic message for optimal financing in the case of increasing returns to scale.

The applications of these theoretical stipulations to policymaking require consideration of some elementary rules for the financing of recurrent education. First, as discussed above, financing at full-cost pricing would exclude a considerable number of potential recurrent students and therefore, is not desirable. Second, the rules of "optimal" finance imply a basic standard contribution in order to balance out the potential deficit. In addition, there should be a fee payable on use, the size of which should be determined by the marginal costs of participation in recurrent education.

The question of what an adequate financing scheme for intermediate bodies would be has not been answered in a rigorous way. The economics of public finance tends to develop coherent frameworks for the finance of public or semipublic bodies either in a territorial or a functional perspective. This has meant that analytical public finance has been developed alongside the description of institutions and agencies.

Following this brief sketch of the analysis of finance, it is only fair to look also at the other strand of development in this area—the institutional findings. Here, a certain, if only partial, recognition of the role of intermediate bodies of finance can be found in Italian, German, and French economic thought—particularly in the concepts of organic finance and parafiscality.

THE MAIN CHARACTERISTICS OF PARAFISCALITY

Without attempting to give a comprehensive picture of fiscal institutions and mechanisms, some characteristic properties should be described (Smekal, 1969; Mäding, 1971; Tiepelmann, 1975). One can begin with their *objectives*. On the whole, parafiscal institutions are expected both to fulfill a public function and to be in accord with the needs of a population grouping. They are assumed to be able to do this more efficiently because of the possibilities of limiting membership or participation (the exclusion principle). They are also expected to realize the aims of decentralization and self-management through a far-reaching autonomy of decision making and action.

The above mentioned objectives cannot be attained without securing some minimum degree of *fiscal distinctiveness*. On the revenue side, traditionally it has been claimed often that one can only speak of a true "parafiscus" if the body in question has the right to levy taxes or contributions. However, strict adherence to this rule would eliminate an interesting range of fiscal institutions and narrow the subject down only to social security, unemployment insurance funds, and some professional corporations that have financial autonomy. Since the purpose here is to cover the areas of intermediate bodies more generally, our broader perspective will focus on intermediate bodies *that rely upon mixed revenues coming from different sources*. These may be state subsidies and transfers, contributions they levy themselves (e.g., through fundraising; Flanagan, 1977), and even revenues from economic activity (Weisbrod and Long, 1977) although the economic activity must not be profit-making. Even the earmarking of funds for specific purposes would not be a reason to exclude it, so long as a certain degree of financial autonomy were maintained (Kirchhoff, 1973).

The recognition of an intermediary sector between the state and private commercial activities and the establishment of criteria under which institutions would belong in this parafiscal area are loose indicators of the types of organizations that are meant to be included.

In order to provide greater specificity about true parafiscal *institutions,* the middle of the spectrum between state and private entities is the easiest to deal with. This covers institutions which are common features of the corporate state such as employers' federations, trade unions, chambers of commerce, and associations of the liberal professions— in short, interest groups and social partners. As one moves from the middle ground to the more governmental institutions, the social security system, public trust funds, and even "quangos" (quasi-autonomous nongovernmental organizations) might fall under the heading of parafisci. Whether or not a specific body should be included under this heading depends on the extent of its financial autonomy and self-ruling capacity.

Moving towards the private sector at the other end of the scale, syndicates, cooperatives, and companies acting for the public interest would not be considered parafisci because in these cases the criteria of raising and managing public finances and providing public goods certainly cannot be applied. The same may be true, if to a lesser extent, of voluntary associations.

Looking at the question of *financial planning,* parafiscal funds are earmarked for specific purposes. This is a major incentive for contributions from those who supply the finances, and it is also probable that the forces of group cohesion would soften if this principle did not hold. As to the relation between the contribution to and the benefits from a parafiscal institution, a certain difference from government taxation may also be discerned. Modern welfare-state budgets generally tax individuals according to their ability to pay and render services according to some principle of equity. While this idea also applies to parafisci, it does so to a lesser extent. One of the very reasons for their creation in the first place is that certain individuals are willing to pay more than the average on the understanding that they will receive an equal or comparable benefit from such a fund.

MAIN FEATURES OF AN INTERMEDIATE (PARAFISCAL) FINANCING SCHEME FOR RECURRENT EDUCATION

GENERAL ASPECTS

To make the principles of group provision and finance more operational, the theoretical rules and considerations need to be translated into criteria that specify how a functioning system actually would look. This cannot be done comprehensively or exhaustively here—the above discussion shows that intermediate schemes cover a widely ranging variety of activities and mechanisms. Not surprisingly, their aims, legal bases, activities, revenue structures, budgeting and bases of fiscal authority, and administrative and decision-making structures differ significantly. What is outlined here is only an overview of some of the more important issues raised under these headings.

THE REVENUE SIDE

Classifying the revenues of intermediate bodies is not difficult: Monies may come from individual contributions or fees, from the state through grants, subsidies, transfer payments, or loans, or from enterprises through voluntary contributions, compulsory levies, or loans. They may also come from the economic activities of the body in question and the management of portfolios. As stated before, the degree of financial autonomy is a central aspect of intermediary bodies of finance and provision. Within this general criterion, classification of revenues can reflect such features as the proportion of general or block grants as compared with earmarked funds, and can distinguish between the suppliers and the distributors of finance, between spending bodies, and between those who receive funds and those who use them (Peacock, 1967).

Taking *individual contributions* first, it is not difficult to see that basing them upon the expected benefits to the individuals of the education or training presents very difficult theoretical and practical problems (e.g., how to disentangle individual from social benefits, or general from vocational elements, or how to impute a precise figure to these benefits).

Moreover, as discussed above, individual contributions based on full-cost pricing would be a particular deterrent to those whose income is low, and any attempt to try to meet the costs fully through some formula for payments based on supposed subsequent pay-offs from the education (e.g., through loans or educational insurance funds) might be unduly discouraging to the would-be student. Therefore, participants' own contributions may only prove to be a marginal source for the necessary finance. Nonetheless, it is probably preferable that a certain portion be raised in this way—both as a reminder of the costliness of education and as a means of revealing actual preferences for education.

Turning to the *state,* it has already been emphasized that it cannot be the major source of the funds. A state contribution may nevertheless be required to ensure a "just representation" among the participants in the intermediate body. A possible upper limit to state grants could be set at the net costs—that is, the costs minus the direct benefits, which are open to approximate estimation.[2] Apart from these financing considerations, it may be stipulated that the state cover the capital expenditures in order to provide the initial capacities. This participation of the state might also be extended to include compensation for salaries foregone or incidental expenses of participation in recurrent education (as is done in Sweden).

Third, there are several reasons why *private firms* should share the financial burden of education and training that is organized and financed in this way. First, it can be assumed that they can afford it (especially if they can pass the costs on in prices) and that they will benefit in any case through productivity gains. But, they will tend to provide firm- or industry-specific skills that limit the value of training and its results to competitors. Insofar as this will lead to an under-supply and unjust distribution of educational provision, it argues for an industry-wide approach and the creation of a fund which is maintained through enterprise contributions to increase the supply of education and training and make the financial burden more equitable.

As to the basis of the levies or fees enterprises would pay, there are a number of possibilities; the choice between them is largely a technical one depending on circumstances. (The factors include the total number of employees or eligible employees, the value-added, the turnover, the profit, and the payroll.) The latter criterion—the payroll—does suffer from the problem of placing labor-intensive firms at a disadvantage (Hegelheimer, 1977). The net costs may prove a fairer basis if equalization of the burden is an aim of the fund enterprises contribute to. A case, then, can be made for the fund compensating firms for this difference, although in practice it may prove to be anything but simple to establish precisely what it should be. Therefore, different kinds of systems have been used such as that of the levy-grant, of the levy-grant-exemption, or the levy-premium systems used in the United Kingdom and France.

THE EXPENDITURE SIDE

The expenditure pattern is closely linked to the costs. These can be broken down as follows: capital-current costs, direct costs (for the participants, the firm, or the state), and indirect costs. The latter includes the foregone income of the participants, the loss of production (if any) due to staff reductions, and possible social costs that occur as negative spill-overs.

Among these, the most important items are the current costs of the teaching personnel and the compensation of trainees for loss of earnings. There is some debate about who should incur the payment of earnings foregone; in international comparisons, income foregone or the maintained payment of the salaries are rarely included at all. Significant differences are thus possible in the relative burdens for the spending bodies. In Britain, for example, it has been said that "at least two-thirds of post-initial vocational expenditures on adults is till financed . . . by employers" (Drake, 1978). In France under the 1971 law, on the other hand, the state assumes two-thirds of the expenditures. Extreme caution, however, is required with this kind of comparison.

Another argument centers around the question of whether the financial resources should be allocated to people or to institutions. This may appear to be a misplaced question since it can be said that it is always people who ultimately receive the money. Yet in practice the difference may be of consequence. When the institution is the primary recipient of the subsidy, the advantage is that educational supply can be created and regulated in certain known ways. The risk, on the other hand, is that needs may be overlooked or provision may prove inadequate. Moreover, there may be risks of institutions behaving as bureaucracies and hence neglecting the consumers of education—the students. Advantages and disadvantages when finance is directed toward individuals are the converse of those just outlined.

DECISION MAKING AND POWER

The issue of the distribution of power is a central one, since parafiscal bodies can be distinguished not only by their relative degree of financial autonomy but also by their degree of self-government. When participation, fundraising, and determination of educational content all rest with the same interest group, there is little question about where the locus of power and control lies. Such a "closed-shop" situation may be justified on its own grounds, but not from a social perspective. Education is seen as a service for the members of the interest group, and sometimes may even be essential to ensure the stability of the group. This is reflected in the British case by the following:

> In the case of qualified manpower, valuable legal or conventional powers over training and access are vested in bodies like the Bar, the Law Society, the Royal Colleges of Medicine and in numerous chartered associations like the associations to which the 300,000 chartered and technical engineers belong [Drake, 1978].

Quite another type of situation arises when interest groups form a coalition and are induced by the state to establish educational provision. In this case, the power structure is usually tripartite and the stability of such a body is dependent upon the observance of the founding agreement (or law). Otherwise, there may be power shifts that would upset any initial balance. In fact, this is probably the most important and widely applied type of intermediate body as it conforms to certain principles of representative democracy. Examples are the Industrial Training Boards in Britain, the FAF (Training Insurance Funds) in France, and, to a certain extent, the *Bundesanstalt für Arbeit* in Germany.

In practice, the network of decision making and control is usually much more complex than is indicated by these general examples. First, there is considerable variety in the extent to which power is exercised over matters of finance alone or as it extends to education as well. Sometimes educational institutions are left relatively free and are financially supported on the basis of some index of man-hours of training delivered. More complicated criteria of support have also included stipulated educational standards (e.g., the system of *baremes* in France; see Glennerster, 1977; Blondel and Le Roux, 1975). An alternative arrangement is one in which control over finance and education is divided—for example, where educational institutions have to be recognized by the state or by some official body and funding is left to variegated schemes. A common arrangement is one in which intervention, information, and finance are examined and controlled through informal channels of different institutional structures. For higher education, a good example is the University Grants Committee in the United Kingdom, but other examples resembling this one also can be found in less mainstream educational settings.

CONCLUDING SUMMARY REMARKS

This chapter starts with the recognition of two very basic points. First, we can observe the fact that intermediate bodies (in education and training as well as in other fields and sectors) occupy a prominent position between purely private and public organizations. That is, they are an existing and very real fact of the world. Second, recurrent education has the properties of a mixed good, and therefore its provision and financing cannot be either exclusively private or public—further reason for seeing intermediate institutions as particularly suited to recurrent education. It can be added that the fact that recurrent education is a mixed good suggests that it is supplied best by groups.

Going beyond these two basic observations, we can observe that in pluralistic societies there are many movements or trends—such as the rise in participation in a variety of fields or the growth of voluntary organizations—that support the call for a truly intermediary sector. The fiscal form of this intermediary sector, organized around groups, would be institutions that are capable of raising funds under their own authority (at least to some degree) and can reflect the preferences of the individuals who comprise the group. The organizational forms this can take are funds, insurance, chartered associations, and voluntary groups. It is crucial to state that as soon as a group provision is recognized (according to educational standards) it may claim its right to be financed through this scheme.

One can foresee objections or potential problems with these proposals. For one thing, such intermediary organizations and financing may hardly provide an adequate basis for extensive recurrent opportunities. Nor, it might be added, do they provide reasonable assurance that various disadvantaged groups, who presently participate the least in adult education, would establish or join groups organizing education and training. Furthermore, except in the case of collective bargaining, national level coordination of group activities would seem unlikely without the assistance of some sort of state intervention.

The response to these potential criticisms reveals the flexibility inherent in such a system of intermediary provision and finance. It must be recognized that there is no one "best" solution to the development of such a sector for recurrent education. Hence an integrated system of education and finance must be sought, in line with the goals, institutions, and traditions of each country. Therefore, the state (for example) may take a role in ensuring that disadvantaged groups face adequate provision or in establishing a suitable mode of coordination without endangering the intermediary status of the bodies concerned. Added to this, it is likely that there may be much more rapid and flexible creation or adjustment of educational supply within such a sector than would otherwise be the case.

There are even grounds for believing that the overall level of provision of recurrent education would be increased if a more thoroughgoing intermediate sector were encouraged and developed. For this to be true, a number of holding conditions would probably have to be obtained. We might say that overall provision would increase if

- people would express and realize their preferences through groups of a convenient size;
- their willingness to do so thereby becomes greater than it is at present;
- sensible economies of scale would reduce the costs of the provision (e.g., through enhanced productivity);
- more people are thereby encouraged to join and participate with sufficient participatory power granted to participants in the management of the body, and in the management of funds in particular.

As with many questions concerning intermediary provision and finance, they have yet to be explored adequately and thoroughly. The fast growing body of literature that has been published since the presentation of a first version of this chapter is proof of the great interest in this area.

NOTES

1. For an overview see Sandler and Tschirhart (1980: 1496) and the literature mentioned there.

2. This is the approach of the German Edding Commission on Costs and Financing of Vocational Education and Training (see Kosten und Finanzierung der ausserseulishen beruflichen Bildung, Bonn, 1974).

REFERENCES

BADELT, C. (1983) "Community action: success, failure, prospects," in M. Pfaff (ed.) Public Transfers and some Private Alternatives During the Recession. Berlin-München: Duncker and Humlot.

——— (1980) Soziookonomie der Selbstorganisation, Beispiele zur Burgerselbsthilfe und ihre wirtschaftliche Bedeutung. Frankfurt, New York: Campus. 120-124.

BENGTSSON, J. and H. G. SCHÜTZE (1979) "Developments in recurrent education and recent economic and social trends," pp. 11-41 in W. Clement and F. Edding (eds.) Recurrent Education and Berufliche Flexibilitätsforschung. Berlin: Duncker und Humblot.

BLONDEL, C. and C. LE ROUX (1975) Le financement de la Politique de Formation professionnelle et de Promotion en France. Paris: JJPE.

BOWEN, H. R. (1977) Investment in Learning: The Individual and Social Value of American Higher Education. San Francisco: Jossey-Bass.

BUCHANAN, J. M. (1965) "An economic theory of clubs," Economics 32: 1-14.

DOWNS, K. (1968) Inside Bureaucracy. Boston: Little, Brown.

DRAKE, K. (1978) "The financial, legislative and regulatory structure of vocational training in the United Kingdom." Prepared for the CEDEFOP, Berlin, April. (mimeo)

FLANAGAN, J. (1977) The Grassroots Fundraising Book. Chicago: Swallow Press.

GLENNERSTER, G. H. (1977) "The existing system of finance," in M. Keynes (ed.) The Finance of Education: Economics and Education Policy IV.

HABERMAN, G. and H. J. LÖSER (1980) Antiburokratie. Munchen: Moderne Verlagsgesellschaft.

HAVEMAN, R. H. and B. A. WEISBROD (1977) "Determining benefits of public programmes: some guidance for policy analysis," in R. H. Haveman and J. Margolis (eds.) Public Expenditure and Policy Analysis. Chicago: Markham.

HEGELHEIMER, A. (1977) Finanzierungsprobleme der Berufsausbildung. Stuttgart: Ernst Klett.

JANNE, H., P. DOMINICÉ, and W. JAMES (1980) Development of Adult Education. Strasbourg: Council of Europe.

KIRCHHOFF, G. (1973) Subventionen als Instrument der Lenkung und Koordinierung. Berlin.

MÄDING, H. (1971) Fondsfinanzierte Berufsausbildung, Gutachten und Studien der Bildungskommission 19. Suttgart.

MUELLER, D. (1979) Public Choice. Cambridge: Cambridge Univ. Press.

OAKLAND, W. H. (1972) "Congestion, public goods and welfare." J. of Public Economics (November): 339-357.

OECD/CERI (1977) "Conference on developments in recurrent education." Paris: Secretariat Synthesis.

——— (1975) Recurrent Education: Trends and Issues. Paris: Author.

——— (1973) Recurrent Education: A Strategy for Lifelong Learning. Paris: Author.

OLSON, M. (1965) The Logic of Collective Action: Public Goods and the Theory of Groups. Cambridge, MA: Harvard Univ. Press.

ORZECHOWSKI, W. (1977) "Economic models of bureaucracy, survey, extensions and evidence," pp. 229-259 in T. E. Borcherding (ed.) Budgets and Bureaucracy: The Sources of Government Growth. Durham: Duke Univ. Press.

PEACOCK, A. (1967) "A conceptual scheme for the analysis of data on educational finance," p. 285 in OECD (ed.) Methods and Statistical Needs for Education Planning. Paris: OECD.

SANDLER, T. and J. T. TSCHIRHART (1980) "The economic theory of clubs: an evaluative survey." J. of Econ. Literature 18 (December): 1481-1521.

SMEKAL, C. (1969) Die Finanzwirtschaft intermediarer Gruppen. Innsbruck: Universität Innsbruck.

TIEBOUT, C. M. (1956) "A pure theory of local expenditure." J. of Pol. Economy 64: 416-424.

TIEPELMANN, K. (1975) "Parafiski." WISU, Das Wirtschaftsstudium, 6: 295-300.

TULLOCK, G. (1965) The Politics of Bureaucracy. Washington: Public Affairs Press.

WEISBROD, B. A. (1978) "Some collective-good aspects of non-government activities: not-for-profit organizations," pp. 163-174 in H. C. Recktenwald (ed.) Secular Trends of the Public Sector, Proceedings of the 32nd Congress of the International Institute of Public Finance. Berkeley: Univ. of California Press.

——— [ed.] (1977) The Voluntary Nonprofit Sector, An Economic Analysis. Lexington: Lexington Books.

——— (1977) "Toward a theory of the voluntary nonprofit sector in a three sector economy," pp. 51-76 in B. A. Weisbrod (ed.) The Voluntary Nonprofit Sector. Lexington: Lexington Books.

——— (1964) External Benefits of Public Education. Princeton: Princeton University, Industrial Relations Section.

——— and S. H. LONG (1977) "The size of the voluntary nonprofit sector, concepts and measures," pp. 11-50 in B. A. Weisbrod (ed.) The Voluntary Nonprofit Sector. Lexington: Lexington Books.

WEISBROD, B. A., J. F. HANDLER, and N. K. KOMESAR [eds.] (1978) Public Interest Law, An Economic and Institutional Analysis. Berkeley: Univ. of California Press.

WEISSHUHN, G. (1980) Probleme ökonomischer und soziler Kosten—Ertragsre chnungen der Weiterbildung, Discussion Paper 54. Berlin: Technical University.

5

FINANCING MECHANISMS
Their Impact on Postcompulsory Education

DIETER TIMMERMANN

This chapter will discuss the effects of various financing systems on recurrent postcompulsory education. First, a number of criteria will be introduced for assessing the probable impact of financing mechanisms on recurrent education. Second, several alternative financing models will be presented. Three models are presented in this volume (see Chapters 2, 3, and 4) so they will not be discussed in detail in this chapter. Other models which have not been proposed explicitly here will be discussed more fully. Third, an attempt will be made to evaluate each of the mechanisms in the light of the criteria—that is, to speculate on whether and to what extent the various systems of financing are likely to satisfy the objectives of recurrent education. One essential part of this discussion will be the identification of possible trade-offs between those objectives. The fourth step will be the attempt to find out which financing mechanism promises to fulfill the criteria most adequately. Such a "best" financing system very well may be a mixed one. Finally, the impact on macroeconomic activities of financing recurrent education as well as some caveats will be discussed.

CRITERIA FOR EVALUATING FINANCING MECHANISMS

In this section various criteria are set out for evaluating financing plans for recurrent education. Although much of the discussion of recurrent education has been limited to equality of educational opportunity and efficiency, several additional criteria will be introduced here.[1]

ENCOURAGING RECURRENCE

The first criterion is to encourage the replacement of traditional schooling patterns with a flexible and recurrent alternation of education, work, leisure, vacation, and retirement. This criterion is referred to as "encouraging recurrence," and advocates in particular part-time work as well as flexible work and vacation schedules. Also considered is the ability of alternative financing schemes to induce educational institutions to offer recurrent education.

INCREASING EFFICIENCY

The second criterion, "increasing efficiency," entails several different aspects of efficiency. The first is *internal efficiency,* which refers to optimizing the organization and mode of production within the educational industry by choosing cost-minimizing combinations of production factors, optimal firm sizes, time-minimizing decisions, and efficient management procedures. Internal efficiency also entails the matter of output quality—in other words, teaching contents. The second aspect is *external efficiency,* which is concerned with the efficient use of educational resources as it affects the functioning of the economic sector (i.e., of the labor market and its branches). While recurrent education is concerned with reducing unemployment, it also aims at preventing it by giving employed workers the opportunity to take part in recurrent education activities in order to alter their skills even before the threat of unemployment occurs. In this sense, external efficiency implies flexibility of the labor force (Clement and Edding, 1979).

As a result of recurrent education activities, productivity of the labor force is likely to increase in two ways: Recurrently educated workers and employees can be expected to be more productive than those who are not; and preventive recurrent education is likely to minimize the costs of structural and technological changes by ruling out or at least mitigating structural disequilibria in the labor market. Beyond this, external efficiency is also affected by the existence of external benefits and costs of education and the way they are taken into consideration by the financing schemes. Finally, achieving greater harmonization of labor markets through avoiding or mitigating cobweb cycles and over- or underinvestment in recurrent education will also enhance the external efficiency of postcompulsory education and training.

ENCOURAGING INNOVATIONS

The third criterion aims at increasing the innovative potential of the recurrent education system. The regulatory and financing mechanisms of the existing postcompulsory education systems are said to prevent drastic innovations in education. Thus scrutinizing the impact of alternative finance systems on educational innovations will be of interest. Some innovations can be easily sold in the educational market place and aim at increasing the market value of human capital (marketable innovations). Others may have a low value in the market place, but they have high social value.

ENCOURAGING MARKETABLE SKILLS

Fourth, a recurrent education system may be designed and financed such that primarily marketable skills and knowledge will be produced while nonmarketable abilities are suppressed, or vice versa. Hence, it is important to assess whether or not financing models for recurrent education foster a system that primarily produces marketable or nonmarketable skills or both in an appropriate mixture.

ENCOURAGING INTEGRATION

One salient feature of current activities in both continuing education and present postcompulsory education is the segregation of vocational training and general education as well as the lack of coordination among the diversity of other educational activities. Recurrent education stresses a systems approach to all recurrent offerings, so it is important to know if the various financing schemes foster the coordination of recurrent postcompulsory educational activities in a holistic and systematic way. It would be desirable to achieve an integration of the present subsystems and offerings of postcompulsory education and training into one general module system of recurrent postcompulsory education and training (Edding et al., 1974: 22). This integration should not be confined to the matter of organization and coordination; it should also refer to the integration of theoretical knowledge and practical know-how as well as of general education and vocational training. This criterion will be called "encouraging integration."

ENCOURAGING INDIVIDUAL CHOICE AND PERSONAL DEVELOPMENT

There is wide agreement among critics that in most countries present educational institutions and processes are marked by authoritarian hierarchical decision structures dominated by the state bureaucracy that do not give any significant decision-making power or influence to their clientele. Virtually all proponents of recurrent education project a system of postcompulsory education and training that will be tailored to the individual needs of learners, most of whom will be adults with some work experience and with specific perceived needs (Lowe, 1975).

For this reason, the criterion of increased individual choice and freedom for the learners is an important one for recurrent education. Hence, the sixth criterion for evaluating the alternative financing mechanisms will be the extent to which individual choice and freedom will be enforced. Such choice should foster personality enrichment and self-development, self-determination and self-responsibility, self-independence and self-control, democratization of educational decisions, and individual participation in shaping recurrent education activities. This criterion will be referred to as "encouraging individual choice and personal development." But note that this criterion (as well as others) very well may be in conflict with other criteria, as will be shown later.

EQUALITY OF EDUCATIONAL OPPORTUNITY

The seventh criterion is to promote equality of educational opportunity and encourage the demand for recurrent education. Here, the question will be whether and to what extent alternative financing modes are likely to encourage participation in recurrent education activities. Although precise information on the contribution of different factors to the demand for postcompulsory education and training does not exist, the available information on recurrent education suggests that several types of variables have an influence on the demand for it (O'Keefe, 1977).

First, there are ascriptive factors like sex, race, ethnic origin, and age. Second, career and promotion perspectives are said to be important determinators of recurrent education demand. This argument refers to the position of the potential learner in the job ladder and the labor market segment in which he or she is situated. In this context, some researchers have introduced the terms "recurrent education value" or "recurrent education closeness" of the respective jobs and work content. A related component is job security or the obligation to reemploy persons who have interrupted their work to undertake recurrent education activities.

A third set of variables likely to affect the demand for recurrent education is related to social background. The most common of these variables seem to be the education, social status, profession, income, and wealth of both the potential learner's parents and the learner as well as the number and kind of recurrent education activities he or she has already experienced.

Fourth, from a human capital theory perspective, the expected economic and noneconomic benefits—that is, the improvement of income or the expected rate of return from an investment in recurrent education—should exert a major influence on the demand for recurrent education. Fifth, the attitude of individuals towards mobility and change might be an important variable of demand. So might the sixth factor, the organization of work with respect to shift work, part-time work, and flexible work-time schedules.

Seventh, the recurrent education activities themselves (their regulatory as well as informational systems) are said to be important in motivating or discouraging demand for recurrent education. Important characteristics in this regard are as follows: the duration of recurrent education units, their contents and curricula, their module character, time schedule (during the day, evening, or weekends, and block or sequential), the regional distribution and the local distance of the recurrent education institutions, the variety of courses with respect to the clientele and their diverse interests, the mode of regulation of access, eligibility and admission rules, the degree of participation and learner influence on the activities, and the certification of performance and transferability of credits. The latter is likely to be of great importance as long as certificates are a prerequisite for entering career tracks and for promotion.

Finally, it is believed widely that the form and amount of financial contribution has a very strong impact on the willingness and ability of individuals to participate in recurrent education. The less the potential participants have to contribute out of their own pockets or through income foregone (at present in fees or in the future through loans) and the higher the subsidies, the more likely they are to demand postcompulsory education and training activities (Jackson and Weatherby, 1975). Encouraging additional demand for recurrent education is seen as an important criterion for assessing the impacts of diverse financing proposals. The view that it is desirable that the demand for recurrent education should behave in an anticyclical fashion reinforces this social perspective. The goal is that when demand for labor is low there will be more participation in recurrent education, and vice versa. Anticyclical behavior in the demand for recurrent education would not only relieve the labor market but also the public budget: It would reduce the need for unemployment compensation during recessions as well as avoid or mitigate "withdrawal effects" (losses of economic growth) in boom phases. Hence, it seems worthwhile to analyze the degree to which the financing schemes in question do initiate or enforce a specific demand behavior as to economic cycles.

Alternative financing mechanisms for recurrent education can affect the demand for recurrent education in two ways: first is the extent to which the potential participant has to pay for the education and has to forego income during the education period; second is variations in the types of recurrent education activities engendered that may result from different financing schemes. In comparison, social background and labor market as variables affecting the demand for recurrent education seem to be least alterable through different funding modes. The criteria of equality of educational opportunity and demand for recurrent education will be referred to as "encouraging demand for recurrent education" and "increasing equality of participation in postcompulsory education and training," respectively.

SOCIAL AND ECONOMIC EQUITY

The eighth criterion is that of "social and economic equity." It is comprised of a number of related aspects. The first one is equity among regions in the distribution of recurrent activities. The second facet has to do with equity of the financial burden between individuals, social classes, and generations, which brings up the "ability-to-pay" versus "pay-as-you-use" controversy. The third concern is directed towards equity of financial support for individuals, social classes, and generations, and the next means equity in the distribution of skills, education, and training between and within generations as well as equivalency of general education and vocational training. Finally, some researchers call for equity of financial and nonfinancial benefits of income, as well as of career outcomes and life chances between and within generations. All these different aspects of equity will be called "equalizing the distribution of recurrent education implications."

DEMOCRATIZATION OF EDUCATION AND WORK

The ninth criterion that is widely discussed in the literature and should be taken into consideration is "democratization" of education and work. However, as employment is beyond the reach of schemes for financing recurrent education, we aim at democratization of education alone, excluding the dominance of particular interests (Edding et al., 1974: 27). Furthermore, we should evaluate whether financing recurrent education models encourages activities and processes in postcompulsory education and training that are likely to endanger or enforce the social cohesion and integration of different social classes, races, or ethnic groups.

Some politicans and researchers are also concerned with the extent to which different financing schemes are likely to increase the total costs of education as well as specifically the burden upon the public budget. These concerns will be considered as the eleventh and twelfth criteria, respectively.

ALTERNATIVE MECHANISMS OF FINANCING POSTCOMPULSORY EDUCATION AND TRAINING

Six basic models for financing a recurrent system of postcompulsory education have been suggested in the past:

model 1: self-financing
model 2: drawing rights
model 3: entitlements (vouchers)
model 4: single-employer financing
model 5: parafiscal funds
model 6: state financing

Three of these models (the drawing rights model by Rehn, the entitlements model by Levin, and the parafiscal funds model by Clement) are presented in this volume. As the other three models (the self-financing model, the single-employer financing model, and the state financing model) have not yet been introduced and may be new to the reader, they will be described briefly before being evaluated.

The impacts of these financing models on recurrent education will be discussed with respect to the criteria introduced above. The discussion is followed by a matrix scheme that will show the impacts of the alternative financing mechanisms on the criteria. This scheme should also allow for a cautious comparison of the impacts of the various models that can then be used to draw some prudent conclusions as to what financing mechanism (a pure or a mixed one) seems to be most promising. These conclusions will clearly depend on value judgments with respect to the weight of the various criteria as well as to the assessment of the impacts; thus each weight-assessment system is likely to come to different conclusions. Hence, the choice or construction of a specific financing scheme for recurrent postcompulsory education and training is not possible without strongly involving personal and political preferences and judgments—in other words, without elements of arbitrariness.

THE SELF-FINANCING MODEL

A system of self-financing recurrent education requires individuals to pay for their own postcompulsory education and training out of their own resources. This can be achieved in a threefold manner: using up former savings, expending current income, or paying through loans which will be repaid out of future earnings. Individuals are assumed to consider themselves as consumers of and investors in recurrent education. In a free educational market, private producers would offer recurrent education services in order to make profits.

Yet it seems unlikely that this kind of free market provision for recurrent education would help meet the objectives that were implied by the preceding criteria. First, there is no reason why the recurrence of education and the alternation of work and education or training should be encouraged in a free market system of education to any considerable extent. Recurrent education is likely to increase the labor costs for employers; hence, they will prefer cheaper (i.e., traditional) forms of education and training, and so the demand for recurrent education by the mass of workers is not likely to emerge.

Second, pressure for internal efficiency can be expected to increase remarkably as consumers insist upon getting efficient services for their money and competition among producers forces them to look for cost-minimizing production. Thus, the production of recurrent education will tend to focus on the short run (and be more expensive for the demanders in the long run) and new production functions may reduce the production to only marketable outputs (i.e., to outputs that have a market value in the first place for the educational firm as well as for the demander). Those outputs that are not of value in the market but are of great value for society are more likely to be ignored.

Given a short-run orientation of a free-market system of recurrent education, overall external efficiency is not likely to improve very much either. First of all, as a response to structural or technological unemployment, recurrent education activities can be expected to be only reactions to unemployment—it is very likely that the motive of prevention will be absent. Second, the short-run market orientation of postcompulsory education will not help to increase flexibility in the labor force and the labor market; instead cobweb cycles of over- and underproduction of specific qualifications in various educational and labor markets are likely to prevail. Moreover, external effects of recurrent education will not be internalized at all, and in the long run private monopolies may emerge within the educational industries.

With respect to innovations, it can be expected that new educational technologies will be developed and used for recurrent education in a free-market system such that the internal efficiency of the education industry will increase as asserted above. Also, innovations in subjects, teaching contents, teaching methods, and so forth will emerge. However, these innovations are likely to be limited to marketable ones rather than be applied to those of high social import but little private demand.

As one consequence, the recurrent education system will focus on the improvement of marketable skills, whereas general education will be neglected widely. However, the integration of general education and vocational training as well as of the various activities of adult and further education in a recurrent education system will be encouraged, and the links between theoretical knowledge and practical know-how are likely to be strengthened (at least within postcompulsory vocational education).

There is no doubt that a free-market and self-financing system of recurrent education will strengthen and widen individual choice and freedom (Friedman, 1962; Coons and Sugarman, 1978; West, 1964) and consumer sovereignty. This will allow for a much broader variety of postcompulsory educational activities than is witnessed at present. It is likely that those broader activities will be shaped more to the specific needs of the buyers of recurrent education. But note that some inefficiencies can also result from individual choices based on individual purchasing power and preferences. First, there is the problem of imperfect information that may lead to "bad" or "wrong" decisions. Second, there is the problem of the short-run orientation in making choices: According to Bohm-Bawerk's law of time preference, the individuals' time preferences tend to overestimate present consumption with respect to a quick pay-off and to underestimate future benefits. This disposition implies a number of consequences which have already been mentioned above: short-run and quick pay-off demands for recurrent education, focus on marketable skills, cobweb cycles in the educational sector as well as in partial labor markets, and underinvestment in recurrent education.

Moreover, we would expect a self-financing system of recurrent education to have a detrimental effect on the demand for postcompulsory education relative to the effects of the subsidies offered by the present system. The increase in direct costs would discourage demand, particularly among disadvantaged and "education-distant" groups. We cannot foresee whether incentives created by increases in career and promotion possibilities, job security, and the "recurrent-education value" of work will occur and encourage demand for recurrent education.

Finally, demand for postcompulsory education and training seems very likely not to behave anticyclically with respect to the business cycle. Those laid off in phases of recession will lack the necessary resources to be able to bear the financial burden of paying for the direct cost of education. Many of those still employed who might be interested in pursuing recurrent education measures are likely to refrain because they may fear losing their jobs. Hence, most of the potential clientele for postcompulsory education and training can be expected to participate in recurrent education in periods of economic prosperity when the labor markets are tight and jobs rather secure. However, during such periods of full employment or even overemployment, withdrawal effects (output foregone) would be high, and wage as well as price pushes might occur in the wake of scarce labor. Generally, from an investment perspective, rational behavior would induce individuals not to postpone their education and training. Rather, to enjoy the maximum pay-off it would seem advisable to demand education in the early years as much as possible in order to get a high entry-level job and then receive on-the-job training afterwards (Stoikov, 1975).

Another important question is whether the self-financing (free-market) model of postcompulsory education and training would tend to reduce social and economic inequality. In this respect there is little reason to be optimistic. A free-market system would tend to enforce the disparities in the regional distribution of recurrent education activities such that the great bulk of offerings would be found in urban areas, where purchasing power and demand is concentrated, rather than in rural areas. Without subsidies,[2] the price of recurrent education, family income, and the expected return from the investment in recurrent education will be the main economic variables determining demand behavior.[3] *Ceteris paribus,* more recurrent education will be demanded by individuals of higher income. Individuals will demand post-compulsory education and training as long as they can pay for it. Therefore, the distribution of demand for recurrent education will probably mirror the present distribution of income rather than be more equal.

The drawing rights model as proposed by Rehn would use social security accounts to enable individuals to finance recurrent education as well as pensions and other periods out of the labor market. Inequal educational opportunities and life chances are very likely to continue from generation to generation. Also, equity of general education and vocational training will not be achieved.

Moreover, democratic participation in the decision and power structures of education as well as in the employment system will not be increased. The market mechanism is likely to reproduce these structures such that powerful interests in the economic sector will tend to dominate the choice of individuals. Self-financing and a market system in recurrent education also may lead to a higher degree of social stratification of the population and to social norms and values that might endanger social cohesion in the long run. While the total cost burden for education might decline substantially in such a financing system, the public sector would, of course, be relieved completely from the burden of financing postcompulsory education and training.

THE DRAWING RIGHTS MODEL

Before going into some detail on the drawing rights approach, two remarks seem necessary. First, the evaluation of the model depends to a great extent on the knowledge of the supply system of recurrent education. Rehn's model restricts itself to the demand side (the principles of raising, administrating, distributing, and using up the drawing rights from, among, and through potential demanders) but says nothing about the supply side of postcompulsory education and training. In particular he leaves open whether recurrent education activities should be offered in a free market by private firms, exclusively in a regulated market by state institutions, or in a partly regulated mixed market of private and public supplies (obviously, the latter currently prevails in most countries).

The structure and ruling principles of the supply system are of great importance for the way in which a recurrent education system functions, and hence for an assessment of it. Since Rehn stresses the freedom and responsibility of individuals for their own lives and the liberation of individuals from the bureaucratic state, it seems logical to assume that a free-market supply system fits best into his financing model. Hence, the completed model is basically a free-market system of postcompulsory education and training, differing from the self-financing model in one major way: Individuals are free to save for later consumption of or investment in recurrent education in the self-financing case, while in the drawing rights system individuals are forced to save a certain amount of their current income in order to acquire drawing rights which they then are free to use (for recurrent education or other activities). The basic contradiction in Rehn's model can be put as follows: Why should individuals gain more freedom for themselves by being forced to save? Why not allow them to decide whether to save or not and, if so, what amount to save?

Second, Rehn's model describes primarily a labor market strategy rather than an educational policy. However, the model can obviously be extended to serve as a strategy for financing recurrent education. The problem here is that Rehn tends to reduce the financing issue to solely a matter of bookkeeping. By doing so he overlooks the fact that shifting a financial amount from one account to another may induce substantial changes in the behavior of the respective account owners.

Generally, the drawing rights model is in many ways very similar to the self-financing model. That is why the following evaluation has been placed closed to the preceding one and, hence, can be shorter. Again, there is no reason to believe that a recurrent alternation of work, education, leisure, and training would emerge solely through the free-market forces. Within a free-market approach to recurrent education, alternation of work and education is more likely to be achieved through collective agreement or legislative actions rather than solely through the market forces which are independent of the way postcompulsory education is financed (i.e., whether through self-financing, drawing rights, or entitlements). As in the self-financing model, recurrent education programs will develop as a response to the respective demand. However, as drawing rights depend directly on earnings, the power for purchasing recurrent education will be distributed as unequally as earnings are. In addition to the remarks in the preceding evaluation, large quality differences within recurrent education are likely to occur in a free-market supply system.

Two other important issues are those of underinvestment in recurrent education and of equality of opportunity and life chances. First, it seems that underinvestment in recurrent education is very likely within the self-financing model. The drawing rights solution will also lead to that tendency because it does not restrict the use of the drawing rights to recurrent education but allows for leisure, early retirement, sabbaticals, vacation, and other activities too. We can expect that a great number of individuals will not use their drawing rights for education and training.

Second, the drawing rights model implies a strong relationship between earnings and the ability to pay for postcompulsory education and training. Earnings being distributed unequally, the opportunity to spend on recurrent education is also distributed unequally. Hence, those with high earnings accumulate more drawing rights than low-earners and are able to purchase more recurrent education. If education affects future earning power, those with high present earnings can increase their future earnings through recurrent education much more than those with low incomes. This mechanism will widen the inequality of educational opportunity as well as of the income distribution. Moreover, we can expect high-earners to be more likely to use their drawing rights for recurrent education than low-earners, who might use most of their drawing rights for leisure, vacation, and so on. Thus, inequality of education and of life chances would increase.

High earners who use most of their drawing rights for recurrent education while they are in their 20s and 30s will not only enjoy growing earnings but also a growing stock of drawing rights from these earnings. This will enable them to enjoy more leisure, sabbaticals, and other types of free time in their 40s and 50s. Moreover, the unemployed are not able to accumulate drawing rights during the unemployment period. This fact reduces their power to purchase recurrent education in the future. Finally, while the public budget will not be burdened in this model, it is impossible to estimate whether the total costs for education would increase or decrease. It is important to note that subsidies might be used to supplement drawing rights in meritorious cases such as those of the poor, as Rehn suggests.

THE ENTITLEMENT MODEL

The entitlement proposal has been introduced and discussed by Levin in this volume. Essentially, the government would guarantee a specified sum or entitlement for each citizen at the end of postcompulsory schooling that could be used for recurrent education. Like the two preceding models the entitlement scheme is a free-market model for the supply of postcompulsory education and training. The main difference lies again on the demand side. While demanders have to raise the budget for recurrent education totally out of their own resources (in the first case voluntarily, in the second case by requirement) in the preceding models, the entitlement solution requires the state to raise most of the financial resources. The state, then, has to transfer these resources to the individuals in the form of entitlements. These individuals are obliged to use them only for postcompulsory education and training but are free to choose among various suppliers.

The main characteristic of the model is the redistribution of income. This can occur through a system of finance that provides larger entitlements to the poor while requiring lower tax contributions from them. Again, as there are a number of similarities resulting from the free-market characteristics of both preceding models, the focus will be on the criteria in which substantial differences occur. Generally, as with the first model, efficiency gains will not be high except those resulting from competition and from a better-integrated approach to recurrent education.

The main effect of the entitlement solution may be the improvement of equality of educational opportunity and social equity. It should be clear that the strength of this effect depends on the size of the entitlement, its composition of grants and loans, and the incidence of the tax system. It seems safe to state that the higher the entitlement and the lower the loan component, the more demand there will be for recurrent education from disadvantaged groups and the less inequality there will be in educational opportunity. We can at least imagine an entitlement system in which educational opportunities and life chances are distributed rather equally. This would include the economic and noneconomic benefits of recurrent education as well as the distribution of skills, knowledge, education, and training within and between generations. However, that system is still likely to focus on vocational training, although this orientation may be weaker than in the two preceding models. The entitlement system is very likely to increase the total costs of education as well as the educational burden of the public budget.

THE SINGLE-EMPLOYER FINANCING MODEL

This model can be seen to be an extension of the on-the-job training system as well as of the apprenticeship system. Within this model, there are two investors: private or public employers who offer their own recurrent education activities to their employees (or apprentices) or pay for comparable activities offered by the (private or public) educational industry, and the employees who invest in their human capital through these activities. Both the employer and the employee enjoy a return on these investments in the resultant productivity growth: The employee experiences an increase of earnings, and the private employer experiences a higher profit. Also, the public employer is assumed to produce better (more productive) services (Becker, 1975: 15-80). Both parties are likely to pay for recurrent education in this system. The employer's expenses are for the direct educational costs and the subsistence of those employees engaged in full-time recurrent education; the employee foregoes income during the training periods and may be paid below his or her marginal productivity afterwards.

It is an open question whether this financing mechanism would encourage a recurrent alternation of work, education, and training. This would depend primarily on the needs of employers for such alternation and, beyond that, on collective agreement or legislative action. However, the educational activities in this system are very likely to be reduced to specific postcompulsory training (as expressed by Becker, 1975: 26) as employeers will aim at capturing the returns to postcompulsory training while trained employees could improve their earnings by changing employers (Mattern, 1979: 122). However, specific recurrent training seems very likely to restrict the mobility of employees: Such mobility might conflict with macroeconomic goals of encouraging shifts from declining industries to expanding ones. Hence, single-employer profitability calculations very well may conflict with labor market needs and reduce the external efficiency of the recurrent education system even though internal efficiency for a particular employer can be expected to be high (Sadowski, 1980: 5).

Employers will probably minimize the necessary time and cost needed for a certain amount of education and training. Moreover, it is likely that the single-employer financing mechanism will induce employers to seek a quick return by placing learners in productive work during their education and training period. Firms that are able to gain net returns from education and training through paying lower wages during the training period will be stimulated to train more individuals than they will be able to employ afterwards. This has been found to be true for most firms in the craft sector in West Germany (Mattern, 1979: 123; Sachverständigenkommission Kosten und Finanzierung, 1974: 93). Also, the large quality differences and the short-run orientation towards specific marketable outputs with respect to labor market changes indicate that a reactive (rather than preventive) policy of recurrent training prevails.

The single-employer financing systems can be seen to suffer from substantial external efficiency losses. Not only may individual profitability calculations conflict with labor market needs regarding the quality and quantity of recurrent training, employers who offer training will enjoy a significant competitive edge over those who do not (Sachverstandigenkommission Kosten und Finanzierung, 1973: 32).

A general tendency of underinvestment in recurrent education can be expected. Overinvestment in areas with positive (high) net benefits during the training periods will occur, while those areas with high net costs probably will be characterized by underinvestment in recurrent training. The inclination of these branches to invest in recurrent training will decline particularly in recession periods, while branches with net benefits will be induced to expand these investments by substituting cheap trainees for expensive workers. Moreover, those who are trained in net-benefit branches that do not find a job there probably will be able to find employment only in an unskilled or semiskilled position within another branch, thus their investment in recurrent training will not pay off. Inflexibility of the trained, cobweb cycles in the markets for trainees, overinvestment in one set of branches, underinvestment in others, a general tendency toward underinvestment, and competition biases will produce structural misallocations in the education and training market as well as in the labor market.

Another serious problem is that the unemployed would not be able to participate in recurrent education. Also, since innovations can be expected to respond to employer-specific marketable offerings, general, political, and cultural education will not be addressed by this financing system. Integration of general education and vocational training also will not be encouraged, while individual choice will be strengthened. There will be only a restricted range of educational offerings, mainly of specific training, and choices will be influenced substantially by employers.

It is hard to see how demand for postcompulsory education and training would be encouraged in this system, and particularly not that of disadvantaged groups. Career and promotion perspectives, job security, and recurrent-education value of work will not be affected to a substantial degree. Employers would restrict postcompulsory education activities to their economic needs. Restricted participation in recurrent education is not likely to reduce inequality in the distribution of skills and knowledge, of education and training between and within generations, of the distribution of career outcomes, or in the distribution of financial and nonfinancial benefits. The individual financial burden of trainees and individual financial support by employers may be subject to large variations. Sectoral, regional, and quality differences are likely to exist, and (an even more serious problem) the system is likely to imply a redistribution of burden and benefits in favor of those who can undertake the postcompulsory education and training activities. By means of a general wage reduction to below marginal productivity, by regressive tax-reduction incidence in the case of tax-deductible training costs for employers, as well as by the shift of training costs to the consumers, all workers and employees (as workers, consumers, and taxpayers) will pay for recurrent training but only a minority will profit. More concretely, those who remain unskilled or semiskilled workers or employees will help to finance the recurrent education of the skilled workers and of highly qualified workers. Hence, a redistribution from those with less recurrent education to those with more training is very likely to take place in the single-employer financing model. As in the first two models discussed, a polarization between qualified and unqualified manpower seems likely to develop. The dominance of particular employers' interests will prevail in the range of offerings. Total costs for education are not likely to increase, and the public budget will only be burdened in the case of tax reduction for training costs.

THE PARAFISCAL FUNDS MODEL

The finaincing mechanism of parafiscal funds has been analyzed in length by Clement in this volume. As should be clear from his analysis, in such a solution private and public employers are required to pay a levy on total wages (a payroll tax) or on value added into a funds system. The funds system can be organized into a central fund or a system of decentralized funds; the criterion of decentralization being alternatively professions, regions, or branches. (For discussion of the funds solution with respect to the German apprenticeship system and these alternatives see Hegelheimer, 1977; *Sachverständigenkommission Kosten und Finanzierung,* 1974: 245; Sadowski, 1980).

There are two possibilties of funding postcompulsory education and training within the model. One—which has not been discussed at all up to now—is an entitlement or voucher version. Under such a solution, the funds would transfer vouchers to employees at the beginning of their careers. Employees would be free to ask for recurrent education in those participating institutions and firms. Those institutions would be reimbursed for their training expenditures by redeeming the vouchers with the funds. The alternative possibility is direct institutional funding: The institutions and firms participating in the funds advance the expenditures themselves and are compensated directly from funding resources according to the regulations.

The parafiscal funds system has a number of favorable characteristics with respect to our criteria, although some serious problems remain. Generally, the funds system can be expected to encourage recurrent alternation of work, education, and training, and to initiate flexible work and nonwork schedules more than any of the models discussed before because a political will for establishing a recurrent education system within the funds is likely to develop. Comprehensive post-compulsory education and training programs may emerge. These programs would not only focus on specific short-run, marketable education and training, but would also stress general education, a long-run orientation toward training, and diversity. Hence, recurrent education could be freed from the cost-benefit calculations of single employers. Internal efficiency of recurrent education within training firms is likely to be high, although the funds may involve time-consuming and costly decision processes as well as high administrational costs, particularly for centralized funds.

As to external efficiency, ultimately postcompulsory education and training under parafiscal funds very likely will raise the flexibility of the labor force, and hence may contribute to the prevention of structural or technological unemployment. Structural disequilibria in the labor market are likely to be mitigated, and productivity gains can be expected.

However, there may be some aspects that would reduce efficiency. Different results may arise between labor-intensive and capital-intensive employers in favor of the latter, as well as between large and small firms in favor of the former. Differing abilities to shift the levy on to the consumers by raising prices will not only boost inflation but also will create new competition distortions. The expectation that the funds revenue will change in cadence with the business cycle (Hegelheimer, 1977: 102) seems attainable as the funds could accumulate a surplus in boom periods in order to support sufficient postcompulsory education and training in recession periods. This could contribute to steady development of recurrent education. But it is hard to foresee whether and (if so) why the funds system would be able to avoid cobweb cycles in recurrent education and the structural misallocations produced by them.

Innovations in postcompulsory education and training will be high within a funds system and will include nonmarketable innovations as the innovational risk will be shared by all institutions and firms. Moreover, by setting certain quality standards for the provision of general and specific education and training, not only marketable skills and knowledge will be improved significantly but also the general, political, cultural, and social qualifications that are desired by the members of the fund. The fund system may also encourage integration of general education and vocational training, theoretical knowledge and practical know-how, and various activities in adult and further education into the recurrent education system.

The major weakness of the parafiscal funds model is its inability to encourage demand for recurrent education and to diminish the inequality of participation in postcompulsory education and training, particularly with respect to disadvantaged groups, as long as job structures, job contents, and employment hierarchies remain unchanged. As long as job security does not exist and the recurrent-education value of work is not achieved for these groups (i.e., for the great majority of employees), the parafiscal funds system will suffer from the "law of participation" mentioned above. Another problem will be the fact that young people leaving the compulsory schooling sector and not finding an entry job, will be excluded from recurrent education.

With respect to the equity issue, the parafiscal funds model will not fare much better than the preceding models, with the exception of the entitlement solution. While the inequality of general education and vocational training might be lessened, and while the inequity in the regional distribution of recurrent education activities might be done away with completely through affirmative actions of the funds (Mattern, 1979: 128), the issue of inequality of educational opportunity and of life, income, and career chances is very likely to remain acute for the very same reasons presented in the context of the single-employers financing model. Through shifting the levy back on wages of all employees, forward on prices for all consumers, and, in the case of tax-reduction possibilities, forward to the tax payers, all employees and workers are condemned to bear the financial burden as wage-earners, consumers, and tax payers while probably only a minority will benefit (at least as long as the "participation with respect to demand law" is effective). Hence, there will be a redistribution over time of income from those who do not participate or who participate only a little in recurrent education to those who participate intensively. More concretely, the disadvantaged (the unskilled and semiskilled, the poor, women, blacks and ethnic minorities, and foreign workers) will pay for the postcompulsory education and training of skilled workers (white men) and particularly of highly qualified manpower. This redistribution effect could be overcome through self-financing contributions or income-contingent loans—funds that could make recurrent education available to those interested in taking part.

While the funds system would not necessarily increase individual choice for trainees, the funds system is likely to exclude the dominance of a particular employers' interest by establishing a kind of group democracy of trainees, employers, unions, parents, educators, and the state (Mattern, 1979: 129). However, this democratic participation in decision processes concerning recurrent education would be restricted to the administration of the funds and would not include the training activities themselves. On the other hand, a polarization between the trained and untrained parts of the labor force and between the disadvantaged and advantaged groups may emerge and grow within a funds system. While it seems difficult to see whether the total costs of education would increase in such a system, the public budget would be substantially relieved by shifting the largest part of the costs for postcompulsory education and training from the state budget to funds budget(s).

THE STATE FINANCING MODEL

The term "state financing model" may seem ambiguous in that the entitlement approach could also be understood to be a state financing mechanism because it is the state who issues the vouchers and redeems them (i.e., supplies the money). However, contrary to the entitlement approach, our state financing model assigns two functions to the state: first, that of financing postcompulsory education and training (as does the voucher approach); second, the function of producing and providing education and training through public institutions (which the entitlement approach does not do). This functional difference between the two models generates a number of differences in their impacts. Hence, our state financing model turns out to be a model for state finance and production of recurrent education. It extends the education monopoly of the state (which prevails in many countries in the schooling and higher education sector) to the whole postcompulsory education and training realm. Such a system could introduce a radically different system of education. The following is a description of one possible method.

(1) Compulsory schooling begins at the age of 6 for each individual and ends after having participated in a comprehensive school system at age 16 with the first high school diploma (high school diploma I). This would qualify a person for both work and for attendance in the second phase of high schools.

(2) The phase of postcompulsory education and training is organized according to the recurrent education concept. One becomes eligible attending the second phase of high school by earning the high school diploma I and accruing a minimum of four years of work experience. By way of exception, only extremely talented persons may be allowed to skip the work experience (in order to recruit scientists). The second high school phase ends after two or three years with the diploma II which again qualifies the individual for work and study. Admission to higher education is only possible for persons with diploma II or for those with diploma I and seven years of work experience. The attendance of high schools in the second phase and of institutions of higher education is possible on either a part time or full-time schedule.

(3) High schools and higher education institutions offer a highly stratified variety of education and training possibilities. These are developed in response to the various needs of individuals according to their work experience, their interests, and their educational prerequisites. Institutions of higher education carry out postgraduate studies in order to recruit young scientists.
(4) The state is the sole agent to offer all education and training activities during compulsory and postcompulsory education and training.
(5) The state bears all direct and indirect costs of education and training through the public budget.
(6) Each person with diploma I (i.e., who has completed compulsory education with success) gets a quota of "life education hours" or "points" in order to keep the demand for recurrent education within reasonable limits. These points can be used according to individual plans and preferences during the postcompulsory period. Only unemployed persons with specific characteristics (e.g., long unemployment) are restricted as to their freedom of choice: Unemployment compensation will be paid on the condition that one takes part in postcompulsory training activities.
(7) The state alone is responsible for the training and recruitment of teachers and trainers as well as for the size, structure and contents of education and training.
(8) Responsibility for the educational system forces the state to undertake research in qualification, technology, education, training, and the labor market in order to be able to carry through a plan of recurrent education. State planning of education is the dominant mechanism of allocation within the system of financing and producing recurrent education through the state.

Such a system could encourage the recurrent alternation of work, education, leisure, and training, and promote a general flexibility of work and nonwork time. Moreover, the integration of general education and vocational training and of theoretical knowledge and practical know-how would be likely to occur. Also, participation of the population in recurrent education can be comprehensive and equitable. Quality differences can be expected to be low, while the minimum standards of general education probably would be high. However, performance in vocational training might not satisfy employers. The regional distribution of activities would be equal, and social cohesion would generally be strengthened (Lowe, 1975: 44).

But note that a comprehensive high standard may imply uniformity instead of variety, and boredom rather than diversity. This characteristic may conflict with the postulate for more individual choice in education. Moreover, the federal structure of the state may be seen to endanger comprehensive solutions while it is feared that state responsibility for all kinds of education and training will reinforce the alienation between education and training on the one side and work on the other (Hegelheimer, 1978; Oberhauser, 1970: 27). We may also question the ability of this financing system to restrain the dominance of particular state interests in favor of the democratic participation of learners (Edding et al., 1974: 131).

The impact of the state financing solution on the efficiency of the recurrent education system is hard to estimate. Improvements of internal as well as innovational efficiency are unlikely to be substantial because of a lack of stimuli and of efficient possibilities of control, and also because of political and bureaucratic slowness in decision processes (Friedman, 1962; Levin, 1976; Weizsacker, 1975). External efficiency effects seem to be more complex: Efficiency may improve by internalizing external effects; these gains, however, may be lost through overinternalization—that is, encouraging overinvestment in recurrent education through a zero-price offer, creating a divergence between private and social rates of return (Friedman, 1962).

While we would expect the coordination between the education and employment systems to improve because of the productivity and flexibility of recurrently educated people and because of preventive training strategies, these efficiency gains may be compensated for (if not nullified entirely) by global and structural misallocations and misplanning by the state resulting from a lack of necessary information or political quarrels. Moreover, business cycles may destabilize recurrent education activities over time, and short-run interests of politicians are likely to cut resources for education in times of growing financial stress. Furthermore, recurrent education may become a victim of political conflicts and political cycles (Widmaier, 1976: 81; Downs, 1972).

The state financing model allows realization of social objectives in recurrent education (Edding et al., 1974: 127)—for example, equality of educational opportunity or similar equity principles—more than other models do. Through the progressivity of the tax system, the financial burden created by recurrent education can be redistributed to the benefit of those with low income. However, the basic question of whether the tax system actually can be constructed to work progressively is hard to answer. Apart from this problem, the lack of direct charges for recurrent education, new and flexible structures for work time, and attractive programs may suffice as incentives to attract those disadvantaged individuals and groups who are said to be education-distant today. Thus the possibility of enforcing equality of educational opportunity and of redistributing economic burdens and benefits in favor of the poor and disadvantaged supports the state financing model. In addition, the model could be extended by income-contingent loans or self-participation of those who are well-off in the case of a nonprogressive tax system. Finally, it seems very likely that such a model would increase the total costs as well as the state budget for education. This may again raise the question of an upper limit for the state budget.

CONCLUSIONS

The evaluation of the different financing mechanisms shows that none of the "pure" models can attain all of the goals. Each is characterized by deficiencies, although they are different for each model. This difference in deficiencies makes a comparison of the models very hazardous, particularly when this comparison is intended to identify the "preferable" financing mechanism. The assessment suggests a general trade-off between economic and noneconomic criteria (i.e., between efficiency and equality or social cohesion)—this trade-off becoming more significant to the degree that individuals are expected to finance recurrent education out of their own resources.

One way to determine the "best" financing system is to comprise a cost-utility analysis for each alternative model. First, this analysis would have to ask specifically which model is most able to meet each particular criterion. Each system would be evaluated on its ability to do the following: to maximize external and internal efficiency, minimize structural misallocations and efficiency losses, internalize external effects, maximize the quality of educational output and guarantee minimum quality standards, maximize innovation efficiency, minimize inequality of opportunity, maximize individual choice, prevent both underinvestment and overinvestment in recurrent education, minimize social and economic inequality, encourage demand for recurrent education, (particularly from disadvantaged groups and classes), maximize democratization and social cohesion, encourage integration, and so forth.

Second, in the course of such an analysis specific weights expressing the preferences of researchers, politicians, and others would have to be assigned to each criterion. This procedure would allow one to establish a definite order among the financing mechanisms and determine which is the "best" one. However, it is likely that there will be as many different orders and "best" financing modes as there are different preference structures.

My own evaluation of the impact of the various financing schemes suggests that a proper financing scheme for recurrent postcompulsory education should focus on entitlement, parafiscal funding, and state financing. These models seem to have a stronger impact on those criteria that should be met by a financing system of recurrent education than do the self-financing, the drawing rights, and the single-employer financing models. However, as the favorable models suffer from serious deficiencies as well, it seems obvious that we should attempt to construct a financing scheme that is composed mainly of various elements of the preferred models, but that capitalizes on their advantages while avoiding their deficiencies as much as possible.

A MIXED MODEL FOR FINANCING POSTCOMPULSORY EDUCATION AND TRAINING

The mixed model of financing recurrent education (model 7) should start with the assumption that the individual learner, the individual employer (public and private), and society in general will accrue monetary and nonmonetary economic as well as noneconomic benefits from postcompulsory education and training. Therefore, individuals, employers, and the state should pay for postcompulsory education and training. However, the extent to which each of these audiences should pay is open to discussions and political dispute since there is no knowledge of the distribution of these benefits among the individual learner, employers, and the society. In order to encourage demand for recurrent education, the contributions of individuals should strictly follow the "ability-to-pay" principle. The basic features proposed for this mixed model of financing recurrent education (model 7) are as follows:

(1) A parafiscal fund will be established, and all public and private employers will be required to contribute to this fund by a levy on their value-added. (A further question is whether a central fund or decentralized funds should be utilized. This question will not be discussed here.)

(2) The state pays a certain amount of tax money into the fund, for example as a fixed proportion of the state budget, with the proportion changing over time as needed. The fund will be administered by an agency, which is governed collectively by representatives of the state, employers' unions, and nonunionized laborers.

(3) Postcompulsory education and training is produced and offered by private as well as state institutions. Both have to meet high minimum standards of program quality and diversity in order to be accredited by the fund.

(4) The fund issues entitlements to every person who has completed compulsory schooling. Everyone is free to use the entitlements for any education or training activities in accredited institutions over their lifetime. The use is limited to recurrent education activities. Completion of compulsory schooling is the only prerequisite for admission.

(5) The entitlements consist of a basic grant for each eligible person and a dual component beyond the basic grant. The dual component generally consists of a grant and a loan element. The partition between the two elements depends on the ability of the eligible person to pay (i.e., based on income and wealth considering family responsibilities). This means that the grant (or loan) component decreases with increasing ability-to-pay (income and wealth), and vice versa, such that a disadvantaged low-income person may enjoy a full grant entitlement while an advantaged person who is more able to pay is likely to be supplemented in the form of a loan. Each person is free to pay out of present resources and refrain from using a loan.

(6) One becomes obligated to pay back a loan on reaching a specified income (for example, one that exceeds the income of a person without recurrent education).

This mixed financing system is likely to develop a comprehensive integrated system of recurrent education and recurrent alternation of education, work, leisure, and training as well as flexible work-time schedules. High minimum standards of output quality as well as a good diversity of programs that are tailored to the interests and needs of the learners seem very likely to emerge. Internal efficiency as well as efficiency in innovation are likely to increase, the latter with respect to nonmarketable as well as to marketable innovations The labor force will gain flexibility whereby labor market disequilibria very well may be prevented. An anticyclical investment strategy may prevail, and external effects will be internalized but not to the point of overinternalization. While the labor force will gain productivity, general over- or underinvestment may be avoided. General knowledge and specific mar-

TABLE 5.1 Impact of Financing Models on Recurrent Education

	Degree of Impact																																		
	Model 1					*Model 2*					*Model 3*					*Model 4*					*Model 5*					*Model 6*					*Model 7*				
Criteria	*vl*	*l*	*p*	*nl*	*c*	*vl*	*l*	*p*	*nl*	*c*	*vl*	*l*	*p*	*nl*	*c*	*vl*	*l*	*p*	*nl*	*c*	*vl*	*l*	*p*	*nl*	*c*	*vl*	*l*	*p*	*nl*	*c*	*vl*	*l*	*p*	*nl*	*c*
Encouraging recurrence				x		x					x							x			x					x					x				
Increasing efficiency			x				x					x							x				x				x				0	0			
internal	x					x					x					x							x					0	0			x			
external			0	0			x					0							0	0			x			0	0				x				
Encouraging innovation	x					0			0		x					x						x						0	0		x				
improving general knowledge				x					x					x					x			x					x					x			
improving marketable skills	x					x					x		0			x					x								0		x				
Encouraging integration				x					x					x					x		x					x					x				
Increasing individual choice	x					x					x							0	0					x					x		0	0			
Encouraging demand for RE and increasing equality of participation				x				0	0		x								x					x		x					x				
Decreasing social and economic inequality				x					x			0	0						x					x				0	0		0	0			
democratization				x				x					x					0	0			x						0	0			x			
Preservation and the enforcement of social cohesion				x					x					x					x					x			x						x		
Increasing total costs of education				x				0	0		x							0	0				x			x					x				
Increasing state budget burden for education				x	0				0	0	x								0	0				0	0	x							x		

1 = Self-financing model
2 = Drawing rights model
3 = Entitlement model
4 = Single-employer financing model
5 = Parafiscal funds model
6 = State financing model
7 = Mixed financing model

x = impact seems clear
0 = impact seems not very clear; either/or

vl = very likely
l = likely
p = possible
nl = not likely
c = contrary

ketable skills will improve within a system that is able to integrate general education, vocational training, theoretical knowledge, and practical know-how.

The entitlement component will enhance individual choice, and state and employers' participation in decision processes is likely to promote social cohesion. Demand for recurrent education will be stimulated, particularly among disadvantaged groups, because there will be no direct charge for recurrent education for those with less ability-to-pay, and also because we may expect strong efforts to change the job structure in order to increase the recurrent-education value of work.

The distribution of education and training as well as knowledge and skills will probably become more equal across regional and generational distinctions. Moreover, burdens and benefits will be distributed less unequally such that an overall drop in the extent of social and economic inequality would be likely. Furthermore, the dominance of particular interests will be broken and be replaced by democratic participation of all relevant social groups and institutions. While the total costs of education and training will increase, under such a system the state budget could be relieved. Generally, this financing model is likely to require the least trade-off between efficiency and equality. Apart from the problems of designing a financing method as well as the regulatory and information systems in detail, and leaving aside the problems of implementation, the mixed model (model 7) seems to be the most promising alternative. This can be seen in Table 5.1, which gives a summary of the model evaluations.

NOTES

1. All criteria are drawn from the literature on recurrent education. The sequence of introduction does not reflect priorities. Various references with respect to the objectives of recurrent education are to be found in Bengtsson and Schutze (1979); CERI (1973); Clement and Sauerschnig (1978: 12); Levin (1977, 1980) Mattern (1979: 9). More specific criteria have been proposed by Edding (1974), and Edding et al. (1974); and recently by CERI (1982), and Schutze (1982). The system of social indicators of performance of educational systems developed by the OECD (1973) is very detailed but has not been tailored to the needs of a recurrent education system. It has been constructed for the purpose of international comparisons in education rather than for comparing alternative financing models.

2. This is true only for public support. Private support (grants) by firms or other institutions might occur but is likely to remain an exception rather than the rule.

3. It does not seem very likely that loans will have a strong effect on demand (Mattern, 1979: 83).

REFERENCES

BECKER, G. (1975) Human Capital. Second edition. (New York and London: Columbia University Press).

BENGTSSON, J., and H. G. SCHÜTZE (1974) "Developments in recurrent education and recent economic and social trends," in W. Clement and F. Edding (eds.) Recurrent Education und Flexibilitätsforschung. Berlin.

BLAUG, M. (1970) An Introduction to the Economics of Education. London: Viking.

——— (1967) "Approaches to educational planning." Economic J. 57: 262-287.

CERI/OECD (1982) The Costs and Financing of Recurrent Education. Paris: Author.

——— (1979) Recurrent Education for the 1980s: Trends and Policies. CERI/CED (79) 12; ED (79) 16. Paris: Author.

——— (1973) Recurrent Education: A Strategy for Lifelong Learning. Paris: Author.

CLEMENT, W., and R. SAUERSCHNIG (1978) Empirische Grundlagen und Konzepte einer Bildungsfinanzierungspolitik in Österreich (Empirical Foundations and Concepts of a Policy for Financing Education in Austria). Vienna: Vertschafts verlag Dr. Anton Orac.

CLEMENT, W., and F. EDDING [eds.] (1979) Recurrent Education und Flexibilitatsforschung (Recurrent Education and Flexibility Research) Berlin: Dunker and Humblot.

COHN, E. (1975) The Economics of Education. Cambridge, MA: Ballinger.

COONS, J. E., and St. D. SUGARMAN (1978) Education by Choice: The Case for Family Control. Berkeley: Univ. of California Press.

DOWNS, A. (1972) "Up and down with ecology: The 'issue-attention-cycle'," The Public Interest 28 (Summer).

EDDING, F. (1976) "Ökonomische probleme des recurrent-education-konzepts," ("Economic Problems of the Concept of Recurrent Education") Jahrbuch für Wirtschafts—und Sozialwissenschaften, Heft 4: 287-301.

——— (1974) "Higher education in a future system of universal recurrent education," Paedagogica Europaea 9, 2.

——— (1974) "Educational Leave and Sources of Funding," in S. J. Mushkin (ed.) Recurrent Education. Washington, DC: NIE, U.S. Department of Health, Education, and Welfare.

EDDING, F., U. BOEHM, G. DYBOWSKY, and H. RUDOLPH (1974) Struktur und Finanzierung der Aus-und Weiterbildung (Organization and Finance of Continuing Education and Training). Gottingen: Verlag Otto Schwartz and Co.

FREEMAN, R. B. (1977) "The decline in the economic rewards to college education." Rev. of Economics and Statistics 59 (February) 1.

——— (1976) The Overeducated American. New York: Academic Press.

FRIEDMAN, M. (1962) Capitalism and Freedom. Chicago: Univ. of Chicago Press.

GLENNY, L. A. "Financing postsecondary education in the USA." Higher Education 5, 1: 103.

HANSEN, W. L., and B. A. WEISBROD (1969) Benefits, Costs and Finance of Public Higher Education. Chicago: Markham.

HEGELHEIMER, A. (1977) Finanzierungsprobleme derr Berufsausbildung (Problems of Financing Vocational Training). Stuttgart: Klett-Cotta Verlag.

JACKSON, G. A. and G. B. WEATHERSBY (1975) "Individual demand for higher education: a review and analysis of recent empirical studies." J. of Higher Education 46, 6: 623-652.

JENCKS, C. et al. (1972) Inequality: A Reassessment of the Effect of Family and Schooling in America. New York: Random House.

O'KEEFE, M. (1977) The Adult Education and Public Policy. Palo Alto, CA: Aspen Institute for Humanistic Studies..

KRELLE, W., M. FLECK, and H. QUINKE (1975) Gesamtwirtschaftliche Auswirkungen einer Ausweitung des Bildungssystems: Abschlussbericht (Macroeconomic Effects of an Expansion of the Educational System: Final Report). Tubingen: Verlag J.C.B. Mohr and Paul Siebeck.

——— (1974) Gesamtwirtschaftliche Auswirkungen von Änderungen der beruflichen Ausbildung und Weiterbildung (Macro-Economic Effects of Changes in the System of Initial and Continuing Training). Bielefeld: Bertelsman Verlag.

KUHLENKAMP, D., and H. G. SCHUTZE [eds.] (1982) Kosten und Finanzierung der beruflichen und nicht-beruflichen Weiterbildung (The Costs and Financing of Continuing Education and Training). Frankfurt Main: Verlag Moritz Diesterweg.

LEVIN, H. M. (1980) Individual Entitlements for Recurrent Education. Paris: OECD, CERI.

——— (1977) "Post-secondary entitlements: an exploration," p. 1 in N. D. Kurland (ed.) Entitlement Studies. NIE Papers in Education and Work 4. Washington, DC: U.S. Department of Health, Education, and Welfare.

——— (1977) "Financing recurrent education with post-compulsory entitlements." Stanford, CA: Stanford University, School of Education.

——— (1976) "Concepts of economic efficiency and educational production," in J. T. Froomkin et al. (eds.) Education as an Industry. Cambridge, MA: Ballinger.

——— (1975) "Educational vouchers and educational equality," in M. Carnoy (ed.) Schooling in a Corporate Society. New York: Longmans.

LOWE, J. (1975) The Education of Adults. Paris: Unesco Press.

MATTERN, C. (1979) Bildungsfinanzierung: Probleme unds neue Ansätze (Financing Education: Problems and New Approaches). Frankfurt-Berlin-München: Verlag Moritz Diesterweg.

MINCER, J. (1974) Schooling, Experience, and Earnings. (New York: Columbia Univ. Press.

MUSHKIN, S. J. [ed] (1974) Recurrent Education. Washington, DC: NIE, U.S. Department of Health, Education, and Welfare.

OBERHAUSER, A. (1970) Finanzierungsalternativen der beruflichen Ausund Weiterbildung (Alternative Financing Schemes for Initial and Continuing Training). Stuttgart: Klett Verlag.

OECD (1977) Learning Opportunities for Adults, Vol. I-IV. Paris: Author.

——— (1973) Indicators of Performance of Educational Systems. Paris: Author.

PECHMAN, J. A. and B. A. OKNER (1974) Who Bears the Tax Burden? Washington, DC: The Brookings Institution.

PFAFF, M., and G. FUCHS (1975) "Education inequality and life income: a report on the Federal Republic of Germany," p. 7 in OECD (ed.) Education Inequality and Life Chances, Vol. 2. Paris: OECD.

REHN, G. (1978) Towards a Society of Free Choice. Stockholm: Swedish Institute for Social Research.

——— (1974) "Towards flexibility in working life." University Q.: 276-286.

Sachverständigenkommission Kosten und Finanzierung der ausserschulischen beruflichen Bildung: Abschlussbericht (Expert Commission on Costs and Financing of Non-School-Based Vocational Training: Final Report) [1974]. Bonn.

Sachverständigenkommission Kosten und Finanzierung der beruflichen Bildung: Zwischenbericht der Kommission (Intermediate Expert Commission Report) [1973]. Bonn.

SADOWSKI, D. (1980) "Finance and governance of the German apprenticeship system: some considerations on market failure and its efficient corrections." Stanford, CA.

SCHÜTZE, H. G. (1982) "Das OECD-Konzept 'Recurrent Education' und Kriterien fur die Finanzierung lebenslangen Lernens" ("The OECD concept of recurrent education and criteria for financing lifelong learning") in D. Kuhlenkamp and H. G. Schütze (eds.) Kosten und Finanzierung der beruflichen und nicht-beruflichen Weiterbildung (The Costs and Financing of Continuing Education and Training). Frankfurt Main.

STOIKOV, V. (1973) "Recurrent education: some neglected economic issues," International Labour Rev. 109: 187-208.

THUROW, L. C. (1975) Generating Inequality: Mechanics of Distribution in the U.S. Economy. New York: Basic Books.

TIMMERMANN, D. (1982) "Das Staatsfinanzierungsmodell als Finanzierungsalternative fur Recurrent Education" ("The state financing model as an alternative to financing recurrent education") in D. Kuhlenkamp and H. G. Schütze (eds.) Kosten und Finanzierung der beruflichen und nicht-beruflichen Weiterbuldung (The Costs and Financing of Continuing Education and Training). Frankfurt Main.

——— (1979) Bildungsmarkte oder Bildungsplannung: eine kritische Auseinanderstzung mit swei alternativen Stuerungssystemen und ihren Implikationen fur das Bildungssystem (Educational Markets or Educational Planning: A Critical Review of Two Alternative Regulatory Systems and Their Implications for the Educational System). Erweitertes Manuskript des Habilitationsvortrags vom 20.6. Bielefeld.

WEIZSACKER, C. C. v. (1975) "Hochschulstruktur und Marketsystem" ("The structure of higher education and the market system") in U. Lohmar and G. E. Ortner (eds) Die deutsche Hochschule Zwischen Numerus clausus und Akademikerarbeitslosigkeit. Der Doppelte Flaschenhals (The German University and the Double Bottleneck of Limited Access and Graduate Unemployment). Hanover-Dortmund-Darmstadt-Berlin: 306.

WEST, E. G. (1964) "Private versus public education: a classical economic dispute." J. of Pol. Economy 5 (October): 465-475.

WIDMAIER, H. P. (1976) Sozialpolitik im Wohlfarhrtsstaat (Social Policies in the Welfare State). Reinbek: Rowohlt Tachenbuch Verlag GmbH.

WINDHAM, D. M. (1976) "Social benefits and the subsidization of higher education: a critique." Higher Education 5, 3: 237.

[illegible]

[illegible] Educational Administration Quarterly [illegible]

[illegible]

[illegible] Review [illegible]

[illegible]

[illegible] Administrative Science Quarterly [illegible]

[illegible]

[illegible] Educational [illegible]

[illegible] Higher Education [illegible]

II

FINANCING RECURRENT EDUCATION IN THE UNITED STATES

6

AN INVENTORY OF PROGRAMS AND SOURCES OF SUPPORT

ALAN P. WAGNER

In 1980, 50 million individuals in the United States participated in at least 1 type of organized postsecondary learning activity, at a total cost of $55 billion. While the actual numbers are imprecise, the volume of and investment in learning beyond high school are impressive. The purposes of this chapter are to estimate the participation in different types of postcompulsory education and training programs in the United States, to compare the costs of and funding for these activities, and to consider differences in the attributes of participants among programs.

As sources of improvements in the productive capacities of workers, all postcompulsory education and training programs merit the attention of policy makers. The more detailed focus on the different types of education and training is important for several reasons. First, efforts to improve productivity through post-high school education and training may be less successful if public policies ignore sources of training outside of postsecondary educational institutions. Beyond identifying the available sources of training, the comparison may reveal which providers tend to be most efficient in producing trained manpower. Second, eligibility for public subsidies might be extended to nontraditional programs as a means of reaching those most in need

---

AUTHOR'S NOTE: *The author appreciates the helpful comments and suggestions of R. Anderson, R. Boaz, W. Bruno, C. Byce, R. Calvert, T. Chase, B. Clayton, J. Green, A. Sinaiko, P. Smith, and F. Woods.*

of training (such as the disadvantaged or the older worker with technically obsolete skills).

For the purposes of this article postcompulsory education and training programs are identified as those that include any formal, organized sessions of instruction. The definition excludes self-directed study, on-the-job training, and programs designed to transmit information only. Even with this restriction, the numbers must be regarded as "order of magnitude" estimates, principally because the data, culled from several published and unpublished sources, are inconsistent and, in some instances, quite dated.

I begin with a discussion of the enrollments in different types of postcompulsory education and training programs. Estimates of the costs of, and sources of funding for, these programs are considered in the next section, and a discussion of differences in the attributes of participants among the programs follows. The last section presents several implications for public policy.

VOLUME AND TYPES OF PROGRAMS

Estimates of the number of participants in postcompulsory education and training programs vary. The Carnegie Commission (1973) estimated that 74 million individuals participated in some organized learning activity in 1970 (projected to 108 million in 1980). This is reasonably close to the ETS estimate of 62 million learners for 1972 (Carp et al., 1974), but much higher than the 27 million reported in companion census surveys (NCES-sponsored Survey of Adult Education and the Census Bureau's own October school enrollment surveys). More recently, Peterson and others (1979) estimated the participation in organized post-high school education and training at 64 million. My own estimate, for 1980, is 75 million (see Table 6.1), although this figure (and the others) probably overstates the unduplicated count of participants by about 30%.

What types of education and training programs are chosen? During 1980, nearly 58% of the enrollees attended programs other than those offered at postsecondary education institutions. This finding is consistent with Peterson's estimate as well as figures cited by Smith (1973).

This and other interesting dimensions of current postcompulsory education and training programs emerge from the detailed distribution of participants by source of program in Table 6.1. As in other studies, the programs shown here are defined largely in terms of the *provider* (such as a four-year college or a tutor). Broschart (1977), among others, notes that this approach is but one of several ways of categorizing postcompulsory education and training.[1] The inventory of programs by provider, however, permits some comparisons with previous studies, reveals some differences in costs of and sources of funding for essentially identical training, and, in some cases, also distinguishes among types of education and training programs. To allow additional comparisons by type of program and funding, I have extended the general approach in two ways. First, estimates of participation by "type of program" (such as full-time, part-time, and noncredit study) are presented for some providers since differences in the type of course and the characteristics of participants are obvious. Second, some essentially similar programs offered within major employment sectors (private business or industry, armed forces, government) are considered separately, since these represent major providers of training.

Although good descriptions of the types of programs appear elsewhere (Fraser, 1980; Peterson et al., 1979; Calvert, 1977), several of the participant estimates merit emphasis. First, to better reflect the level of resources required to provide postcompulsory education and training, the participant data have been converted to equivalent class hours for each program. These estimates are shown in the last two columns of Table 6.1. Here, contrary to the distribution of participants, providers other than postsecondary educational institutions account for less than 30% of the total class hours devoted to postcompulsory education and training. Clearly, much of the training outside of postsecondary educational institutions is less extensive (fewer courses per participant) and relatively short term (fewer hours). As a result, those attending courses at postsecondary educational institutions spend over 200 hours in class, on average, while their counterparts receiving training from other providers average less than 100 hours in class.

Second, part-time (including correspondence) and noncredit enrollments represent about two-thirds of the 31 million enrolled in all postsecondary educational institutions. According to these figures, although full-time enrollment of 7.9 million students at a four-year institutions clearly dominates, part-time and noncredit enrollments represent a sizable proportion of this sector's clientele. These observations become all the more significant when viewed in light of recent enrollment trends: full-time enrollments rising at about 1% per year, part-time enrollments at about 6% per year, and noncredit enrollments (regis-

TABLE 6.1 Participation in Postcompulsory Education and Training Programs by Source, 1980

	Participants		*Participant Class Hours*	
	Number[a] *(thousands)*	*Percentage*	*Number (millions)*	*Percentage*
TOTAL	74,850	100.0	8,950	100.0
POSTSECONDARY EDUCATIONAL INSTITUTIONS	31,350	41.9	6,350	71.0
Four-Year Colleges and Universities				
Full-Time	7,900	10.6	2,600	29.0
Part-Time	3,500	4.7	525	5.9
Non-Credit	3,100	4.2	75	.8
Two-Year Colleges				
Full-Time	2,000	2.7	650	7.3
Part-Time	2,700	3.6	350	3.9
Non-Credit	3,450	4.6	100	1.1
Vocational				
Full-Time	600	.8	450	5.0
Part-Time	3,000	4.0	550	6.1
Proprietary				
Full-Time	600	.8	450	5.0
Part-Time	3,000	4.0	550	6.1
Correspondence (civilian)	1,500	2.0	50	.6
OTHER POSTCOMPULSORY EDUCATION AND TRAINING	43,500	58.1	2,600	29.0
Elementary and Secondary Schools	2,400	3.2	150	1.7
Business or Industry				
Apprenticeships	700	.9	100	1.1
Other organized instruction (off-the-job)	7,400	9.9	400	4.5
Professional Associations	5,500	7.3	125	1.4
Labor Unions	100	.1	25	.3
Armed Forces				
Initial training	1,050	1.4	500	5.6
Other organized instruction	750	1.0	150	1.7
Correspondence	1,000	1.3	50	.6
Prisons	75	.1	25	.3
Other Government Programs				
Manpower training	975	1.3	325	3.6
Cooperative extension	5,100	6.8	75	.8
Other organized instruction (off-the-job)	1,300	1.7	75	.8

(continued)

TABLE 6.1 Continued

	Participants		*Participant Class Hours*	
	Number[a] *(thousands)*	*Percentage Percentage*	*Number (millions)*	*Percentage*
Other Organized Programs (churches and synagogues, community organizations, libraries and museums, etc.)	16,000	21.4	575	6.4
Tutors	1,150	1.5	25	.2

SOURCES: Numbers represent best estimates, using published available data from census, private association, agency, and other surveys. Rounded to nearest 25 thousand of million. See text.
a. Overstates number of participants by about 30% due to multiple program enrollments.

trations) at about 7% per year over the 1976-1978 period (NCES, 1980; Dearman, 1980).

Third, nearly 15% of all participants in postcompulsory education and training receive off-the-job, classroom instruction provided by employers.[2] Although the estimates are "best guesses," these programs train 7.4 million persons in the private sector, plus 1.8 million in the armed services, plus 1.3 million in the public sector (federal, state, and local). According to Lusterman (1977) and the U.S. Office of Personnel Management (1980), this training takes place on or near the job site and tends to be job related.

Fourth, federal, state, and local governments *directly* provided postcompulsory education and training to over 25 million individuals in 1980. In addition to the armed forces and public employee training just discussed, the programs are quite diverse: adult and vocational education at elementary and secondary schools, CETA vocational training for the disadvantaged and unemployed or underemployed workers, a growing set of education programs in prisons (particularly at the postsecondary level), cooperative extension meetings, and programs of public community organizations, libraries, and museums. These programs are examined in more detail in other studies (see, for example, Congressional Budget Office, 1980b; Bell et al., 1979; U.S. Department of Agriculture, 1980; Kay, 1974; Peterson et al., 1979), but the nature and range of the learning activities should be obvious.

COSTS AND SOURCES OF FUNDING

In 1980, the instructional costs of postcompulsory education and training programs exceeded $55 billion (see Table 6.2). Although the figures are not strictly comparable, the Carnegie Commission (1973) estimated the 1970 costs at $28 billion. The 1980 figure excludes the indirect costs of the participants' time. If these are included, the total exceeds $100 billion in instruction and individual time resources devoted to post-high school education and training.

Selected measures of instructional costs by source of program are shown in Table 6.2. Particularly for programs provided outside educational institutions, the figures represent "best guesses." Again, however, some broad generalizations are possible.

First, the largest share of total cost, by far, appears in four-year colleges and universities ($24.5 billion, or 43.4% of the $56 billion expended). Perhaps the single most important reason for this result is the relatively high number of participant class hours at these institutions. In fact, over 70% of the dollars for postcompulsory education and training are spent by postsecondary educational institutions.

Second, employer-sponsored, off-the-job training programs account for over $11 billion in instructional costs, or about 20% of the total. In particular, private industry spent $7.2 billion for classroom instruction at the job site. The armed forces allocated over $2.8 billion for initial training and $8 billion for advanced instruction at military installations and schools. Instructional costs for government employee training came to an estimated $.6 billion in 1980.[3] One should recall that these cost figures *exclude* employee wages. From the employer's point of view, the wages of trainees represent a sizable part—perhaps as much as 50%—of the costs of their training programs.

Third, sizable differences emerge in direct costs per participant and per participant class hour. These figures control, to some extent, for the size of the programs offered by each provider, and hence give a better indication of differences in the cost of providing training. However, even these cost measures conceal important differences. For example, the high cost per class hour in postbaccalaureate study has been averaged with relatively low cost per class hour in noncredit courses. Further, flight programs in proprietary or vocational schools, or in the armed forces, tend to be considerably more expensive than other programs offered by these providers.[4]

Even with the "concealed" differences, the range of instructional costs per student is revealing: from $2675 for initial training in the armed forces to about $1700 in four-year college and university programs to less than $100 per participant for extension, tutored, and other organized community programs.[5] Differences remain even when costs are measured per participant class hour, although the ranking of providers is somewhat altered. University or four-year college programs run almost $8.00 per hour compared to $5.00-$5.50 in armed services training. Principally because few class hours are required, correspondence courses are estimated to cost over $18.00 per hour. This finding is also consistent with the Carnegie Commission's (1973) estimate for 1970.[6]

How are these costs of instruction met? Data on all sources of funding for all providers are quite sketchy, but enough information exists to suggest relative differences among programs in sources of funding. The amounts from each funding source used to meet the costs of instruction for each provider are shown in Table 6.3. Public funding consists of: (1) appropriations made to the provider from federal, state, or local governments; (2) grants and scholarships awarded through federal, state, or local government programs; and (3) tax expenditures for tuition aid, charitable contributions, and spending for training (private providers only). Private sources of support include: (1) employer tuition aid and expenditures on in-house training (net of tax expenditures); (2) other support derived from charitable giving (net of tax expenditures), or through nonprofit organizations; and (3) out-of-pocket spending by participants and their families (a residual). Many of the published figures on sources of support for individual programs were adjusted to include only the amounts used to defray instructional costs. Thus I have attempted to exclude, among others, the wage costs of participants (and the employers' support of these costs), and student aid used primarily to support living costs. Obviously, these adjustments required strong, somewhat arbitrary assumptions.[7] Given these cautions, several useful patterns in sources of funding emerge.

Taken together, public funding (including tax expenditures) provides $34.2 billion, or about 60% of the total cost of instruction of postcompulsory education and training programs in 1980.[8] Even though the larger amount of this public subsidy ($24.0 billion) is allocated to postsecondary educational institutions, the *share* of instructional costs met through public funding for nonpostsecondary school providers (61% of the $16.9 billion expended) is about the same as in the postsecondary education sector.

However, wide differences in the form of the public subsidy do appear. Postsecondary educational institutions receive $18 billion in institutional appropriations, compared to a little over $7 billion allocated to other providers. Even considering the larger costs of instruction in the postsecondary education sector, the difference is large: Institutional appropriations meet 49% of costs at the schools, while providing only 43% for other sponsors.[9] A similar difference in levels of support occurs in the distribution of student aid grants. Here, the $4.8 billion awarded to students meets 12% of instructional costs at postsecondary institutions. The $.05 billion in grants awarded to participants in nonschool programs represents less than a 1% share of costs.[10]

Third, the sectors also differ in the amount of support received from private sources. Here, almost 90% of the $5.4 billion provided by employers goes to support nonpostsecondary school programs of post-compulsory education. The $5.05 billion supporting these other providers of training meets 30% of the instructional costs in this sector. This also helps explain the $2.7 billion in tax expenditures ($2.5 billion for employer-provided in-house training alone), as private sector employers, treating training costs as a business expense, reduce their taxable income by the total cost of their programs.

Fourth, the share of all costs of instruction undertaken by employees primarily at their employers' expense exceeds $10 billion, or almost 20% of the total. Included here are all private sector employer spending ($5.4 billion), plus armed forces training (total: $4 billion), plus government employee in-house training (at $.6 billion).

Finally, some interesting differences emerge in sources of funding for different types of postsecondary education. University and four-year college programs meet about 40% of costs ($10.3 billion) through institutional appropriations, and perhaps 12% through public and private grants. At 2-year or vocational institutions, 70% to 80% of the funding ($3.9 billion and $3.4 billion, respectively) comes from institutional appropriations, with student aid grants and out-of-pocket family support accounting for another 15% each. This pattern is reversed for proprietary and correspondence school programs, where 80% to 85% of costs are met through the participants' own resources.[11]

CHARACTERISTICS OF PARTICIPANTS

Whether differences in public funding across providers serve to meet public policy goals depends, in part, on the extent to which particular types of individuals participate in the training. In Tables 6.4 through 6.8, participants are distributed by age, race, sex, employment status, income, and provider. These comparisons suggest which providers currently serve (or do not serve) potential target groups, and which programs are likely to grow or contract.

Differences in the distribution of participants by age suggest the providers that best meet the concept of recurrent education, and, importantly for policy purposes, which programs are likely to grow most rapidly through the 1980s. Table 6.4 presents the approximate age distribution of participants in each type of postcompulsory activity. From the estimates, those providers and programs serving the middle-aged group (age 35 to 54) include part-time postsecondary education (where 30% to 36% of the provider's participants come from this age group). Private employee in-house organized training, professional association training, and government employee in-house training draw even more heavily from the middle-aged group, accounting for 39% to 42% of the participants in these programs. As might be expected, younger learners represent the largest shares in full-time postsecondary education (ranging from 90% at four-year colleges and universities to 46% at proprietary schools), initial training in the armed forces (92%), and government manpower training (56%). Significantly, these programs serving younger age groups tend to utilize public funding, while the programs serving the middle-aged groups rely more heavily on private sources of funds.

Differences in the distribution of participants by race and ethnic group and by sex seem to indicate differences in the level of subsidy and in the type of training received by these groups. As shown in Table 6.5, although whites are heavily represented in postsecondary education, they also constitute a larger than proportional share in private employer in-house organized instruction (93%), professional association (94%), and public employee organized instruction (93%). On the other hand, blacks, accounting for 10% of the civilian adult population, tend to be more heavily represented in armed forces and government manpower training (at 16% and 34%, respectively). These training programs rely exclusively on public funding.

TABLE 6.2 Selected Measures of Instructional Costs of Postcompulsory Education and Training Programs by Source, 1980

	Total Cost[a]		*Per Program Participant*[b]	*Per Participant Class Hour*[c]
	Dollars (millions)	*Percentage*	*(in Dollars)*	*(in Dollars)*
TOTAL	56,475	100.0	750	6.25
POSTSECONDARY EDUCATIONAL INSTITUTIONS	39,600	70.1	1,275	6.25
Four-Year Colleges and Universities	24,525	43.4	1,700	7.75
Two-Year Colleges	5,675	10.0	700	5.25
Vocational Schools	4,300	7.6	1,200	4.25
Proprietary Schools	4,050	7.2	1,125	4.00
Correspondence Schools (civilian)	1,050	1.8	700	18.25
OTHER POSTCOMPULSORY EDUCATION AND TRAINING	16,875	29.9	400	6.50
Elementary and Secondary Schools	350	.6	150	2.75
Business or Industry				
Apprenticeships	350	.6	475	3.25
Other organized instruction (off-the-job)	7,200	12.7	975	18.00
Professional Associations	550	1.0	100	4.50
Labor Unions	25	*	225	7.25
Armed Forces				
Initial training	2,825	5.0	2,675	5.50
Other organized instruction	775	1.4	1,000	5.00
Correspondence	700	1.2	700	18.25
Prisons	100	.2	1,225	4.50
Other Government Programs				
Manpower training	1,475	2.6	1,500	4.75
Cooperative Extension	350	.6	75	5.75
Other organized instruction (off-the-job)	575	1.0	450	6.50
Other Organized Programs (churches and synagogues, community organizations, libraries and museums, etc.)	1,500	2.6	100	2.75
Tutors	100	.2	100	4.00

SOURCES: Numbers represent best estimates, using published available data from census, private association, agency, and other surveys. See text.

a. Rounded to nearest 25 million.

b. Rounded to nearest 25 dollars.

c. Rounded to nearest 25 cents.

*Less than .1%.

The differences in the distribution of participants by sex and provider (Table 6.6) suggest that women may be less likely to receive employment-related training than men. In particular, men make up the majority of participants in apprenticeship, professional association, and both private and public employee organized training. The latter programs are particularly important, since they may facilitate promotion in the company or agency. Elementary and secondary school, cooperative extension, and community-based programs—programs that are more likely to be avocational—enroll larger proportions of women.

Finally, participation in all programs tends to be linked to employment and income, as can be seen in Tables 6.7 and 6.8. However, those not working represent a majority of the participants in full-time study (50% to 70%) and in manpower training programs (96%). Similarly, over 90% of the trainees in government manpower training programs come from the lowest income quartile.

CONCLUDING REMARKS

The $55 billion spent in postcompulsory education and training programs in 1980 represents an important investment in probably the most important factor of production: human resources. Yet the data presented in this article suggest that sizable differences exist in the types of, costs of, and sources of funding for these programs. Three findings with broad implications emerge.

First, although over half of the participants enroll in programs offered outside of postsecondary educational institutions, the major portion of postcompulsory education and training costs are incurred in the postsecondary education sector. In part, this reflects the amount of participant time devoted to the learning activities. However, even though similar proportions of the instructional costs in both sectors appear to be met through public funding, this parity disappears when government-provided programs (armed forces, manpower training, public employee training) are separated out of the nonschool sector. This contrast suggests potential administrative and financial barriers to providing further education and training outside of schools. If these barriers were eased (through voucher or institutional funding), larger numbers of individuals might be able to participate in types of programs of particular importance to policymakers (such as job-related training provided by employers and professional associations).

TABLE 6.3 Costs and Sources of Funds for Postcompulsory Education and Training Programs, 1980

	Cost of Instruction (millions of dollars)	Sources of Funds (millions of dollars)					
		Public			Private		
		Institutional Appropriation[a]	Student Aid Grants[b]	Tax Expenditure[c]	Employer[d]	Private Other[e]	Student[f] and/or Family
TOTAL	56.475	25.425	4.850	3.875	5,425	2,000	14,950
POSTSECONDARY EDUCATIONAL INSTITUTIONS	39.600	18.050	4.800	1.150	375	1.500	13,775
Four-Year Colleges and Universities	24.525	10.300	2.900	1.050	200	1,400	8,675
Two-Year Colleges	5.675	3.925	850	50	75	50	775
Vocational Schools	4.300	3.450	600	25	50	25	150
Proprietary Schools	4.050	275	400	25	50	25	3.725
Correspondence Schools (civilian)	1.050	100	50	–	–	–	–
OTHER POSTCOMPULSORY EDUCATION AND TRAINING	16.875	7.375	50	2.725	5.050	500	1.175
Elementary and Secondary	350	300	–	–	–	–	50
Business or Industry							
Apprenticeships	350	150	–	75	125	–	–
Other Organized Instruction (off-the-job)	7.200	–	–	2.525	4.675	–	–

Professional Associations	550	–	50	50	125	100	225
Labor Unions	25	–	–	–	–	25	–
Armed Forces							
Initial Training	2,852	2,825	–	–	–	–	–
Other Organized Instruction	775	775	–	–	–	–	–
Correspondence	700	700	–	–	–	–	–
Prisons	100	100	–	–	–	–	–
Other Government Programs							
Manpower Training	1,475	1,475	–	–	–	–	–
Cooperative Extension	350	350	–	–	–	–	–
Other Organized Instruction (off-the-job)	575	575	–	–	–	–	–
Other Organized Programs (churches and synagogues, community organizations, libraries and museums, etc.)	1,500	125	–	75	125	375	800
Tutors	100	–	–	–	–	–	100

SOURCES: Numbers represent best estimates, using published available data from census, private association, agency, and other surveys. Rounded to nearest 25 million; amounts less than 12.5 million are omitted. See text.

a. Includes institutional appropriations from federal, state, and local jurisdictions allocated to provider.

b. Includes public grants and scholarships awarded directly to students through basic grants, supplemental grants, state grants, and 25% of Veterans Administration benefits (an estimate of the proportion of VA benefits covering tuition and fees expenses). Tuition waivers are funded by institutional appropriations (and included there).

c. Tax expenditures consist of reduced tax liabilities resulting from private tuition-aid plans, corporate and individual support of educational and training programs, and the implicit tax subsidy for programs offered in private industry.

d. Includes support of tuition-aid, on-site training programs in the private sector, and programs offered by other providers, net of tax expenditures.

e. Includes corporate, nonprofit, and individual support of educational and training programs, either to institutions or to students (excluding tuition aid).

Second, with the aging of the U.S. population, participation in programs outside of postsecondary educational institutions will continue to increase at a faster rate than full-time postsecondary education enrollments. Here the growth of noncredit, community-based, and

TABLE 6.4 Participants in Postcompulsory Education and Training Programs by Age and Source, 1978 (in percentages)

	Total 17 Years and Over	*17-24 Years*	*25-34 Years*	*35-54 Years*	*55-64 Years*	*65 Years and Over*
TOTAL CIVILIAN ADULT POPULATION[b]	100	20	22	30	13	15
POSTSECONDARY EDUCATIONAL INSTITUTIONS						
Four-Year College or University						
Full-Time[a]	100	90	8	3	–	–
Part-Time[b,1]	100	17	47	30	5	1
Two-Year College and Vocational-Technical Institution						
Full-Time[a]	100	84	12	4	–	–
Part-Time[b,1]	100	26	36	30	6	2
Proprietary						
Full-Time[b,2]	100	46	33	18	2	1
Part-Time[b,1]	100	22	35	36	6	1
Correspondence[b,3]	100	19	39	33	7	3
OTHER POSTCOMPULSORY EDUCATION AND TRAINING						
Elementary and Secondary Schools (part-time)[b]	100	23	34	34	7	2
Business or Industry						
Apprenticeships	na	na	na	na	na	na
Other Organized Instruction (off-the-job)[b,4]	100	15	37	39	7	1
Professional Associations[b,5]	100	9	36	42	10	2
Labor Unions	na	na	na	na	na	na
Armed Forces						
Initial Training[c,6]	100	92	7	1	–	–
Other Organized Instruction	na	na	na	na	na	na
Correspondence	na	na	na	na	na	na
Prisons[d,7]	100	38	38	21	3	–
Other Government Programs						
Manpower Training[e]	100	56	27	10	3	–
Cooperative Extension[f]	100	13	25	29	16	10
Other Organized Instruction (off-the-job)[b,4]	100	15	37	39	7	1

(continued)

TABLE 6.4 Continued

	Total 17 Years and Over	17-24 Years	25-34 Years	35-54 Years	55-64 Years	65 Years and Over
Other Organized Programs[b,8] (churches and synagogues, community organizations, libraries and museums, free universities, etc.)	100	17	35	33	9	5
Tutors[b]	100	20	33	32	10	4

SOURCES:

a. U.S. Bureau of the Census (1979c: Tables 6, 17, 19).
b. Boaz (1980); based on those 17 years old and older.
c. Defense Manpower Data Center (1980)
d. Bell et al. (1979: 15-18); U.S. National Criminal Justice Information and Statistics Service (1979: Table 2; 1980: Tables 1, 2, 3, 6, 9).
e. U.S. Department of Labor (1979: 20, Table 2); U.S. Department of Labor, Employment and Training Administration (1980a).
f. U.S. Department of Agriculture (1980: Table 7); the Gallup Organization (1979).

1. Includes noncredit enrollments.
2. Based on respondents enrolled full time in an occupational program of more than 6 months.
3. Based on distribution of course registrations.
4. Based on "labor/professional organization" distribution.
5. Based on "labor/professional organization" distribution.
6. Based on distribution of accessions.
7. Based on distribution of prisoners.
8. Based on "private organization" and "other" distributions.

employer training programs might be expected. The role for public policy in this area is not clear. Public funding for these nontraditional programs might be channeled to sponsors or to students. A voucher scheme would put funds at the disposal of potential participants, removing at least part of the financing constraint. Further, educational institutions may be encouraged to continue to expand their offerings into these nonacademic program areas.

Finally, although the level of public funding is substantial, the distribution across programs and hence across subpopulations is far from even. Currently, the major proportion of public funding supports programs serving younger, minority, male, and employed participants. Opportunities for supporting other postcompulsory education and training activities clearly exist, and should be explored.

(notes begin on page 154)

TABLE 6.5 Participants in Postcompulsory Education and Training Programs by Race and Ethnic Origin and Source, 1978 (in percentages)

	Total	*White*	*Black*	*Hispanic*	*Other*
TOTAL CIVILIAN ADULT POPULATION[a]	100	83	10	5	2
POSTSECONDARY EDUCATIONAL INSTITUTIONS					
Four-Year Colleges and Universities					
Full-Time[b]	100	84	8	3	3
Part-Time[a,1]	100	91	5	2	2
Two-Year Colleges and Vocational-Technical Institution					
Full-Time[b]	100	76	13	6	5
Part-Time[a,1]	100	89	5	4	2
Proprietary					
Full-Time[a,2]	100	76	16	6	2
Part-Time[a,1]	100	90	5	4	1
Correspondence[a,3]	100	93	5	2	–
OTHER POSTCOMPULSORY EDUCATION AND TRAINING					
Elementary and Secondary Schools (part-time)[a]	100	82	7	8	3
Business or Industry					
Apprenticeships[c]	100	82	9	5	4
Other Organized Instruction (off-the-job)[a,4]	100	93	4	2	1
Professional Associations[a,5]	100	94	3	2	1
Labor Unions	na	na	na	na	na
Armed Forces					
Initial Training[d,6]	100	75	16	4	4
Other Organized Instruction	na	na	na	na	na
Correspondence	na	na	na	na	na
Prison[e,7]	100	51	37	10	2
Other Government Programs					
Manpower Training[f]	100	48	34	13	4
Cooperative Extension[g]	100	95	4	1	–
Other Organized Instruction (off-the-job)[h]	100	82	11	3	4

(continued)

TABLE 6.5 Continued

	Total	*White*	*Black*	*Hispanic*	*Other*
Other Organized Programs[a,8] (churches and synagogues, community organizations, libraries and museums, free universities, etc.)	100	93	3	2	2
Tutors[a]	100	95	1	2	1

SOURCES:

a. Boaz (1980); based on those 17 years old and older.
b. Dearman and Plisko (1980: Tables 3.5, 3.6).
c. U.S. Department of Labor, Employment and Training Administration (1980b); data refer to registered apprenticeships (about 60% of the total).
d. Defense Manpower Data Center (1980).
e. Bell et al. (1979: 15-18); U.S. National Criminal Justice Information and Statistics Service (1979: Table 2; 1980: Tables 1, 2, 3, 6, 9).
f. U.S. Department of Labor (1979: 20, Table 2); U.S. Department of Labor, Employment and Training Administration (1980a).
g. U.S. Department of agriculture (1980: Table 7); the Gallup Organization (1979).
h. U.S. Office of Personnel Management (1980: Charts 13, 15) and unpublished tabulations.

1. Includes noncredit enrollments.
2. Based on respondents enrolled full time in an occupational program of more than 6 months.
3. Based on distribution of course registrations.
4. Based on "business or industry" distribution.
5. Based on "labor/professional organization" distribution.
6. Based on distribution of accessions.
7. Based on distribution of prisoners.
8. Based on "private organization" and "other" distributions.

TABLE 6.6 Participants in Postcompulsory Education and Training Programs by Sex and Source, 1978 (in percentages)

	Total	*Male*	*Female*
TOTAL CIVILIAN ADULT POPULATION[a]	100	47	53
POSTSECONDARY EDUCATIONAL INSTITUTIONS			
Four-Year College or University			
Full-Time[b]	100	53	47
Part-Time[a,1]	100	45	55

(continued)

TABLE 6.6 Continued

	Total	*Male*	*Female*
Two-Year College or Vocational-Technical Institution			
Full-Time[b]	100	50	50
Part-Time[a,1]	100	37	63
Proprietary			
Full-Time[a,2]	100	50	50
Part-Time[a,1]	100	46	54
Correspondence (civilian)[a,3]	100	68	32
OTHER POSTCOMPULSORY EDUCATION AND TRAINING			
Elementary and Secondary Schools (part-time)[a]	100	28	72
Business or Industry			
Apprenticeships[c]	100	97	3
Other Organized Instruction (off-the-job)[a,4]	100	62	38
Professional Associations[a,5]	100	56	44
Labor Unions	na	na	na
Armed Forces			
Initial Training[d,6]	100	87	13
Other Organized Instruction	na	na	na
Correspondence	na	na	na
Prisons[e,7]	100	96	4
Other Government Programs			
Manpower Training[f]	100	46	53
Cooperative Extension[g]	100	32	68
Other Organized Instruction (off-the-job)[h]	100	65	35
Other Organized Programs[a,8] (churches and synagogues, community organizations, libraries and museums, free universities, etc.)	100	35	65
Tutors[a]	100	27	72

SOURCES:

a. Boaz (1980); based on those 17 years old and older.
b. Dearman and Plisko (1980: Tables 3.5, 3.6).
c. U.S. Department of Labor, Employment and Training Administration (1980b); data refer to registered apprenticeships (about 60% of the total).
d. Defense Manpower Data Center (1980).
e. Bell et al. (1979: 15-18); U.S. National Criminal Justice Information and Statistics Service (1979: Table 2; 1980: Tables 1, 2, 3, 6, 9).

TABLE 6.6 Notes Continued

f. U.S. Department of Labor (1979: 20, Table 2); U.S. Department of Labor, Employment and Training Administration (1980a).
g. U.S. Department of agriculture (1980: Table 7); the Gallup Organization (1979).
h. U.S. Office of Personnel Management (1980: Charts 13, 15) and unpublished tabulations.

1. Includes noncredit enrollments.
2. Based on respondents enrolled full time in an occupational program of more than 6 months.
3. Based on distribution of course registrations.
4. Based on "business or industry" distribution.
5. Based on "labor/professional organization" distribution.
6. Based on distribution of accessions.
7. Based on distribution of prisoners.
8. Based on "private organization" and "other" distributions.

TABLE 6.7 Participants in Postcompulsory Education and Training Programs by Employment Status and Source, 1978 (in percentages)

	Total	*Employed*	*Not Employed*
TOTAL CIVILIAN ADULT POPULATION[a]	100	60	40
POSTSECONDARY EDUCATIONAL INSTITUTIONS			
Four-Year College or University			
Full-Time[b]	100	50	50
Part-Time[a,1]	100	87	13
Two-Year College and Vocational-Technical Institution			
Full-Time[b]	100	57	43
Part-Time[a,1]	100	77	21
Proprietary			
Full-Time[b]	100	42	58
Part-Time[a,1]	100	82	19
Correspondence (civilian)	na	na	na
OTHER POSTCOMPULSORY EDUCATION AND TRAINING			
Elementary and Secondary Schools (part-time)[a]	100	65	35

(continued)

TABLE 6.7 Continued

	Total	*Employed*	*Not Employed*
Business or Industry			
Apprenticeships[c]	100	100	–
Other Organized Instruction (off-the-job)[a,2]	100	91	9
Professional Associations[a,3]	100	94	6
Labor Unions[c]	100	100	–
Armed Forces			
Initial Training[c]	100	100	–
Other Organized Instruction[c]	100	100	–
Correspondence[c]	100	100	–
Prisons[d,4]	100	69	30
Other Government Programs			
Manpower Training[e]	100	4	96
Cooperative Extension[f]	100	30	70
Other Organized Instruction (off-the-job)[c]	100	100	–
Other Organized Programs[a,5] (churches and synagogues, community organizations, libraries and museums, free universities, etc.)	100	67	32
Tutors[a]	100	63	37

SOURCES:

a. Boaz (1980); based on those 17 years old and older.
b. Smith et al. (1980) and unpublished tabulations.
c. Author's estimate.
d. Bell et al. (1979: 15-18); U.S. National Criminal Justice Information and Statistics Service (1979: Table 2; 1980: Tables 1, 2, 3, 6, 9).
e. U.S. Department of Labor (1979: 20, Table 2); U.S. Department of Labor, Employment and Training Administration (1980a).
f. U.S. Department of Agriculture (1980: Table 7); the Gallup Organization (1979).

1. Includes noncredit enrollments.
2. Based on "business or industry" distribution.
3. Based on "labor/professional organization" distribution.
4. Based on distribution of prisoners prior to incarceration.
5. Based on "private organization" and "other" distributions.

TABLE 6.8 Participants in Postcompulsory Education and Training Programs by Family Income and Source, 1978 (in percentages)

	Total All Income Quartiles	*Income Quartile* Lowest	Lower Middle	Upper Middle	Highest
TOTAL CIVILIAN ADULT POPULATION[b]	100	23	28	28	20
POSTSECONDARY EDUCATIONAL INSTITUTIONS					
Four-Year College or University					
Full-Time[a]	100	17	21	26	35
Part-Time[b,1]	100	7	24	36	33
Two-Year College and Vocational-Technical Institution					
Full-Time[a]	100	26	26	25	22
Part-Time[b,1]					
Proprietary					
Full-Time[a]	100	36	28	20	15
Part-Time[b,1]	100	12	28	35	25
Correspondence (civilian)[a]	100	16	23	34	28
OTHER POSTCOMPULSORY EDUCATION AND TRAINING					
Elementary and Secondary Schools (part-time)[b]	100	14	27	32	27
Business or Industry					
Apprenticeships	na	na	na	na	na
Other Organized Instruction (off-the-job)[b,2]	100	6	23	37	34
Professional Associations[b,3]	100	5	18	34	33
Labor Unions	na	na	na	na	na
Armed Forces					
Initial Training[c,4]	100	91	8	1	–
Other Organized Instruction	na	na	na	na	na
Correspondence	na	na	na	na	na
Prison[d,5]	100	79	12	7	3
Other Government Programs					
Manpower Training[e]	100	91	9	–	–
Cooperative Extension[f]	100	18	25	30	27
Other Organized Instruction (off-the-job)[g]	100	12	27	41	20

(continued)

TABLE 6.8 Continued

Other Organized Programs[b,6] (churches and synagogues, community organizations, libraries and museums, free universities, etc.)	100	11	26	33	30
Tutors[b]	100	12	21	30	37

SOURCES:

a. U.S. Bureau of the Census (1979c: Tables 6, 17, 19).
b. Boaz (1980); based on those 17 years old and older.
c. Defense Manpower Data Center (1980).
d. Bell et al. (1979: 15-18); U.S. National Criminal Justice Information and Statistics Service (1979: Table 2; 1980: Tables 1, 2, 3, 6, 9).
e. U.S. Department of Labor (1979: 20, Table 2); U.S. Department of Labor, Employment and Training Administration (1980a).
f. U.S. Department of Agriculture (1980: Table 7); the Gallup Organization (1979).
g. U.S. Office of Personnel Management (1980: Charts 13, 15) and unpublished tabulations.

1. Includes noncredit enrollments.
2. Based on "business or industry" distribution.
3. Based on "labor/professional organization" distribution.
4. Based on distribution of accessions.
5. Based on distribution of prisoners prior to incarceration.
6. Based on "private organization" and "other" distributions.

NOTES

1. For example, one could distinguish between job-related and avocational training. Unfortunately, the available participant and cost data do not permit these comparisons. Whether the participant's "purpose" should influence public support for the activity is, of course, a policy decision. Current policies are somewhat contradictory, and indirectly applied. For example, college students enrolled less than half time are generally ineligible for federal financial aid (in part because they are presumably less serious about their schooling). On the other hand, local governments underwrite a substantial share of the costs for avocational programs sponsored by community organizations.

2. This estimate excludes employees attending college or university courses, professional association training, and labor union classes at the employer's expense (that is, "sponsored" by the employer). It includes courses taught by consultants or other instructors, as well as in-house training staff, provided that the course is conducted at or near the job site. Anderson et al. (forthcoming) caution that some employer-provided "courses" serve purposes other than training, including evaluation of personnel, dissemination of product information, and executive perquisites (particularly when the "training" occurs in exotic locales).

3. The figures here are imprecise, for two major reasons. First, many firms simply do not know how much they spend for training employees in-house. Second, the definitions of formal training differ: Some include on-the-job learning as well as off-the-job class-

room instruction. As part of a broader project on financing adult education, Anderson et al. (forthcoming) are attempting to measure costs of training programs in firms, unions, community organizations, and other sponsors. Their findings may help to gauge more accurately the level of investment in training outside of schools. See also Goldstein (1980) and Smith (1980).

4. Most postsecondary educational institutions also impose higher fees for flight programs. However, only a few colleges or universities now charge graduate students (or upper-division undergraduates) higher tuition than lower-division undergraduates. Anderson et al. (forthcoming) have found a wide variation in instructional costs per class hour among employee training programs.

5. The cost per student estimates given here differ from those reported elsewhere (Bowen, 1979; Hyde, 1976), since my enrollment figures include those attending degree or nondegree credit courses anytime during the calendar year (rather than only fall degree credit enrollments), and my instructional costs are limited to those allocated for instruction.

6. I also find that per hour instructional costs tend to be somewhat lower in proprietary school programs than for the roughly comparable offerings in vocational schools. See Wilms (1975) for a further discussion of this point.

7. An earlier version of this article included 50 appendices, which spelled out the assumptions made. The appendices are available, upon request, from the author. Several examples will illustrate key assumptions: (1) I allocated institutional appropriations to postsecondary institutions among the teaching, research, and service functions in proportion to their shares of expenditures. (2) Under student aid grants, I exclude all social security benefits, three-fourths of the Veterans Administration benefits paid to postsecondary training participants, and all proceeds from subsidized work or loan programs. As noted in the text, I am assuming that these funds go primarily to support living costs, rather than instructional costs. (3) In the area of private programs, I assume an average 35% corporate tax rate.

8. Across all programs, Christoffel (1978) has estimated that programs for which *adults* (age 25 and over) are eligible were budgeted at $14 billion in federal aid in 1977.

9. In part-time or continuing education programs, Anderson et al. (forthcoming) note large differences in the level of public institutional subsidies by type of course (for example, continuing education at medical schools versus part-time undergraduate study) and among states.

10. These grants would meet the costs of public sector employees participating in professional association training programs (teachers, government employees, and members of the armed forces).

11. These overall averages mask important differences in the receipt of student aid. As Wagner (1978), the Committee on the Financing of Higher Education for Adult Students (1974), and Van Dusen (1975) document, the part-time postsecondary student is less likely to receive aid.

REFERENCES

ANDERSON, R. E., E. S. KASL, J. R. APPEL, S. VARDEN, and L. WEINSTEIN (forthcoming) The Costs and Finance of Adult and Continuing Education in the United States. Lexington, MA: D. C. Heath.

BELL, R., E. CONRAD, T. LAFFEY, J. G. LUTZ, P. VAN REED MILLER, C. SIMON, A. E. STAKELON, and N. J. WILSON (1979) Correctional Education Programs for Inmates. Phase I Report. Washington, DC: Government Printing Office.

BROSCHART, J. R. (1977) Lifelong Learning in the Nation's Third Century. Washington, DC: Government Printing Office.

BOAZ, R. L. (1980) "Participation in adult education, 1978." National Center for Educational Statistics. (unpublished)

——— (1978) Participation in Adult Education: Final Report 1975. Washington, DC: National Center for Educational Statistics.

CALVERT, R. , Jr. (1980) Noncredit Activities in Institutions of Higher Education for the Year Ending June 30, 1978. Washington, DC: National Center for Educational Statistics.

——— (1977) "Participation in adult education: United States," in Learning Opportunities for Adults, Vol. IV. Paris: Organization for Economic Cooperation and Development.

Carnegie Commission on Higher Education (1973) Toward a Learning Society. New York: McGraw-Hill.

CARP, A., R. E. PETERSON, and P. J. ROELFS (1974) "Adult learning interests and experiences," in K. P. Cross et al. (eds.) Planning Non-Traditional Programs: An Analysis of the Issues for Postsecondary Education. San Francisco: Jossey-Bass.

CHRISTOFFEL, P. H. (1978) "Current federal programs for lifelong learning: a $14 billion effort." School Review 86 (May): 348-359.

College Board (1980) "Students may apply for more aid funds as a result of expanded eligibility guidelines." College Board News 8 (March): 6.

College Scholarship Service (1980) Student Expenses at Postsecondary Institutions, 1980-81. New York: College Board.

Committee on the Financing of Higher Education for Adult Students (1974) Financing Part-Time Students: A New Majority in Higher Education. Washington, DC: American Council on Education.

Congressional Budget Office (1980a) Tax Expenditures: Current Issues and Five-Year Budget Projections for Fiscal Years 1981-85. Washington, DC: Government Printing Office.

——— (1980b) Youth Employment and Education: Possible Federal Approaches. Washington, DC: Government Printing Office.

CROSS, K. P. and A. ZUSMAN (1979) "The needs of nontraditional learners and the response of nontraditional programs," in C. B. Stalford (ed.) An Evaluative Look at Nontraditional Postsecondary Education. Washington, DC: Government Printing Office.

DEARMAN, N. B. nad V. W. PLISKO [eds.] (1980) The Condition of Education. Washington, DC: National Center for Educational Statistics.

Defense Manpower Data Center (1980) "FY79 officer and enlisted accessions." Unpublished tabulations. Defense Manpower Data Center, Alexandria, Virginia.

FRASER, B. S. (1980) The Structure of Adult Learning, Education, and Training Opportunity in the United States. Washington, DC: National Institute for Work and Learning.

FROOMKIN, J. and R. J. WOLFSON (1977) "Adult education 1972: reanalysis." Joseph Froomkin, Inc., Washington, D.C. (mimeo)

Gallup Organization (1979) The Gallup Study of Participation and Awareness of the Agricultural Extension Service. Detailed Tabular Analysis. Princeton, NJ: Author.

GOLDSTEIN, H. (1980) Training and Education by Industry. Washington, DC: National Institute for Work and Learning.

HALSTEAD, D. K. (1979) Higher Education and Price Indices. 1978 Supplement. Washington, DC: National Institute of Education.

HYDE, W. D., Jr. (1976) Metropolitan Vocational Proprietary Schools. Lexington, MA: D. C. Heath.

JOHNSON, S. E. (1979) "Education enrollment statistics," in Inmate Programs Reporting System Cumulative Activity Counts Report 72.90 (and earlier numbers). Federal Bureau of Prisons. (unpublished)

KAY, E. R. (1979) Enrollments and Programs in Noncollegiate Postsecondary Schools. Washington, DC: Government Printing Office.

——— (1974) Adult Education in Community Organizations 1972. Washington, DC: Government Printing Office.

LUSTERMAN, S. (1977) Education in Industry. New York: Conference Board.

National Center for Educational Statistics [NCES] (1980a) "Opening fall enrollment, 1979." (unpublished)

——— (1980b) "College and university financial growth outpaces inflation in fiscal year 1979," in Early Release, NCES 80-345. Washington, DC: Author.

——— (1979) Financial Statistics of Institutions of Higher Education, 1977. Washington, DC: Government Printing Office.

National Home Study Council (n.d.) "Nearly three and one-half million Americans study by correspondence." (mimeo)

——— (n.d.) A Report on Current Educational Practice in NHSC Member Institutions. Washington, DC: Author.

PETERSON, R. E., K. P. CROSS, T. W. HARTLE, J. B. HIRABAYASHI, M. A. KUTNER, S. A., POWELL, and J. R. VALLEY (1979) Lifelong Learning in America. San Francisco: Jossey-Bass.

PUMA, M. J., S. MILLER, W. DELLEFIELD, D. GOEKE, and T. MUSSO (1980) "Study of the impact of the Middle Income Student Assistance Act (MISAA)." Office of Evaluation and Dissemination, U.S. Office of Education. (mimeo)

SMITH, G. B. (1980) Employer-Sponsored Recurrent Education in the United States: A Report on Recent Inquiries into Its Structure. Stanford, CA: Institute for Research on Educational Finance and Governance, School of Education, Stanford University.

SMITH, P. A., P. R. KNEPPER, J. P. JACKLEY, and C. HENDERSON (1980) "Financing undergraduate education in 1978-79." Division of Policy Analysis and Research, American Council on Education. (mimeo)

SMITH, V. (1973) "Restructuring education and its timing," in S. J. Mushkin (ed.) Recurrent Education. Washington, DC: Government Printing Office.

U.S. Bureau of the Census (1979a) CPS Tables—October 1978. (unpublished)

——— (1979b) Current Population Reports. Series P-20, no. 333. Washington, DC: Government Printing Office.

——— (1979c) Current Population Reports. Series P-20, no. 346. Washington, DC: Government Printing Office.

U.S. Department of Agriculture, Science and Education Administration-Extension (1980) Evaluation of Economic and Social Consequences of Cooperative Extension Programs. Washington, DC: Government Printing Office.

U.S. Department of Defense (1980) Military Manpower Training Report for FY 1981. Washington, DC: Author.

U.S. Department of Labor (1979) WIN: 1968-1978: A Report at 10 Years. Washington, DC: Government Printing Office.

——— Employment and Training Administration (1980a) "Quarterly progress reports and summary reports." (unpublished)

——— (1980b) "More women are now apprentices, BAT reports." ETA Interchange 6 (March): 8.

U.S. Department of Health, Education and Welfare, Office of Evaluation and Dissemination (1980) Annual Evaluation Report on Programs Administered by the U.S. Office of Education, Fiscal Year 1979. Washington, DC: Government Printing Office.

U.S. National Criminal Justice Information and Statistics Service (1980) Prisoners in State and Federal Institutions on December 31, 1978. Washington, DC: Bureau of Justice Statistics, Department of Justice.

——— (1979) Profile of State Prison Inmates: Washington, DC: Government Printing Office.

U.S. Office of Personnel Management (1980) Employee Training in the Federal Service, Fiscal Year 1979. Washington, DC: Author.

VAN DUSEN, W. D. (1975) "Financial aid for part-time students: status and issues." College Entrance Examination Board, Washington, D.C. (mimeo)

Veterans Administration, Office of the Controller, Reports and Statistics Service (1980) "Veteran's benefits under current educational programs." Information Bulletin 04-80-2.

WAGNER, A. P. (1978) "Financing postsecondary learning opportunity through existing federal student aid programs." School Rev. 86 (May): 410-435.

WILMS, W. W. (1975) Public and Proprietary Vocational Training: A Study of Effectiveness. Lexington, MA: D. C. Heath.

YOUN, T.I.K. and R. THOMPSON (1974) "A summary and analysis of the national commission's survey of noncollegiate institutions," in G. B. Weathersby and D. Nash (eds.) A Context for Policy Research in Higher Education. Washington, DC: Government Printing Office.

YOUNG, A. M. (1977) "Going back to school at 35 and over." Monthly Labor Rev. 100 (July): 43-45.

7

EMPLOYER-SPONSORED PROGRAMS

GREGORY B. SMITH

The purposes, forms, effects, and magnitude of private sector spending for work force education and training have become in recent years, for many and varied reasons, subjects of intense interest and speculation. Demand for detailed and accurate information on these subjects has arisen within industry itself, government agencies, education and research institutions, and organized labor. Stimulating that demand are a diverse array of interests and concerns. Among them:

- continuing anxiety about a declining rate of of productivity growth, and its effects on inflation and our competitive position in the world economy, combined with an appreciation that past and future levels and kinds of investments in skill and knowledge formation might well be part of the cause and solution of present problems;
- concern about the ways and means by which equal employment opportunity gains for minorities, women, older workers, handicapped, and other groups can be advanced or, more probable, sustained in the years ahead;
- concern about whether our public education and training establishments and practices are up to the task of accommodating, quickly enough, the changing skill and knowledge formation needs of our economy, especially in the face of a rapidly altering demography in the work place;
- concern about whether the aspirations and expectations of the work force of the 1980s can be accommodated within traditional pyramidal occupational structures and attendant rewards, in the absence of other human-growth options; and
- an emerging appreciation that to achieve mastery over the demands of everyday life and to participate in an informed way in political affairs require of Americans an increased sophistication obtained only through continuing learning, and in many instances only through organized learning.

We know now that during the past 30 years a vast and diverse educational enterprise has emerged within private industry—particularly large firms. We suspect that how and how well it functions and what kinds of opportunities it entertains will importantly condition how these concerns and national challenges are met.

What are the origins of the present-day structure of employer-sponsored recurrent education, of what Lusterman (1977) has called the "shadow education system"? What functions is this structure intended to perform, and what is its rationale from the viewpoint of management and the stockholder? What methods and modes of education are employed? What kinds of workers are reached by the recurrent education opportunities now offered? Which are left out? Where is equity's place in this system? How substantial are the costs of the present structure? What do we know about the effects of the levels and kinds of expenditures currently being made? What are some salient implications of the shadow education system for public policy in this new decade?

This is an attempt to speak to these questions and, in a few instances, to answer them through two separate but related discussions: the first a brief examination of the whole of the structure of employer-sponsored recurrent education, and the second a closer look at a wing of that structure—tuition assistance programs.

A central question examined here is how large the employer-sponsored recurrent education enterprise is in numbers of participants and in dollars spent. This question has inspired much conjecture. For the whole of recurrent education (deliberate education and training), reasoned estimates range from 37,215,000 to a high of 73,253,000 participants (Fraser, 1980: 11). For industry-sponsored recurrent education the numbers range from 2,605,000 to 16,000,000 participants. We shall look closely at this. On the matter of expenditures, the same enthusiasm for diversity obtains. Estimates of annual employer expenditures range from $2 billion to $100 billion. We will ponder these great differences, as well.

DIMENSIONS OF EMPLOYER-SPONSORED RECURRENT EDUCATION

IN THE BEGINNING

Employer-sponsored recurrent education, in its contemporary configuration, has its recognizable beginnings in the awesome crucibles of the Great Depression and World War II. Despite a rich history in the United States of progressive enlargement of educational opportunity for adult workers,[1] it is true, as Stewart (1980: 9) has observed, that prior to the early 1930s "a policy of no policy describes public policy as to worklife education for adult workers, while little other than formalization of on-the-job training was apparent in private company practice—this despite the much admired rationalization of the American productive mechanism in the prosperity of the Twenties as the United States assumed economic leadership in the world."

The first of these systemic shocks, the Great Depression, displaced and dislocated millions of American workers from industrial jobs and from the soil. The prevailing processes and structures of industrial skill and knowledge formation—the special American blend of "comprehensive" public education, vocational training (formal, informal on-the-job, and apprenticeships), and work experience—were overtaken by events and rendered incapable of sustaining the needs of the economy as industrial production began to rise again in the late 1930s. One reason for the obsolescence of prior skill formation processes was, of course, the fact that human capital accumulation by adult workers became static or indeed declined during the period between 1930 and 1940. Apprenticeship stopped. Formal training in industry was abandoned. Skill acquisition through work experience declined, simply because 1929 levels of employment were not regained until 1940-1941 (Stewart, 1980: 10) As late as 1938, well after human resource development programs such as the CCC and WPA were in full swing, unemployment (and skill atrophy) remained high: 10.4 million workers, 19% of the total labor force, stood idle (Wool, 1947: 638; cited in Stewart, 1980: 10).

The first event conditioned importantly the peculiar ramifications for industry of the second event, World War II. Between 1940 and 1945, the standing military forces grew by about 12 million and civilian employment increased by 7 million. Civilian labor force growth was nearly treble the expected growth of 3 million workers. School- and college-age youth, women 25-54, and men and women over 55 accounted for the 8 million additional workers (Jaffe and Stewart, 1951: 176-182; cited in Stewart, 1980: 10). In the main, these persons had no occupational experience or training, and only irregular work experience or exposure to work discipline.

At every occupational skill level, and in an array of new occupations, demands for labor grew. Every possible training facility was brought into use. With the advent of the Vocational Education for National

Defense Act (VEND Program), $80 million were invested annually in established state vocational systems, with the result that over 7 million prospective war production workers received institutional training at a cost of about $400 million (Venn, 1970: 151; cited in Stewart, 1980: 11). Of greater significance by most estimates was the radical alteration of industrial skill training on the job.

> Jobs were broken down so that workers with a few weeks training could perform the simplified single skill tasks. Supervisory training was especially emphasized so that skilled workers might be more effectively used [U.S. Department of Labor, Bureau of Labor Statistics, 1945; Woytinsky et al., 1953; cited in Stewart, 1980: 12].

The public policy aftermath of these major events is well explored. The unemployment insurance and social security systems were Depression-born initiatives that have played and may yet again play important roles in connection with expanded work life or recurrent education opportunity in the United States. Out of the war experience and immediate postwar concerns emerged the Servicemen's Readjustment Act of 1944, a most important legacy of World War II. The GI Bill of Rights afforded 7.5 million adults new work life education opportunities at a cost of $13 billion in the period from 1944 to 1956. One-half of World War II veterans exercised the education and training option (Stewart, 1980: 12). Then, too, came the Employment Act of 1946, Congress's reaction to the perceived threat of a serious recession from expected reductions in military spending. This act, while in the main procedural and hortatory, established the dominance of macro (demand management) fiscal and monetary policies in postwar management of the economy.

The private policy response—though by no means as separate and insulated from the public policy response as we might think in our more laissez-faire moments—is a far less visible and well-examined matter. We do know that many of the employee education programs of the major U.S. companies, such as tuition assistance programs, began during and just after the war years (Bureau of National Affairs, 1978). We do know that in many high-technology areas developed or refined during the war, industry stepped in with its own technical/functional skills training programs, in part to protect industrial secrets from unscrupulous competitors, but also because the apparatus required for training were often unique and highly expensive.

FUNCTIONS AND NEEDS

Skill and knowledge formation occurs through three modes: (1) general education; (2) vocationally oriented education at all levels, including professional; and (3) learning opportunities provided by employers either on the job or in special programs. The individual, the occupation, the industry, and the social milieu dictate how these three modes are combined. Employer-sponsored education is the capstone of the other modes. In the United States, its main function remains to adapt previously acquired general knowledge and skills to the needs of the job. It also serves, with increasing frequency, the function of compensating for the deficiencies of both general and vocational education. In both cases, employer-sponsored education must often provide general knowledge.

The employer's needs are dominant in the American arrangement. Among the needs that recurrent education offerings are designed to meet are:

- supplementing and focusing the general skills of new workers to adapt to the way work is done in the enterprise;
- orienting new workers to the policies, rules, and organization of the enterprise;
- upgrading employee skills for promotion;
- retraining employees where new production methods and processes have been introduced;
- equipping managerial personnel to deal with new products or new factors affecting the business, such as government regulations in occupational health and safety, environmental governance, and affirmative action;
- compensating for serious deficiencies in the work skills of current employees, such as special training programs for DC-10 maintenance workers following the O'Hare Airport crash of 1979, and establishment of the Nuclear Operations Institute to train operating staff of nuclear electric generating plants following the Three Mile Island incident;
- assuring or achieving occupational vitality, particularly as it relates to managerial and professional employees;
- stabilizing employment, reducing turnover, and filling needs for shortage skills from within;
- enhancing the recruiting capacity of the firm (Goldstein, 1980: 7-14).

The occupation and industry of the worker importantly determine what recurrent education opportunities are available. There are significant differences in the education and training opportunities afforded managerial employees, sales employees, supervisory personnel, craft and operative workers, clerical workers, and professional and technical workers.

The structure and technology of industries similarly affects their needs and the modes of education available to them. In certain high-technology sectors, the telecommunications industry for example, employers can hire trained workers in only a few occupations. Career ladder structure is another decisive factor. Industries with well-articulated promotional sequences and ladders have few hiring points or entry portals except at the bottom rung. Workers advance to skilled production or maintenance jobs through recurrent education opportunities of varying kinds in such industries as steel, automobile, petroleum, and chemical. In the health care industry, a two-tier system obtains. Hospitals employ many occupations for which training is provided by schools. Little or no posthiring education is provided by the employer. The employer-provided education that does occur has the limited purpose of qualifying untrained workers (some 60%-70% of hospital personnel in large cities) for employment upgrading within job groupings where some promotional opportunities exist (Kimmerly, 1979; cited in Goldstein, 1980: 11).

METHODS AND FORMS

Employer-sponsored recurrent education takes many forms, employs an array of methods, and includes a wide range of content depending on the skills to be imparted and the purpose of the education. It ranges from the most informal training to highly formalized academic instruction.

The traditional and probably dominant form of skill acquisition is through informal, on-the-job training using the buddy system or supervisor-monitor trial and error method. More formal training, emphasizing the why as well as the how, may be employed for complex organizations and jobs. This may consist of individual or small-group instruction held in a classroom at the work place, offering programmed learning or audiovisual aids such as electronic blackboards. Or it may entail programs located away from the work site at a school or other community setting, possibly involving some form of tuition assistance or paid release time (Goldstein, 1980: 14-15).

Of the various types of on-the-job skill training processes, apprenticeship is among the most systematic and venerable. While only about 1.5% of new workers complete formal registered or unregistered apprenticeship programs, apprenticeship is the preferred choice in many industries, particularly the unionized sector. (Swerdloff, 1978; cited in Goldstein 1980: 15).

Each method, each form, has benefits and costs, assets and liabilities worked out according to the employer's preference, in most instances, although not necessarily on the basis of any refined tradeoff calculus. There is some evidence that the incidence of formal training programs has risen on the whole.

TELLING TREES FROM FORESTS

Agencies charged with the deep reading of present and future dispositions and capabilities of other countries, allies and adversaries alike, closely watch the processes and structures of skill and knowledge formation. Extensive records are kept concerning at least some aspects of two legs of the knowledge/skill formation triad in the United States—general education and vocational training. However, for the third leg, employer-sponsored education and training, the knowledge base is slim and fragmentary. This is a curious state of affairs in view of the millions of Americans involved in the recurrent education system, the estimated billions of dollars spent, and the consequences hoped for in terms of firm productivity, worker income, U.S. economic competitiveness in the global economy, and occupational and social mobility.

That our knowledge base is so limited is in large part a reflection of the historical separatism between the public and private sectors in the United States and the prevalent opinion shared by both sectors that education in industry is "a private affair." Both that understanding and historical separatism have undergone substantial modification in recent years, in part because of the growing areas of interface between public policy and private policy in the human resource development area. Equal employment opportunity is one major avenue of public policy intervention into that "private affair." Others include the significant evolution of public-private interaction in the employment and training arena since the Area Redevelopment Act of 1961, including the more significant Manpower Development and Training Act of 1962, and, more recently, the Private Sector Initiatives Program under the amended Comprehensive Employment and Training Act of 1973.

Our present knowledge base about the central questions—who is providing how much of what kinds of recurrent education to whom and with what effect—is constrained largely by four factors: (1) National surveys of education and training activity in the economy have been infrequent and irregular; (2) the mode of education that appears to be most prevalent, informal learning under the tutelage of a supervisor or worker, is not captured in surveys because records of such training are simply not kept—even more structured modes of training, such as systematic rotation of workers in skilled crafts areas, are not surveyed for the same reason; (3) few surveys contain a representative sample of companies—many of the studies that have been done involved respondent firms whose interest in training was such that it led them to join associations concerned with training; and (4) despite the fact that nonresponse in surveys usually indicates lack of interest in or lower incidence of the behavior or characteristic being measured, neither of the two most recent surveys of employer-sponsored education (Lusterman, 1977; U.S. Department of Labor, Bureau of Labor Statistics, 1977; cited in Goldstein, 1980) used information obtained from nonrespondents or adjusted reported findings to account for the nonresponse (Goldstein, 1980: 22-23).

THE SIZE OF IT ALL

The first general survey of employer-sponsored education was conducted by the U.S. Department of Labor in 1962. This establishment survey showed that only one enterprise in five sponsored any type of formal training. Only 7% of workers were enrolled in formal programs. Half of the enrollees were in safety training. Only 40% of the enrollees or 3% of all employed workers were receiving skill improvement education. Of these, 10% were taking administrative and advisory training, 7% sales training, and 6% training for the skilled trades. Importantly, this survey captured sharp differences in the incidence of training on the basis of establishment size (U.S. Department of Labor, 1965; cited in Goldstein, 1980: 26).

In a 1957 survey of the top 500 corporations listed by *Fortune* magazine, 85% of the responding companies reported some sort of sponsored education program. Of these, 67% conducted both internal and external programs; 28% conducted only internal programs. The most common type of education was supervisory skills training, offered by 92% of the firms. Education programs for professionals followed, offered by 71% of the respondent firms. Education programs for factory operatives were provided by 45% of respondents and programs for clerical workers (mainly female workers) by 31% of responding companies (Clark and Sloan, 1958: 13-24; cited in Goldstein, 1980: 27).

The most frequently cited study of employer-sponsored education is the Conference Board's survey of all firms with 500 or more employees for the period 1974-1975. The sample included firms together employing about 32 million persons, or about half the wage and salary workers in private nonfarm establishments at the time. The response rate was 22%.

Given the importance attached to the Conference Board survey by industry researchers and public policy analysts, I quote at length here from the analysis of this study's findings and flaws offered by Dr. Harold Goldstein (1980: 27-31):

> In this survey the formal training modes were structured as follows: (1) *Company courses,* whether conducted by company personnel or outside institutions and contractors, and whether they are held on or off the company's premises; . . . (2) *Tuition aid programs* selected and arranged for by employees, who are reimbursed fully or partly by the firm; . . . (3) *Other outside courses* offered by such organizations as the American Management Association, the Conference Board, professional societies, trade associations or corporate suppliers of training. They are open to employees of more than a single firm and are taken during working hours.
>
> Among the 22 percent of firms responding, the following percentages reported having various types of training programs (Lusterman, op. cit., Table 2.6):

Tuition aid (for after-hours courses)	89%
Other outside courses (during work hours)	74%
Company courses (during work hours)	70%
Company courses (after hours)	39%

> The largest firms had the highest incidence of each type of program. . .
>
> On the critical question of the number of employees receiving training, their occupations, and the kinds of training they got, the survey report is unclear. It is possible, however, to piece together a rough estimate of the total incidence of training. Employees who had participated in company courses in the previous year totaled 4.4 million, or 13 percent of all workers in firms employing 500 or more; 3.7 million (11 percent) had participated in programs during hours, and only 700,000 (2 percent) in after-hours programs (Lusterman, p. 11). In addition to those participating in company courses, there were 1.3 million participants annually in

tuition aid programs, or 4 percent of all workers, according to a rough estimate by the author of the study based on a 1970 Conference Board survey (Lusterman, p. 11). To this must be added the employees who participated in courses other than tuition-aid provided by non-company sources. The report gives no estimate of the number involved, but this form of training absorbed 9 percent of the training expenditures (Lusterman, Table 2.7). Making a rough estimate on the basis of the cost figures, this group of workers may have added about 10 percent to the numbers receiving training, or about 600,000. If we assume that none of these four groups of workers participated in more than one type of course, the total number of workers involved in formal training was about 6.3 million, or about *one out of five of the 32 million workers employed in firms with 500 or more employees.*

The percentage of employees participating in company courses (13 percent, overall) was fairly uniform in the larger size companies (14-16 percent), but in the smallest size firms it dropped to 10 percent (Lusterman, Table 2.2). By industry there was less uniformity; manufacturing firms had only 7 percent participation, finance and insurance as high as 20 percent, and in the other sectors, the range was 12 to 15 percent. Most of the participation was in courses during work hours (Lusterman, Table 2.7).

Another measure of the relative emphasis among programs is the distribution of expenditures (Lusterman, Table 2.5):

Company courses	80%
Outside courses	
Tuition aid	11%
Other	9%

Smaller firms depended more on outside courses for their training: in firms in the 500-999 and 1,000-2,499 size groups, between 50 and 60 percent of the expenditures were for outside courses, while in the largest size group, 87 percent was spent in-house (Lusterman, Table 2.5).

In terms of expenditures and employee involvement, therefore, the most prevalent mode of employer-provided training in firms employing 500 or more workers was through company courses during work hours. The kinds of training given in such programs are shown in [the table].

The functional-technical category included such areas as production, maintenance, marketing, sales, service, office administration, internal systems, finance and personnel—i.e., mostly managerial and white-collar skills. Comparing these figures with the occupational distribution of the work force in the reporting companies—11 percent managerial, 12 percent professional and technical, 10 percent sales and marketing, and 67 percent all other occupations (Lusterman, Table 2.11)—the conclusion is inescapable that training through company courses in working hours, the most prevalent mode, was disproportionately concentrated on providing managerial and other white-collar skills. This was less true in the largest companies (those with 10,000 or more employees) where 81 percent of the expenditures were on functional-technical training, while in companies with 500 to 4,999 employees about half the expenditures were in such courses (Lusterman, Table 6.6). In only 21 percent of the companies—and in only 36 percent of the largest size firms—did hourly-paid employees participate in functional-technical courses, however, and low-salaried employees participated in 22 percent of all firms and 43 percent of the largest ones (Lusterman, Table 6.7).

Tuition aid programs, although found in 89 percent of the companies reporting and therefore the most widespread mode of employer-provided training, involved only a small proportion of employees; all after-hours programs, of which tuition aid is one component, involved only 2 percent of the employees of reporting firms. . . . As noted above, tuition aid and other outside courses were favored by smaller firms, who did not have the "critical mass" to make it worthwhile to employ training staffs or to offer courses in occupations with few workers.

THE COST OF IT ALL

In the absence of any systematic record keeping within industry it is not surprising to find earnestly proffered estimates of annual costs ranging from $2 billion to $100 billion.

In an attempt to estimate the costs of education and training to business and industry, Tracey (1974) enumerated previous estimates, ranging from Machlup (1962), $3 billion for 1958; Decarlo and Robinson in a Chase Manhattan Bank report (1962), $17 billion; Boozer (1971), $20 billion; to Otto and Glaser (1970), $25 billion. Tracey went on to report that in 1972 Willard estimated total training costs of $700 annually per employee in large firms—$200 in direct training and $500 in indirect costs (including lost productivity). Using the 1971 annual average number of employees of private, nonfarm, nongovernment establishments (57,836,000), Tracey (1974: 11) assumed that if 2 out of 3 employees received some training at an average cost of $700, total industry expenditures would be about $27 billion; if 3 out of 5 received training, the cost would be approximately $24 billion. One estimate of total costs of employer-provided education and training in the United States (including government employees) runs as high as $100 billion during 1975 (Gilbert, 1976). This represents 12% of all wage and salary payments that year. (All of these estimates are presented in Fraser, 1980: 37-38.)

Lusterman (1977) estimates direct costs were about $2 billion ($1.6 billion for internal programs and $.4 billion for external offerings) for the large firms surveyed. Goldstein estimates an additional $1 billion in direct training costs for the rest of the private sector and adds about $2 billion in salary costs of trainees. After figuring in overhead costs and additional salary costs for managerial and professional workers who receive the bulk of training, Goldstein (1980: 35) estimates a total training expenditure of approximately $10 billion.

Per capita education spending varies significantly by size of firm and type of industry. The median (per capita) direct expense in the Conference Board survey was $16. The mean direct expense was $60 annually. A small number of companies with high expenditures were responsible for pulling up the mean. Transportation, communications, utilities, financial, and insurance companies spent more than the average, while wholesale and retail firms were well below the mean.

One employer, the Bell System, reports that it spends $1 billion per year on employee education, including the salaries of trainees. With nearly 1 million employees, its annual per capita expenditure is therefore $1000. This is estimated to be in the neighborhood of 5% of its total wage and salary bill. Such an apparently atypical company gives currency to an estimate such as that of Gilbert, that is, $100 billion total industry spending.

AND WHAT DOES IT DO?

Whichever estimate one accepts, the conclusion is unmistakable that employer-sponsored recurrent education is a massive enterprise that provides significant learning opportunities for many American workers. At the same time it is clear that opportunity is unevenly available, and that there is nothing approaching a consensus within industry that education for employees is in the employer's interest. Part of the reason for this latter condition most assuredly is the absence of any clear measure of the value or yield of education investments or, more precisely, the ratio of benefits to costs. The condition appears to remain as reported by Clark and Davis (1975: 186; cited in Goldstein, 1980: 50):

> Surprisingly little progress has been made toward developing techniques for comparing the benefits of training with its cost. While many studies

> have shown the returns to investments in formal schooling, a survey of 100 large corporations by the authors turned up no instances (among the 50 replies received as this chapter is written) of business being able to gauge the returns to investments in training with the same financial analysis that it uses before deciding to build a new plant or when choosing between alternative pieces of equipment. While some companies may be conducting formal financial analysis of their training, our findings reveal that business, in general, lacks sophisticated guidance in cost-effectiveness analysis.

This assessment has been confirmed in numerous conversations with industry education and training officials over the past 24 months. It is worth noting that both the Bell System and IBM Corporation have significant research projects under way to measure performance changes (the critical variable for evaluation research).

IN SUM

From these diverse surveys this shadowy picture emerges: Formal education opportunities are provided by fewer than half of all firms, but by more than 4 out of 5 of the larger firms. Among these larger firms about 1 in 5 workers is involved in education during any given year, with a much smaller proportion for all industry. Most education opportunities are provided during working hours in company-sponsored courses. Education for skill and general knowledge development (as distinct from company or product orientation, safety, or the like) is only a modest part of the total. Many of the formal skill training and education opportunities are for management and other white-collar skill areas, particularly professional and technical. Manual workers receive a disproportionately small share of formal training. Educational expenditures were probably in the range of $10-$20 billion dollars in the mid-1970s. Because training is often constrained during downsurges in the economy, expenditures may be lower currently than they were during 1975-1976. The effects of these investments on individual or firm performance are not now measured. In the absence of such measures, one can anticipate that the ambivalence toward education and training observed in many conversations and in industry behavior today will continue.

This is a picture of the whole. What of that category of employer-sponsored recurrent education most prevalent in American firms today?

How significant is it? What are its implications for the financing of work life or recurrent education opportunity in the years ahead?

TUITION ASSISTANCE PROGRAMS: PROBLEMS AND PROSPECTS

From the public policy vantage, one of the more intriguing and enigmatic elements of employer-sponsored recurrent education is tuition assistance. As indicated above, it is the most widespread mode of employer-sponsored education. Tuition-assistance programs represent a private basis for financing those education experiences most in keeping with the image of recurrent education, that is, a curriculum inclusive of, if not principally concerned with, liberal learning and general knowledge areas, from Plato to polymers, Socrates to cybernetics.

Until recently, little attention had been given tuition assistance in the United States by either education policy circles, union officials, or the training and development community within industry. (Some elements of the latter appear to remain especially chary of tuition assistance.) Four years ago the National Institute of Education contracted with the National Institute for Work and Learning (formerly the National Manpower Institute) to examine the prevalence, content, and objectives of negotiated tuition assistance programs in the private sector and the obstacles to worker utilization of them. The overall study was subsequently broadened to include a series of case studies of successful (highly used) tuition-assistance plans, a series of model work place demonstration projects, a policy development initiative, and other activities in the general area of recurrent or work life education. Thus, tuition assistance is a dimension of employer-sponsored recurrent education about which our knowledge is a bit more complete.

The data presented below were gathered in 1976-1977 through mail surveys and direct interviews with 51 company and 52 union officials and 910 unionized workers, and analysis of 79 major contracts containing negotiated tuition assistance provisions.

DESCRIPTION

Tuition assistance is an educational finance mechanism, nothing more nor less. The operational definition for the National Manpower Institute's 1976-1977 study follows:

> A tuition assistance program is any formal program through which a company offers financial assistance to some or all of its employees to encourage them to complete courses of study either at outside educational institutions or through other educational vendors [LeBel, 1977: II-27].

Negotiated tuition assistance is an unusual subphylum. The operational definition of negotiated tuition aid (from the same study) follows:

> Any formal plan in which a company has agreed within terms of a company union contract, to pay all or part of the tuition and related financial expenses incurred by employees covered under the agreement, while pursuing courses of study offered on or off company or union premises [LeBel, 1977: II-26].

Four distinct types of negotiated tuition assistance plans were identified in this study of collective bargaining agreements covering 1000 or more workers. In rank order of incidence, and by definition, these four types are described below.

Tuition Reimbursement and Tuition Advancement Plans

Tuition reimbursement plans are by far the most common form of tuition assistance negotiated between companies and unions in the United States. Tuition reimbursement and advancement plans pay all or part of tuition and related costs for enrollment in education and training programs outside the company.

- Employees are usually reimbursed by the company after submitting evidence of satisfactory course completion and of tuition payment. "Satisfactory" usually means a passing grade, although in a significant number of plans a specific grade requirement is established.

- Plans usually cover all or part of registration fees, student activities fees, laboratory fees, and graduation expenses. Other costs sometimes covered are books, supplies, CLEP fees, transportation, and meals. The prevailing practice is to allow higher payments for diploma or degree courses and for job-related education.
- Common eligibility criteria are the worker's job classification, accrued seniority, and satisfactory course completion. Most are open to all active employees who are working at least half time and who have six months or more of service.
- The plans usually specify acceptable institutions and courses of study. Often these institutions include colleges and universities, community colleges, technical and vocational schools, high schools, professional societies, labor unions, trade associations, and correspondence schools. In a large number of plans, courses must be for credit and/or must be job-, career-, or degree-related. (Only 3.9% of the NMI sample provided coverage for other than job-, career-, or degree-related courses.)
- Time off for course attendance or study is not allowed in most plans. Course work is not supposed to affect job performance. In several plans, however, employees may trade shifts or adjust work schedules to accommodate courses.

The criteria for eligibility, institution, and course approval and the application procedures mentioned above obtain for the other three types of plans as well.

Educational leave is granted to a worker for educational purposes for a specified period during working hours; *educational leave of absence* is granted for a more extended period of time. Either may but does not necessarily involve full or partial tuition payment. Under the *educational leave of absence,* leave time is usually credited as continuous company service for pension rights, and many companies will reinstate the worker at the individual's previous job classification (7.8% of the NMI sample had educational leave provisions).

Under *training fund* plans, employers contribute fixed amounts of money per employee into a central fund to finance employee education and training. Usually training fund plans are administered by a board of trustees as part of an industrywide or areawide program. Often the fund is used to underwrite the operational and fixed costs of training institutes or schools. The objectives of training fund plans are to improve job performance, upgrade skills, retrain workers, and reduce workers' educational outlays.

Scholarship and educational loan plans are the least commonly encountered form of negotiated tuition aid (NTA). Under scholarship plans, eligible workers are given funds to cover educational costs. Loan plans provide loans that require repayment according to an agreed-upon schedule. (In the NMI sample 9.8% had scholarship provisions and 15.7% had loan provisions.)

PERCEPTIONS

Management and labor share positive attitudes as to perceived *objectives* and *impacts* of NTA use. Both management and labor overwhelmingly concur that updated knowledge and skills, improved worker performance, and personal development and growth are each important objectives. In addition, 92% of the company officials surveyed view preparation for future assignments to be an important objective. Over 65% of the union officials surveyed consider as other important objectives preparing union members for job mobility and responding to local membership concerns. In sum, both companies and unions with NTA plans view tuition aid as a means for improving the position of workers in terms of their skills, personal development, and future occupational assignments.

As to *impacts*, company and union officials share the view that the three major potential outcomes of NTA are greater worker effectiveness on the job, heightened career development and job mobility, and increased worker satisfaction.

The workers surveyed by NMI share the views of company and union officials regarding the objectives and impacts of NTA benefits mentioned above. Most workers of the 910 in the survey consider further education and training to be important for many diverse reasons, such as degree completion, improved basic skills, better job performance, preparation for another job, and so on.

The consensus among company and union officials and workers disintegrates over the question of what factors prevent fuller participation by workers in tuition-assisted education and training. Through its study, NIWL sought the views of these groups on the relative significance of 20 structural, social, and psychological conditions that previous studies indicated to be of possible importance.

Conditions posited included:

(1) The company does not give time off or adjust schedules to promote participation.

(2) Workers' interest in attending courses on their own time is low.
(3) Insufficient incentives are used to reward participants.
(4) Management does not encourage participation sufficiently.
(5) The range of courses offered by local educational institutions is too limited.
(6) Supervisors do not encourage workers or employees under them to participate.
(7) Counseling services in the company or union are not sufficient.
(8) Workers do not have enough information about the program.
(9) Course schedules offered by local educational institutions are not flexible enough.
(10) Shop stewards do not encourage workers under them to participate.
(11) Eligibility criteria in the plan are too restrictive.
(12) Support services, particularly child care, are inadequate to give workers enough free time to participate.
(13) Workers lack information about educational opportunities in the community.
(14) The locations of classes are not convenient for workers.
(15) Plan application and approval procedures are too complicated.
(16) Workers object to paying income tax on tuition-aid payments.
(17) Workers feel inadequate to understand or complete courses that are available.
(18) Workers are unwilling or unable to pay the costs of courses.
(19) Workers do not participate because of social pressure from other workers.
(20) Sex, age, ethnic, or racial discrimination restrict participation.

Company officials tend to discount the importance of all of these conditions except one: low worker interest in education. Union officials, on the other hand, cite workers' inability to take time off or make schedule adjustments, low worker interest in education, and insufficient encouragement by management as important obstacles to fuller participation. Workers cite lack of company encouragement, inadequate information about available courses, lack of adequate promotional or income incentives, inflexibility of work schedule, and restrictiveness of course eligibility criteria.

On the matter of information, about one-third of the workers surveyed did not know or were not sure about either their eligibility for the NTA program or the approval process. All were eligible. Workers themselves overwhelmingly reject the idea that low worker interest in education is a major barrier to education.

THE EXTENT OF TUITION ASSISTANCE

NIWL estimates that 1 in 10 major private sector collective bargaining agreements in 1977 contained tuition-assistance provisions. Expressed differently, we estimate that in 1977 there were approximately 200 NTA plans covering nearly 2 million workers. Found in all types of industries, the incidence of NTA plans approximates the distribution of unionized workers, with the largest proportion in manufacturing. There is limited evidence that the number of these NTA plans is growing.

Of the 79 plans closely studied, tuition reimbursement or advance provisions are present in 60 (75%) of the agreements. Of the 60, 54 offer tuition reimbursement exclusively. Only 6 of the 60 contain tuition advance provisions. Educational leave plans appear in 13 (16%) of the agreements. Training fund plans appear in 22 (27%) of the agreements, and scholarships and loans are provided for in only 6 (7%) of the agreements studied.

The Bureau of Labor Statistics estimate of a 4% participation rate in NTA plans nationally in the mid-1970s has been supported by a number of other proximate studies in the 1970s (O'Meara, 1970; Bureau of National Affairs, 1978). Applying this 4% use rate to the total population covered (2,000,000 workers), and assuming a per capita annual expenditure rate of $250, one can estimate *annual outlays* under NTA of about $20 million. *On-paper commitments* under NTA programs are quite probably in the range of 1 billion dollars (2,000,000 workers × $500 average maximum allowance).

What do we know about the reach and characteristics of tuition-assistance programs of the more common nonnegotiated variety? We know very little for certain. Available evidence suggests that they conform closely in basic features and nomenclature to what was described above in the NTA plans. Available evidence also indicates that the use rate is in the 4% range for these plans and that it is the younger, better educated, higher paid, typically white, male worker who takes greatest advantage of these plans (for a detailed discussion, see Charner, 1979, 1980).

Several recent surveys suggest significant growth in the number of tuition-assistance plans on the American scene during the past 15-20 years. If estimates such as those of O'Meara (1970) and Lusterman (1977) are correct, there has been an increase. If these estimates are correct, then we have a situation in which over 80% of all establishments with over 500 employees have tuition-aid plans.

Using data from Lusterman, I have made some rough "guestimates" on the dimensions of tuition-assistance plan prevalence in the United States and the implications for enrollments in adult education resulting from incremental increases in the average utilization rate for TA plans. These guestimates will gain moment in the context of the brief discussion of participation rates achieved in several U.S. companies' tuition-assistance plans; they appear in the Appendix, with necessary caveats. In brief, I estimate that in 1975 between 17 and 24 million U. S. workers in private establishments were eligible to participate in tuition-assistance plans and that approximately 818,000 did so. If participation rates were increased by 1%, nearly one-quarter million additional adults would be participating in recurrent education programs.

The average maximum coverable education expense under the 79 plans examined in the NIWL study was approximately $500. If we assume that all plans have an annual per capita ceiling of half that amount, and if we simply multiply that sum by the number of potentially eligible workers, the upper and lower limits of *paper commitments* for tuition assistance in the private sector were $6.1 and $4.2 billion in 1976 (see Appendix).

THREE PROGRAMS THAT WORK

The 4% participation rate is by no means constant across programs. In 1978-1979, NIWL examined three programs that boast relatively high rates of worker utilization. The purpose was to attempt to identify factors in the program structure and administration, in the work force, and in the contextual environment (industry, community, education infrastructure, and so on) that seem to account for above-average participation rates.

A synopsis of each of the 3 programs examined in these case studies follows. These synopses suggest that every large employer in the country has available the wherewithal, via direct policy action, to enhance employee participation in voluntary education and training programs by a factor of 5 to 10.

The Kimberly-Clark Corporation's Educational Opportunities Plan (EOP), which originated in 1974, is regarded as the leader in innovative company-sponsored tuition-assistance plans. The introduction of this progressive plan, which has a participation rate of over 35%, was a dramatic departure from the previously limited and restrictive tuition-aid program at Kimberly-Clark (K-C), which claimed a participation rate of only 1%.

Kimberly-Clark, headquartered in Neenah, Wisconsin, is a fast-growing, worldwide marketer of fiber-based personal care products.

The EOP, which provides benefits to workers *and* their families for courses that do not have to be job-related, is open to nearly half of the almost 16,000 U.S. employees. Many of the eligible employees are concentrated around Neenah, an area rich in educational institutions. The majority of eligible employees are white-collar workers. The participation rates of hourly workers under the plan are lower than the overall 30+ percentage rate. The EOP was introduced by the top corporate leadership as a way to recruit, develop, and maintain a highly qualified and satisfied work force and to evidence K-C's commitment and trust in its employees.

The EOP includes the following major components:

- *Kim Ed account*—a personal "bank account," determined by formula, allotted to each employee for his/her educational use. After submitting a "self-development plan," the employee may draw on this account throughout the year. (The typical Kim Ed allotment in 1978 was approximately $450.) Kim Ed includes a provision for up to ten days of educational leave per year.
- *Fam Ed account*—financial assistance provided to employees *and* their families, based on a formula allotment, for current or future educational expenses. The company makes annual deposits to the account, and there are financial incentives for employees to save for the future.
- *extended educational leave*—a limited number of paid leaves for up to one year. Reportedly, this component of the EOP is rarely utilized.

While notable for the care and detail with which it has been designed, the EOP is also unusually flexible, with deliberate attempts having been made to include structural features that would maximize employee use of the plan. The most striking among these include:

- *liberal eligibility*—unlike many plans, the EOP is not limited to professional or salaried employees. There is a six-month seniority requirement.
- *coverage of non-job-related and cultural activities*—again, a rarity. Courses and institutions must be approved.
- *advance payment*—for tuition and other educational expenses.
- *no grade requirement or proof of course completion.*

- *unit coordinators*—in addition to full-time, high-level administration, a network of local coordinators provides crucial support services, including information on the plan and local educational opportunities.
- *extensive plan promotion and publicity*—through employee orientation, special announcements, bulletins, supervisors, and word of mouth.

Plan officials view the high participation rate as the best measure of EOP success.

The Kimberly-Clark Educational Opportunities Plan is a carefully designed program offered to employees within a corporate context of strong support for self-development in an area rich in educational opportunities. Many of the plan's features directly reduce or eliminate the structural barriers that commonly inhibit workers from using educational assistance (Rosow, 1979).

District Council 37 of the American Federation of State County and Municipal Employees in New York City offers an unusual array of educational programs and services to a large and diverse group of municipal employees. DC 37's Education Fund (EF) stands out because it is overseen by a board of union members and operates out of the union's headquarters. Fund programs are not only highly subscribed (the overall participation rate is about 10%-12% and many programs have waiting lists); they have managed to attract most heavily those groups normally viewed as least likely to take advantage of educational opportunities—lower-skill and lower-paid employees.

With over 110,000 members, DC 37 is the largest council of AFSCME. Known as a progressive, service-oriented union, it offers a wide range of benefits for its members, including a health plan, legal services program, retirees' association, and political action program. Through an agreement negotiated in 1971, the City of New York provides $25 annually for each of over 76,000 eligible employees to be used to meet a general set of educational objectives. The total annual fund budget is nearly $2 million.

The Education Fund evolved out of the union leadership's attempts, in the 1960s, to meet the perceived needs of workers for education and training that would lead to job upgrading and promotional opportunities within the city's civil service system. Because of the enthusiastic response of the membership, the initial emphasis on career development has continued and is evident in the focus of Fund programs today. Whether by learning English, passing a civil service test, or obtaining a diploma or college degree, career advancement is the primary objective of most participants and in the selection of course offerings.

In an attempt to fulfill the learning needs of a very diverse population, the Fund has, over the years, developed a wide range of educational programs and offerings. Most of these offerings are in basic *skills development programs* (including, for example, high school equivalency, English as a second language, and reading improvement), *college degree programs* (DC 37 campuses of Hofstra University and the College of New Rochelle, labor/liberal arts for women, and the tuition refund program), and *career-related programs* (clerical skills, test-taking preparation, accounting, nursing, and so on).

Key provisions and features of Education Fund programs attempt to reduce barriers to participation in education faced by working adults who are returning to school after a long absence. These features and provisions include:

- *Flexible, simplified admissions procedures* with a minimum of the bureaucracy and red tape that students reported encountering at other schools.
- *Scheduling arrangements* enabling many students to attend classes on their way home from work. Most classes are held evenings or Saturdays at union headquarters, and alternative arrangements often exist to accommodate work shifts. Students gain support from attending classes with their coworkers in the union setting.
- *A diversified, nonrestrictive curriculum.* Programs are designed to meet a variety of learning needs and styles, and degree programs are not required to be job-related.
- *Little or no out-of-pocket expenses* for students, made possible through the existence of a fund that is to be spent *only* on education programs, unlike some arrangements in which education is seen as a cost item for the sponsoring organization.
- *An accessible network of support services,* including widely available group and individual educational counseling, a learning lab for tutoring and individual instruction in basic skills, a library, and a staff of faculty and administrators who reportedly often act as advisors to students.
- *Widespread publicity* of the Fund and its programs, through the highly popular union newspaper, word of mouth, referrals, notices, and so on. Especially because of the former, there is a high level of awareness of the existence of Fund programs.

Overall, the fund is seen by the union as successful because it meets its stated objectives and succeeds in attracting large numbers of students, most of whom have positive reactions to its programs. In addition to career development, other reported major outcomes of

Fund use are: improved job performance; increased self-esteem, interpersonal skills, and self-confidence; improved family relations; greater readiness to pursue further education (in the psychological sense or in terms of credentials or skills); and increased involvement in the union as a whole.

As with Kimberly-Clark, the success of the Ed Fund can be attributed to an interplay of environmental and programmatic factors. Many Fund-eligible workers have a strong, clear need for education in order to advance within the civil service system or even to maintain their jobs. Thus, when faced with a highly promoted education program tailored to their particular social/psychological and learning needs and offered within a union that strongly encourages them to "own" and use such programs, many DC 37 workers choose to return to the classroom (Shore, 1979).

The importance of leadership commitment and innovation emerges again in an account of the successful *Tuition Assistance Plan of Polaroid Corporation.* The creation of a learning environment was central to the vision of Dr. Edwin Land, the unique founder of this unusual and successful corporation, headquartered in Cambridge, Massachusetts, an area brimming with educational opportunities. Ever since Land's founding of Polaroid's education program in 1957, the company has placed high value on maintaining a cadre of highly trained and skilled employees who will advance in the Polaroid system.

As a result, the Polaroid education program today is noted not only for its liberal Tuition Assistance Plan (TAP), but for an extensive and highly utilized internal education and training system. The effect of all this, reports one employee, is that "education is just in the air at Polaroid." The numbers are a striking testament to this. Fully *50%* of the corporation's approximately 12,000 domestic employees participated in 1 or more internal or external educational opportunities in 1977-1978. TAP was utilized by 10% of the eligible work force and, of these participants, *40%* were hourly employees. These figures stand out for two reasons, in addition to the unusually high 50% figure. First, as is the case of DC 37, TAP manages to attract significant proportions of users from the ranks of those considered least likely to utilize education and, second, TAP sustains a high level of participation despite the existence of a comprehensive internal education program.

Why does TAP do so well? Again, a look at the key features of the program reveals provisions that do much to overcome major barriers to participation. TAP is an integrated component of the overall employee development program, which includes skills training, management and organizational development, technology-based seminars, and career counseling. It exists to finance both independently undertaken external education programs and company-initiated programs that require use of outside educational institutions.

Of crucial importance is the fact that TAP *prepays 100%* of the costs of approved educational programs successfully completed by employees (the money must be refunded if the employee fails the course or does not complete it). The plan formerly paid only partial tuition costs. Through an "equity provision," hourly and salaried employees are entitled to the same tuition-assistance benefits. The plan, with an annual budget of approximately $450,000, is open to all half- and full-time employees on a prorated assistance basis. Acceptable courses and programs are those defined, *very* broadly, as job-related. In this case, the term encompasses not only those programs related to the employee's current or future job at Polaroid but also basic skills courses and several degree programs.

TAP is widely publicized in a variety of ways—brochures, handbooks, supervisors, word of mouth—and the application process is easy and convenient. Furthermore, not only is educational counseling made *available* to employees at their work site, but it is required before financial assistance is granted, so as to ensure that the best educational match is made between student and course to meet the objectives of both Polaroid and the employee.

Available anecdotal evidence suggests that the education program at Polaroid, and TAP within it, does in fact meet its fundamental objective of promoting advancement within the company.

One begins to sound repetitive when outlining TAP's other success factors. Again, what emerges is a combination of contextual and programmatic features. Counseling, publicity, full prepayment, and simplified and liberal requirements and procedures all tailor the plan to the needs of working adults. Furthermore, Polaroid's "corporate personality" has exhibited a clear and continuing commitment to the education and development of all its employees (Knox, 1979).

Taken together, the three programs described here point to a number of actions that, if adopted by other employers, would significantly enhance the attractiveness and utility of their tuition-assistance plans. These are: (1) advance funds, eliminating or reducing employee out-of pocket expenses; (2) broaden the eligible course criteria (in Kimberly-

Clark's open program, 90% of courses taken are job- or career-related); (3) simplify admissions and approval procedures; (4) provide such support services as career counseling, education advisement, and educational brokering; (5) keep constant the flow of information on the plan and on education and training options.

Wirtz (1979: 31) offers a fitting summary to this discussion of the tuition-aid element of employer-sponsored recurrent education:

> The real reason, though, for restrained reaction here is that these tuition aid and broader worker education developments, especially as they are reflected in cases such as these three, appear to offer such almost limitless prospects that the most serious danger may be in expecting too much from them too quickly. It is hard even to conceive of the changes that might come, in terms of everything from productivity per person hour to people's higher use of the human experience, from breaking out of the time-trap illusion that education is for youth and work for adults and never shall the two worlds overlap. It has been a mistake to assume that the "bridges between the two worlds of education and work" are properly built only from the school side of the gap. Worker education, including tuition-assistance as part of its curriculum, could be as important a development in the 1980's as the community colleges were in the 1960's—or even as the land grant colleges were a century ago.

APPENDIX

Tuition Assistance in the Private Sector: Estimates of Its Coverage and Potential Implications for Adult Education

Size of Establishment by Number of Employees	*Number of Establishments*[1]	*Number of Employees*[1]	*Estimated Percentage of Establishment with Tuition Aid Plans*[2]	*Estimated Percentage of Employees Eligible to Participate*	*Estimated Number of Eligible Employees*	*Estimated Number of Employees Participating at Average 4% Rate*	*Estimated Effects on Number of Employees Participating in Adult Education Resulting from a Participation Rate Increase of:*				
							1%	*2%*	*3%*	*5%*	*10%*
1,000 and more	4,702	9,240,672	92 (90%-95%)[+]	70% (65%-75%)	(6,583,978) high 5,950,992 @ 70%	238,039	+ 59,509	+119,019	+178,529	+ 297,548	+ 595,097
500-999	7,298	5,053,493	82 (30%-85%)	70% (65%-75%)	(3,221,601) high 2,900,704 @ 70%	116,028	+ 29,007	+ 58,014	+ 87,021	+ 145,035	+ 290,070
100-499	71,898	14,429,095	60 (55%-65%)	65% (60%-70%)	(6,565,238) high 5,627,347 @ 65%	225,093	+ 56,273	+112,546	+168,819	+ 281,366	+ 562,732
1-99	4,059,541	33,955,586	32 (25%-40%)	55% (50%-60%)	(8,149,340) high 5,976,182 @ 55%	239,047	+ 59,761	+119,523	+179,285	+ 298,808	+ 597,617
				TOTALS	(24,520,157) high 20,455,225 (17,039,658) low	808,207	+204,550	+409,202	+613,654	+1,022,757	+2,045,516

WARNING: The data in this table are no more than informed guesses about the reach of tuition-assistance programs in the private sector. Survey research on the subject of tuition assistance plan incidence in the private sector has been made up of infrequent and by and large limited surveys of the largest employer establishments. Thus, we have no empirical basis for the assumptions made regarding plan incidence or percentage of eligible employees for establishments under 500 employees, wherein the majority of the American work force is to be found. These "guestimates" are based on an "if this is so, then this is so" logic. They should be viewed and used accordingly.

1. Data are from U.S. Department of Commerce (1978: Table 1B). These data exclude government employees, self-employed persons, farm workers, domestic service workers, railroad employees, and merchant fleet and foreign-based workers.
2. Estimates are based on Lusterman (1977: Table 2.1). For the 500-999 group and the 1000+ group Lusterman's estimates are used. No serious survey data are available on tuition-aid incidence in establishments below 500. Estimates here assume, based on anecdotal evidence, a lower incidence the smaller the establishment size. We estimated a constant intergroup drop of 20% below the 500 employee size level.
3. Estimates are based on O'Meara (1970: Tables 8, 9). The first of these tables examines categories of employee eligible, and the latter examines length of service criteria. These are the key determinants of eligible populations. O'Meara estimates, based on his sample of 200 large companies, that 84% are open to all employees and that 65% have no service time stipulation. For the top 2 establishment size groupings we assume a 70% eligibility. We estimate progressively lower percentages of eligibility for the smaller employer groupings, assuming that because of higher turnover rates in smaller establishments fewer employees would meet service time requirements.

NOTES

This article leans so heavily on the fact gathering and analyses of Dr. Harold Goldstein, Dr. Charles Stewart, Ms. Bryna Shore Fraser, Ms. Jane Shore, Ms. Leslie Rosow, Messrs. Willard Wirtz, Paul Barton, and Ivan Charner, and Dr. Herbert Levine that any claim to authorship of more than a fraction of what appears here would constitute utter fraud. This article's existence is properly understood as a budgetary convenience, nothing more.

The works drawn upon are, in the main, policy research monographs commissioned by the Project on Worker Education and Training Policies, with which it was my good fortune to be associated from 1978 to 1980. This project is one of several current activities of the National Institute of Work and Learning; it was made possible through funding support from the National Institute of Education. Ms. Nevzer Stacey has served as the NIE project officer since 1976, and is, as much as anyone, responsible for its being.

1. To be reminded one needs to note only a few examples: the Carnegie and other public libraries, Samuel Gompers's work place-based training programs for cigar makers, correspondence and proprietary schools, county extension agents, the workers' education programs of unions and radical political groups, debating societies and the nineteenth-century Chatauquas, and literacy classes for immigrants.

REFERENCES

Bureau of National Affairs (1978) Training Programs and Tuition Aid Provisions. Personnel Policies Forum, Survey 123. Washington, DC: Author.

CHARNER, I. (1980) Patterns of Adult Participation in Learning Activities. Washington, DC: National Institute for Work and Learning.

——— (1979) "Workers' educational benefits: an exploration into the non-use of tuition aid programs." Worker Education and Training Policies Project, National Manpower Institute.

CLARK, H. F. and J. C. DAVIS (1975) "Training in business and industry," in M. E. Strong (ed.) Developing the Nation's Workforce. Yearbook 5. Washington, DC: American Vocational Association.

CLARK, H. F. and H. S. SLOAN (1958) Classrooms in the Factories: An Account of Educational Activities Conducted by American Industry. Rutherford, NJ: Fairleigh Dickinson University.

FRASER, B. S. (1980) The Structure of Adult Learning and Education and Training Opportunity in the United States. Washington, DC: National Institute for Work and Learning.

GOLDSTEIN, H. (1980) Training and Education by Industry. Washington, DC: National Institute for Work and Learning.

JAFFE, A. J. and C. D. STEWART (1951) Manpower Resources and Utilization.

KNOX, K. (1979) Polaroid Corporation's Tuition Assistance Plan: A Case Study. Washington, DC: National Manpower Institute.

LeBEL, A. A. (1977) Final Task A Report: A Description of Existing Negotiated Tuition Aid Plans. Washington, DC: National Manpower Institute.

LUSTERMAN, S. (1977) Educational in Industry. New York: Conference Board.

O'MEARA, J. R. (1970) Combatting Knowledge Obsolescence: II, Employee Tuition Aid Plans. New York: Conference Board.

ROSOW, L. A. (1979) Kimberly-Clark Corporation's Educational Opportunities Plan: A Case Study. Washington, DC: National Manpower Institute.

SHORE, J. (1979) The Education Fund of District Council 37: A Case Study. Washington, DC: National Manpower Institute.

STEWART, C. D. (1980) Worklife Education and Training and the Ordeal of Change. Washington, DC: National Institute for Work and Learning.

SWERDLOFF, S. (1978) Report on Project to Develop Data on Nonregistered Apprentices, by Occupation and Industry. Washington, DC: U.S. Department of Labor, Employment and Training Administration.

TRACEY, W. R. (1974) Managing Training and Development Systems. New York: American Management Association.

U.S. Department of Commerce (1978) County Business Patterns 1976. Washington, DC: Author.

U.S. Department of Labor, Bureau of Labor Statistics (1945) Improvement of Labor Utilization Procedures. Washington, DC: Author.

VENN, G. (1970) Man, Education and Manpower. Washington, DC: American Association of School Administrators.

WIRTZ, W. (1979) Tuition Aid Revisited. Washington, DC: National Institute for Work and Learning.

WOOL, H. (1947) "Recent trends in the labor force." Monthly Labor Rev. (December).

WOYTINSKY, W. S. et al. (1953) Employment and Wages in the United States.

8

UNIONS AND POSTSECONDARY EDUCATION

NEVZER STACEY
IVAN CHARNER

During the past two decades, the United States has witnessed a significant growth in the participation of adults in postsecondary education. Moreover, there has been a parallel growth in the awareness of the needs and desires of adults for education. As a result, new programs for adults are being developed at postsecondary educational institutions and through business, community-based organizations, and unions.[1]

Although the overall rate of adult participation in education increased from 7.6% in 1957 to 11.6% in 1978 (Momeni, 1980), significant variations exist among population groups. Generally, younger, white, well-educated, higher-income, higher occupational status adults have the higher rates of participation in education (Charner, 1980c). This variation has maintained and in many cases furthered the inequity between groups in the U.S. population.

Organized labor in the United States has a long history of support for equality of educational opportunity. While the early support focused on educational opportunities for school-aged children, since the early 1900s unions have been interested in education for their members. Organized labor's interest in education of unionized workers began with a concern for social change. It then turned to more utilitarian objectives that reflected the practical needs of the union movement. Finally, the worker education movement settled on the more general concern of providing higher education to union members.[2]

Unlike most Western European countries, the United States does not have any federal or state legislation regarding educational leaves or tuition assistance, nor is any legislation envisioned in the near future. In the United States, workers must rely on company-sponsored educational plans that are unilaterally offered or collectively bargained for. Organized labor, through its collective bargaining efforts and through its own financial support, has created a variety of mechanisms to allow members and their families to pursue education.

Our interest in this article is with union programs that provide educational opportunities to their members. While there are a large number of programs available to nonunion working adults, this article will focus only on union programs. We focus on union programs for two reasons. First, unions represent almost one-quarter of the paid work force and, second, unions play a strategic role in representing the long-range interests of their members, of which education is clearly one.

In 1977, labor unions represented 23.8% of the 81.3 million employed workers. Of these unionized workers 56% are blue-collar workers, 35% are white-collar; and 10% are service workers. Manufacturing and services industries account for 58% of the workers represented by labor unions (U.S. Department of Labor, Bureau of Labor Statistics, 1979).

As far as earnings are concerned, workers who are represented by labor unions earn more than those who are not; in 1977, on the weekly average, unionized workers earned $41 more, due primarily to higher earnings by blue-collar workers. The widest earnings margin between unionized and nonunionized workers is achieved by skilled workers in the building trades. For example, construction carpenters and craft workers in 1977 made on the average, $119 and $116 more per week than their nonunionized counterparts (U.S. Department of Labor, Bureau of Labor Statistics, 1979).

While unions have helped workers maintain and increase their salaries, they have also been concerned with skill upgrading and mobility potential of their members. As such, they have negotiated for and provided educational opportunities for their members. In this article we examine the history and present status of educational programs created by labor unions and collective bargaining agreements and explore the possibilities of developing further opportunities for union members to acquire postsecondary education. By "postsecondary" education we mean education that is beyond the age of compulsory schooling. We include any formal or organized activity undertaken with the intent of bringing about changes in information, knowledge, understanding, or skills. This definition includes courses offered by unions and employers as well as the more traditional education providers. For workers the pursuit of postsecondary education may be job-related, for career change, for personal development, or for social or political reasons.

THE ROLE OF UNIONS

As suggested earlier, labor unions have always supported education. Union involvement has taken several routes. As early as 1829, the New York Workingmen's Party urged the creation of a public school system in New York City open to all. In 1903, at the Twenty-Third Convention of the American Federation of Labor (AFL), the first permanent Committee on Education was established. The committee urged the introduction of textbooks that "will be more in accord with modern thought, social and political economy." It was during the early 1900s that educational departments were established in several unions, including the International Ladies Garment Workers' Education Department in 1917 and the Amalgamated Clothing Workers' Education Department in 1919. In the 1930s workers' education began to respond to the needs of immigrant workers, taking on an added role of providing education for union organizing and day-to-day union work.

Labor unions have played a major role in shaping federal educational legislation. The 1917 Vocational Education Act and the 1963 Amendments to the Vocational Education Act are among the benchmarks of union involvement in shaping educational policy in the United States. The 1917 Act gave the states federal funds to establish vocational education programs in industry, agriculture, and home economics for high school students, to train teachers, and to buy equipment. The amendments of 1963 extended vocational education to students in all vocational fields and gave the states and the federal government the responsibility to review vocational education programs periodically to determine whether programs matched projected manpower needs and job opportunities (United Auto Workers, 1974).

While a review of labor union history reveals that education has been and is a concern for the American labor movement, the emphasis of union education activities has changed in response to the changing needs of members. When unions experienced rapid expansion they focused their educational activities on teaching the fundamentals of trade union organizing and leadership. After the 1940s, when expansion slowed, the unions began to establish relationships with institutions of higher learning in pursuit of access to postsecondary education for their members. These relationships of unions with a variety of educational institutions have taken several forms.

UNION INVOLVEMENT IN POSTSECONDARY EDUCATION

Through funds provided in collective bargaining agreements and through their own financial support, unions have created a variety of mechanisms to allow members and their families to pursue additional education. There are two major approaches: direct subsidy and indirect subsidy. Direct subsidy is usually provided through funds allocated directly from the union's treasury to an individual or to an institution to support educational activities. Indirect subsidies involve employers or other sources of funding (Charner, 1980b).

DIRECT SUBSIDIES

Unions provide scholarships and loans so that members and their families may attend institutions of their choice. The United Auto Workers (UAW) alone spent $848,500 on scholarships in 1979. Some union scholarships pay for tuition only, while others pay a host of education-related expenses (books, stipends for living costs, and so on). Most union scholarships are awarded on the basis of economic need or on a first-come, first-served basis. In relation to total expenditures for postsecondary education, direct subsidy to individuals through scholarships constitutes the smallest single program, and most union scholarships are awarded to members' children, although some have gone to workers.

Another financing mechanism is direct union support of educational institutions where members attend prearranged programs. There are two types of arrangements under direct institutional support. In the first arrangement a specific union (or group of unions) makes educational programs available to its members through an agreement with a college, university, or other educational institution. There are several very successful programs of this kind in operation today. Programs that offer degrees in labor education are currently available in 47 institutions of higher learning. They have "open" admission policies and are strongly supported and advertised by the unions. Students are mostly adult union members. Programs include specific labor-related courses for workers and are run on both full-time or part-time bases. These programs provide bachelor's and some master's degrees to participants in union-related subjects. The Rutgers University Labor Education Center, the New York State School of Industrial and Labor Relations at Cornell (ILR), Empire State College, the College of New Rochelle's campus at the union headquarters of District Council 37 of the American Federation of State, County and Municipal Employees (AFSCME) in New York City, and Wayne State University's Weekend College are among the outstanding programs in this category.

A second type of direct institutional subsidy is the education center that is run as well as funded by a union. One outstanding example of this type of arrangement is the UAW's Family Education Center. The Walter and Mae Reuther Family Education Center, which is not affiliated with any formal higher education institution, spent $5,350,000 in providing education and training to members of the UAW in 1979. While the George Meany AFL-CIO Labor Studies Center and the Labor College in New York have affiliations with other institutions, the programs are designed exclusively for union members and are supported by the unions.

In the third kind of direct subsidy, members' dues support union education departments. The majority of courses offered by union education departments focus on teaching union skills ranging from collective bargaining to fiscal management. Although most of the union officials who take advantage of these courses do not receive credits for these courses, they are provided with opportunities to be better skilled and knowledgeable in understanding economic, social, and political issues.

In direct subsidy programs, the unions play an advocacy role and are closely involved in the management, administration, and curricular aspects of the programs. The participation of union members in these programs is high; in fact, most of them are oversubscribed.

INDIRECT SUBSIDIES

Unions and management establish collaborative relationships to provide education and training to their members through contract provisions that range from simple on-the-job training periods (for both entry-level jobs and promotions) to elaborate apprenticeship programs.

According to the most recent information available from the Bureau of Labor Statistics (BLS) of the United States Department of Labor, as of June 1980 there were 153 collective bargaining agreements covering 1000 or more workers that include in the contract a provision for *educational leaves of absence*, 788 contracts for *apprenticeship* programs, 705 contracts for *on-the-job training*, and 103 contracts providing *tuition aid*. These contracts cover over 7 million workers and represent over four-fifths of all the private sector contracts covering 1000 or more workers. The steelworkers, auto workers, and electrical workers, in particular, are parties to a significant number of contracts that include negotiated training and retraining provisions. Let us examine some examples of the arrangements through which unions provide postsecondary educational opportunities to their members through collaboration with management.

Educational Trust Funds

In this arrangement labor and management establish a trust fund into which employers pay a fixed sum of money on a specified basis. This payment varies based on cents/dollars per hour, or per worker, or may be a total lump sum for the length of the contract. The funds may be administered by the union alone, as in the case of District Council 37 of AFSCME in New York City, or by a board composed of management and union officials. In the case of District Council 37, the City of New York contributes $25 per employee per contract term. There are currently 76,000 covered employees in this contract, so fund contributions total almost $2 million per year. Courses offered under this arrangement range from college-level studies to vocational and career training. According to a survey conducted in 1973, 60% of the District Council participants had not previously gone to college and one-fifth had not finished high school; 60% of the workers earned less than $16,000 per year and 40% less than $12,000.

Recent interviews conducted under a study done by the National Institute for Work and Learning (NIWL)[3] with funding from the National Institute of Education (NIE) revealed that the majority of the participants in the District Council 37 program are females, clerical and hospital workers, who are in lower economic status positions. Attractions of this program are the location of the educational facilities at the union hall, the flexible scheduling arrangements, the close ties of the curriculum to state licensing requirements, and the perception it has instilled in participants that this is the workers' own program, designed and administered to meet their needs. The program also includes counseling to help workers overcome their fears about returning to school. With an estimated 10% participation rate among eligible workers, its developers consider the program highly successful (Shore, 1979).

A similar program is run by Local 3, International Brotherhood of Electrical Workers and New York Electrical Contractors. According to an agreement signed on 1 July 1964, between Local 3 and industry representatives, all employers remit to an educational and cultural trust fund an amount equal to 2% of their gross weekly production payroll. This fund supports a variety of activities, including a year-round residential education program at Bayberry Land, New York, and subsidizes the New York City Labor College associated with Empire State College.

Participants in education programs at Bayberry Land attend courses without loss of income for time away from work. The fund also provides scholarships to the children of members as well as opportunities for workers to take part in cultural activities in New York. In addition, for eligible employees and their spouses who meet certain criteria, the trust fund provides a college tuition reimbursement program. During fiscal year 1978-1979, the fund spent $408,160 on tuition reimbursement.

Tuition Aid

Originally conceived as an employee benefit provided unilaterally by the employer, tuition-aid programs are now also covered by many collective bargaining agreements. According to a recent study conducted by NIWL for NIE, there are approximately 198 plans in firms with 1000 or more employees, covering a total of about 1.6 million workers. Such plans vary with respect to the amount of reimbursement and types of courses, institutions, grade requirements, and eligibility requirements (Charner et al., 1978).

These plans are found in all types of industries: 54% of all plans are in manufacturing, 18% are in transportation and utilities, 19% are in service industries, and 9% are in construction. However, in all usage is low; only approximately 4%-5% of eligible workers and 2%-3% of hourly wage employees attend. Although the amounts negotiated for tuition vary from contract to contract, the General Motors and United

Auto Workers contract, for example, pays $900 per year per worker, whereas a contract between the State of Connecticut and the Connecticut Employees Union pays only $50 per course.

The barriers to participation in tuition-aid plans do not seem to be only financial. The NIWL study on "Work Life Education and Training Policies" (Charner, 1980a) identified perceived barriers to education as:

- inadequate employee information about tuition aid;
- inadequate counseling of employees;
- reimbursement rather than advance payment for courses;
- nonresponsiveness of postsecondary institutions to workers' needs; and
- difficulty in getting courses approved.

Apprenticeship

Another category of programs under direct subsidy to individuals is that of apprenticeship training arrangements. Apprenticeship programs provide credentials to individuals that entitle them to specific wage rates. Apprenticeship training is now available in the 415 recognized skilled occupations. Almost all large craft unions, including United Auto Workers (UAW), International Brotherhood of Electrical Workers (IBEW), International Union of Operating Engineers (IUOE), Sheet Metal Workers Union, and International Brotherhood of Painters and Allied Trades, have successful apprenticeship programs.

The financing schemes of trust funds for apprenticeship programs differ from union to union. An example of a joint labor-management program is the National Training Fund created by the Sheet Metal and Air Conditioning Industry and the Sheet Metal Workers Union. It was established in 1971 and is administered jointly by a committee of union and industry officials. The industry pays 4¢ an hour per employee. On the other hand, the National Joint Apprenticeship Training Committee for Operating Engineers receives no regular contributions. It is supported entirely from the sale of its training curriculum, workbooks, and materials. However, the local Joint Apprenticeship and Training Committees (JATCs) are financed by contributions negotiated under collective bargaining agreements whereby the employer contributes a set amount into the training trust fund for each hour worked by persons covered by such agreements. Such contributions range from 3¢ to 29¢ per hour worked and are considered to be tax exempt as educational institutions by the Internal Revenue Service.

There are currently 73 local apprenticeship programs administered by JATCs for Operating Engineers, representing over 336,000, or 81%, of the IUOE membership. It costs between $3,000 and $8,000 to train an apprentice over the designated period of his or her indenture (Israel, 1981).

An innovation in apprenticeship programs worth mentioning is the Operating Engineers' "Dual Enrollment Programs" sponsored by IUOE through its National Joint Apprenticeship Training Committee. This program combines apprenticeship with college study, thus enabling an individual to receive an associate degree at the end of his or her training. The operation of each local dual enrollment program is locally financed, and some even offer financial assistance to individuals, mostly in the form of a tuition reimbursement after successful completion of a course.

DEMOGRAPHIC CHANGES AND IMPLICATIONS FOR TRAINING AND EDUCATION

Having discussed briefly the existing programs in which unions play a significant role in providing postsecondary education to adults, we now turn to some of the possible advantages to union members if they participate in education and training programs. Although it is risky to rely too heavily on projections, we know that several demographic, technological, skill, and value changes will affect work places and organizations.

Over the last decade, large numbers of people joined the labor force for the first time, and an increasing proportion of these workers were women. In addition, the average age of the labor force is continuing to rise. The number of young people seeking jobs is likely to drop, especially after 1985. These developments point to the declining capacity of public and private pension and social security plans to support retirees. An aging work force also suggests a greater need for retraining. Coupled with these demographic changes, an increasing percentage of poorly skilled, non-English-speaking individuals will enter the labor force. As a result of these developments, the labor force will be highly heterogeneous and will contain an increasing number of workers with poor prospects for upward mobility. The demographics of the future suggest that mobility within internal labor markets will be limited and that education and training of the work force may be especially important for minorities, women, and older workers.

Another reason to suspect that worker training will be needed increasingly in the years ahead is the decline in the growth of American productivity. The causes and possible remedies of this slow but steady decline in the productivity growth rate are of the utmost importance to the economic well-being of the United States and its position in the world market. Although the effect of training on productivity has not been established empirically, there is evidence that productivity is related to rising educational levels (Goldstein, 1980). If general education contributes significantly to rising output per worker (Denison, 1976), then training that enhances work skills may also contribute. Large investments in research and development, more rapid application of new technology to industry, more rapid retraining of workers, and different styles of management to increase worker participation in decision making are also being investigated as possible remedies for declining productivity.

Two technological trends also suggest the increasing significance of employee training and education: technological changes in existing industries, and rapid technological innovations resulting in the creation of new industries. Technological changes generally require retraining of production workers, and most large high-technology companies are already spending large sums of money for this purpose.

The shift in the United States toward high-technology industries is requiring more skilled workers even at lower-level jobs. Some of the industries that reflect these changes are data and word processing, communications, pharmaceutical manufacturers, energy, transportation, heavy equipment manufacturers, and marketing. In the electronics field, the extensive use of micro chips will change the function of jobs by decreasing the need for workers at one level and increasing it at other levels. For office work, word processing machines and electronic filing systems are expected to cut the demand for secretaries and clerks. In the health sector, increasing labor costs will probably bring about the widespread use of electronic diagnostic machines operated by technicians rather than by physicians. These are some examples of innovations that will substantially change the nature of many jobs in the future, eliminating some repetitive, manual tasks and increasing the demand for workers with higher levels of technical knowledge. Such predicted changes in the nature of jobs will necessitate more training and education for workers in the future.

Both basic skill levels and work values have changed in the last decade. Although educational levels attained by individuals are higher then they have ever been, many employers are finding that new workers have inadequate reading, writing, and math skills. In addition, some new workers appear to have different expectations and motivations than their predecessors.

RECOMMENDATIONS

Since these changes will probably take place in the coming decade, it seems that workers who are members of unions must reexamine their education and training opportunities from a different perspective. Once the reasons to acquire further education and training become clear, alternative routes to provide mobility must be made available. What is vitally important to note is that not only should the programs be attractive to workers, but they must also be of high quality.

To be accessible, programs have to be offered at convenient times, based on the type of jobs the worker carries out. Second, education for workers should be at no cost to the workers, at least initially. Reimbursement at the completion of a course or partial payment prior to completion constitute barriers to participation. Third, support services for special groups are essential. For example, for single-parent families it is difficult enough to find child-care facilities during work hours, let alone to make arrangements for their children so that they can take courses after work. Fourth, workers have to feel secure in their learning environment. Adults who have been out of school for many years find it very difficult to compete with traditional students. It is important to conduct courses where workers feel comfortable, in their union halls or other places where the majority of the students are workers with similar problems or academic needs.

The programs that are made available to workers must have high academic standards. It would be a tremendous disservice to workers to raise their aspirations and help them overcome their fears of returning to school only to have them realize at the end of their course of study that their institution or course of study is viewed as less than desirable by others. With the mushrooming of educational providers, unions and workers are faced with myriad institutional options. Employers, too, are confronted with a variety of marketing approaches that make purchasing education not unlike purchasing cosmetics. Workers need counseling and advising services, not only in assessing their own career aspirations and past education and work experiences, but also the quality of courses they are about to take. Such counseling can only be done by individuals who know the work place and are not part of the educational "establishment." If union officials and managers were to provide assistance, the workers may have a real chance to pursue education and training worth their time and energy.

If workers state that their reason for pursuing education and training is to improve their career options, then they should be given training for occupations in which there are likely to be real job openings. Horizontal job mobility must be discussed with workers, and education and training to facilitate the "crossing" to a new occupation must be supported by unions. From the examination of recent data on tuition aid we know that use of educational entitlements dramatically increases in programs where tuition is allowed for courses that are not strictly job-related, but rather *career-related* (Rosow, 1979).

In recent years, organized labor has put a priority on increasing educational opportunities for workers. Through collective bargaining, cooperation with colleges and universities, and their own educational departments, unions have supported the higher education of workers through financial subsidies and program delivery. Union education programs for workers can affect the character of organized labor, the quality of the work force, and the higher education system. Their success is dependent on the ability of unions to cooperate with industry and education and to increase the participation of workers in these programs by overcoming the barriers faced by workers and responding to the diverse educational and training needs of workers.

If union leadership is able to do this, we would expect their ties to workers would be strengthened and their role in society would be enhanced. Involvement in the education of their 20 million members would revitalize their role in our changing society and regain for them the status they rightfully deserve.

NOTES

1. Charner (1980c) examines the possible reasons for this growth.
2. Dwyer (1977) provides a more complete historical delineation of union education.
3. The National Institute for Work and Learning was formerly the National Manpower Institute.

REFERENCES

BOAZ, R. (1978) Participation in Adult Education, Final Report, 1975. Washington, DC: Government Printing Office.

CHARNER, I. (1980a) "Investing in your employees' future." Training and Development J. (May): 100-104.

——— (1980b) "Union subsidies to workers for higher education," in H. Tuckman and E. Whalen (eds.) Subsidies to Higher Education: The Issues. New York: Praeger.

—— (1980c) Patterns of Adult Participation in Learning Activities. Washington, DC: National Institute for Work and Learning.

——— K. KNOX, A. LeBEL, H. LEVINE, and J. SHORE (1978) An Untapped Resource: Negotiated Tuition-Aid in the Private Sector. Washington, DC: National Manpower Institute.

DENISON, E. F. (1976) "Some factors affecting productivity growth," in The Future of Productivity. Washington, DC: National Center for Productivity and the Quality of Working Life.

DWYER, R. (1977) "Worker's education, labor education, labor studies: a historical delineation." Rev. of Educ. Research 47 (Winter): 179-207.

GOLDSTEIN, H. (1980) Training and Education by Industry. Washington, DC: National Institute for Work and Learning.

ISRAEL, P. H (1981) "Education and training programs of the International Union of Operating Engineers," in P. Doeringer (ed.) Work Place Perspectives on Education and Training. Boston: Martinus Nijhoff.

LEVINE, H. and M. FRIED (1978) "Expanding options for worker education," in P. Barton (ed.) Implementing New Education-Work Policies. San Francisco: Jossey-Bass.

MOMENI, J. (1980) Adult Participation in Education: Past Trends and Some Projections for the 1980's. Washington, DC: National Institute for Work and Learning.

——— and I. CHARNER (1979) Tuition-Aid Plans for Workers: Characteristics, Operations and Consequences. Washington, DC: National Manpower Institute.

ROSOW, L. (1979) Kimberly-Clark Corporation's Educational Opportunities Plan: A Case Study. Washington, DC: National Manpower Institute.

SHORE, J. (1979) The Educational Fund of District Council 37: A Case Study. Washington, DC: National Manpower Institute.

United Auto Workers (1980) Annual Report. Detroit: Author.

——— (1974) Labor's Historic Support of Public Education: A Chronology. Detroit: Author.

U.S. Department of Education (1980) The Condition of Education. Washington, DC: Government Printing Office.

U.S. Department of Labor, Bureau of Labor Statistics (1979) Earnings and Other Characteristics of Organized Workers, 1977. Report 556. Washington, DC: Author.

9

TAX LIMITATION MEASURES
Their Impact in California

HAROLD E. GEIOGUE

This chapter will discuss the impact of voter tax limitation initiatives in California on public postsecondary recurrent education efforts. Proposition 13, Proposition 4, and the influence of Proposition 9 are forcing policymakers to order priorities for public expenditures both among and within program areas—where will recurrent education fall on the priority list?

This article will first present background on the structure and scope of California's public postsecondary education system, followed by:

- recurrent education within this system;
- a discussion of the recent "taxpayers revolt";
- the impact of Proposition 13 on recurrent education; and
- the difficult position occupied by education, particularly recurrent education, in the alignment of public expenditure priorities in the 1980s.

CALIFORNIA'S PUBLIC POSTSECONDARY EDUCATION SYSTEM

STRUCTURE

California's system of public postsecondary education is the largest in the nation. It currently consists of 135 campuses serving over 1.4 million students. This system is separated into three distinct public segments—the University of California, the California State University and Colleges, and the California Community Colleges. (In addition to the public system, there are approximately 300 independent colleges and universities serving 185,000 students.)

To provide guidelines for the orderly development of three public segments, the Master Plan for Higher Education in California was developed and its recommendations were largely incorporated into the Donahoe Higher Education Act of 1960. The purpose of the act was to define the function and responsibilities of each segment and to establish a systematic approach to the needs of higher education. A coordinating agency, the California Postsecondary Education Commission (CPEC) was established to assist in meeting the objectives of the act.

The University of California (UC). The UC system consists of 8 general campuses, 5 medical schools, and numerous special research facilities located throughout the state. To govern the University of California, the state constitution grants full power of organization and governance to a 26-member Board of Regents, the members of which serve 12-year terms. The regents have substantial freedom from legislative or executive control.

In addition to the function of instruction, which is basic to all three segments of public higher education, the University of California is designated as the primary state-supported agency for research. Instruction is provided to both undergraduate and graduate students in the liberal arts and sciences and in the professions, including teaching. The University has exclusive jurisdiction over graduate instruction in the professions of law, medicine, dentistry, and veterinary medicine. It has sole authority for awarding the doctorate degree, with the exception that in selected fields joint doctoral degrees may be awarded with the California State University and Colleges.

The UC regents have established their admission standards in conformity with guidelines in the original Master Plan that called on the University to limit admissions to the top one-eighth of California's high school graduates.

The California State University and Colleges (CSUC). This system comprises 19 campuses and is governed by a statutory 23-member Board of Trustees generally serving 8-year terms. Although the Board of Trustees does not have the constitutional autonomy of the UC regents, the Donahoe Act of 1960 did provide for centralization of policy and administrative functions that are carried out by the Chancellor's Office.

The primary function of CSUC is to provide instruction to both undergraduate and graduate students in the liberal arts and sciences, in applied fields, and in various professions, including teaching. The granting of bachelor's and master's degrees is authorized, but doctorate degrees may not be granted except under the joint doctoral program with UC. Faculty research is authorized only to the extent that it is consistent with the instruction function. Admissions are limited to the top one-third of California's high school graduates.

The California Community Colleges (CCC). A 15-member Board of Governors was created by statute in 1967 to provide direction to the 70 community college districts (with 106 campuses) that constitute the system. Unlike UC and CSUC, community colleges are administered by local boards and derive some funds from local property taxes.

Instruction in public community colleges is limited to lower-division levels (freshman and sophomore) of undergraduate study in the liberal arts and sciences and in occupational or technical subjects. The granting of the associate in arts or the associate in science degree is authorized.

Admission to the community colleges is open to any high school graduate or person over 18.

SCOPE

The statement that this is the largest public higher education system in the United States is supported by both enrollment and fiscal data. In the fall of 1978, UC enrolled 8% of the state total, CSUC enrolled 21%, and the CCC enrolled the remaining 71%. Part-time enrollees represented 73% of the CCC figures but only 7% of UC undergraduates (see Table 9.1).

A summary of estimated expenditures for 1979-1980 is shown in Table 9.2. total support for all higher education in 1979-1980 amounted to nearly $5.6 billion. Of the total support budget, the state general fund provided $2.8 billion, or 50%.

Considering there are a total of 135 institutions, 1.4 million students, and an annual state expenditure of $2.8 billion, there is indeed a large recurrent education movement.

RECURRENT EDUCATION IN CALIFORNIA

UNIVERSITY OF CALIFORNIA

Traditionally, off-campus instructional activities of the University of California have been associated with UC Extension and UC Agricultural

TABLE 9.1 California Public Postsecondary Education Enrollment (Headcount), Fall 1978

Segment	Full-time Number	Full-time Percentage	Part-time Number	Part-time Percentage	Total Number	Total Percentage
University of California						
Undergraduate	84,305	93	6,656	7	90,961	100
Graduate	35,067	95	1,853	5	36,920	100
					127,881 (8%)	
California State University						
Undergraduate	167,752	70	70,508	30	238,260	100
Graduate	15,065	22	52,850	78	67,915	100
					306,175 (21%)	
California Community Colleges	285,133	27	762,034	73	1,047,167 (71%)	100
Totals	587,322	40	893,901	60	1,481,223 (100%)	100

SOURCE: CPEC (1979).

Extension. In contrast to CSUC Extension activities, UC Extension operates relatively independently of UC on-campus programs. A very small proportion of UC faculty teach in its programs. The majority of instructors are either working professionals or are employed in one of the other educational segments. UC considers its extension program to be chiefly a noncredit program. Matriculated students constitute a minor role in UC Extension. UC Extension course credit may be applied to a degree program if the student makes special arrangements with his or her academic department, but such arrangements are relatively rare. UC Extension enrolled an estimated 375,000 people in 1979-1980.

UC enjoyed state general fund support for administrative and development costs for extension programs until 1968-1969, when state support was withdrawn. (At its apex the share of state support was approximately 16%.)

Unlike some public institutions that historically have served large numbers of matriculated part-time students and offered extensive pro-

TABLE 9.2 Summary of Estimated 1979-1980 Budget for California Higher Education (in millions)

	State General Fund	*Federal*	*Other*	*Total*
University of California	$964.3	$1,151.5	$854.9	$2,970.5
California State University	821.5	53.2	292.7	1,167.4
Community Colleges	1,000.2	92.5	270.5	1,363.2
Miscellaneous	55.0	15.4	–	70.4
Totals	$2,841.0	$1,312.6	$1,417.9	$5,571.5

SOURCE: California State Department of Finance (1980-1981).

grams in the evening, the University of California over the years has focused primarily on full-time students and has made no scheduling or tuition arrangements designed expressly to serve part-time students. While the University has always had students who did not carry a full-time academic load, it had no programs for part-time students, as such.

One exception to this policy occurred in 1971 when the University developed plans for the UC Extended University (EU). Its first pilot programs were implemented in 1972. The Extended University was planned as a three-year pilot program designed to help the University learn how to serve a new group of qualified, part-time, older, working citizens by increasing opportunities for them to participate in UC degree programs—off campus as well as on campus. The Extended University was established as an entity separate from UC Extension and was placed under the administration of a university vice president headquartered at the systemwide administration building in Berkeley. Although extension personnel were involved on two of the campuses that participated in the EU program, the Extended University did not function as part of the self-supporting UC Extension program. During 1973-1974 the Extended University received $806,949 from the state general fund. In 1974-1975 the amount was increased to $1,312,434.

Students in Extended University pilot programs attended classes in the evening or on weekends. About half of the programs were offered off campus, emphasizing the point that some of the access barriers that had been lowered were not associated with geographic location. Because of the amount of funding granted the Extended University, it was in a position to make more extensive use of the media. Lecture demonstration courses were recorded on videotape for some programs; modules of instruction were on video cassettes in the nursing program; and microwave TV communication was utilized to beam courses to various cities.

In 1972-1973 the Extended University offered 7 graduate and undergraduate programs; 19 were offered in 1973-1974; 23 in 1974-1975. Over 1600 Extended University students were enrolled in the 23 degree programs offered that year by 7 of the UC campuses. More than half were enrolled at 33 off-campus locations.

All programs were regular University of California degree programs developed and offered by regular campus departments following regular academic procedures and regulations.

State funding of the Extended University was discontinued by the governor in 1975-1976 on the grounds that the University should maintain the program, beyond its initial phase, from the regular University budget. The regents' 1976-1977 budget included a request for \$2.6 million for the Extended University as an augmentation (not within the regular budget) but the request was not included in the governor's budget. The state legislature passed a bill that appropriated \$2.6 million, but the bill was vetoed by the governor. The Extended University is currently being phased out.

There is considerable evidence to support the view that the University's effort to extend its traditional approaches into nontraditional and off-campus areas was a partial response to criticism that the University was an "elitist" institution, unconcerned with new instructional techniques, with part-time study, and with older and underrepresented clientele. Another reason for the establishment of the Extended University undoubtedly was the genuine concern among many members of the University community that the criticism had some validity.

What also seems clear, however, is that the University's commitment to the concept of the Extended University was not strong. The fact that the decision was made to phase out the program once state funding was terminated, rather than attempt to continue it under an alternate funding arrangement, such as higher student fees or the use of internal University resources, indicates that the program occupied a relatively low priority within the University family. The fact that University Extension was so well established, and the fact that much of what the Extended University purported to do could also be done through Extension, probably contributed to the decision to abandon the program. At this time, there is little desire at the official levels of the University to continue formal degree programs beyond the confines of the traditional, campus-based setting dealing with top quality undergraduate and graduate students.

Despite this, California has developed a large recurrent education activity in its other two public segments—the CSUC and the CCC.

CALIFORNIA STATE UNIVERSITY AND COLLEGES

The California State University and Colleges offer four distinct approaches to off-campus and extended degree opportunities: (a) State University Extension; (b) miscellaneous courses provided at off-campus locations; (c) external degree programs; and (d) the Consortium of the CSUC. Administratively, extended degree programs and extension offerings are operated under the auspices of State University Extension, miscellaneous courses through the campuses, and the Consortium through its own administration in the systemwide Chancellor's Office.

State University Extension. Begun in 1932, this program is quite similar to most university extension operations. A variety of courses are offered featuring fee support, short duration, a focused audience, and little degree credit. As of 1978-1979, CSUC Extension enrolled 73,526 people, or the equivalent of 5,693 full-time students.

Miscellaneous courses. Conducted at off-campus locations, these courses, both degree-related and non-degree-related, are a rubric within which fall the thousands of efforts to reach adult learners who are isolated from a campus by either distance or time. These courses are classified separately because they are not related to a formal, organized, degree program. Unlike Extension, they do not require special fees. In 1979-1980 it is estimated that 4000 people will enroll almost equally in the degree- and non-degree-related miscellaneous courses.

External degrees. The CSUC system embarked on major efforts to establish formal degree programs for the on- and off-campus recurrent education student through external degree programs and the Consortium of the CSUC.

In 1971, the CSUC chancellor called for a major expansion of off-campus and extended educational opportunities. Noting the perceived "rigid system," which primarily served students in residence, he called for an alternative that included "television, correspondence courses, self-study combined with short-course on-campus programs, taped lectures with study guides to comprise programmed learning, as well as classroom instruction on or off campus," all to be on a self-supporting basis.

The proposed expansion in the nontraditional sector was endorsed by the Board of Trustees with the establishment of the Commission on External Degree Programs, which was charged with the establishment, on a pilot project basis, of policies and procedures for implementing off-campus degree programs. The activities of the commission resulted in the concept of the "1000-mile campus" and the CSUC system now has established policies that govern the development of external degrees.

At present, external degree programs are developed by the individual campuses and, after review by the Chancellor's Office, are forwarded to the commission for approval. These programs are fully self-supporting, although a small amount of funding is provided for fee waivers. By the fall of 1975, enrollment in these programs was 3733.

The Consortium of the California State University and Colleges was established in 1973 as the result of a recommendation by the Commission on External Degree Programs. Its purposes were to:

- serve the needs of highly mobile adult students who through circumstances are required to transfer from one college to another, thereby losing degree credit;
- develop statewide or regional external degree programs to serve sparsely populated geographical areas, or students with special interests who are dispersed over a wide area;
- conduct programs in geographic areas where the local CSUC campus is unable to meet the need with its own resources;
- encourage reciprocity of residence credit and core degree requirements between campuses and to begin building toward the development of a common "credit bank" or curricular records for students; and
- develop strategies for assessing the prior learning experiences of adult students, whose varied backgrounds of work and schooling make admissions decisions more complex.

TABLE 9.3 CSUC Recurrent Education Activity FTE, 1977-1978 to 1980-1981

	1977-1978	*1978-1979*	*1979-1980*	*1980-1981*
Extension	6,112	5,693	5,288	4,942
Miscellaneous Courses	1,002	819	816	816
External Degree	2,122	793	830	835
Consortium	423	318	225	375
Total	8,659	7,623	7,159	6,968

SOURCE: CSUC, Office of Institutional Research (personal communication).

As of 1977-1978, total FTE enrollment in the Consortium was approximately 500, a figure that was reduced to an estimated 300 for the 1979-1980 fiscal year. Although originally supported by the legislature ($46,252 in 1972-1973, with increasing amounts to $200,000 in 1976-1977), it is currently self-supporting. The Western Association of Schools and Colleges granted full regional accreditation to the Consortium in 1976.

A summary of full-time equivalent (FTE) enrollment in all four CSUC recurrent education activities is shown in Table 9.3.

CALIFORNIA COMMUNITY COLLEGES

Of all students enrolled in recurrent education in California's 3 public segments, the majority in the inventory of off-campus locations and programs in fall 1978 (62.4% of the off-campus locations and 81.3% of the course registrations) were in the CCCs. Although this is a decrease from 1976 figures of 67.7% and 84.8%, respectively, the community colleges are clearly the principal providers of recurrent education services.

The figures are also dramatically higher than the total reported in the fall of 1972. At that time, there were 1,363 off-campus locations with an enrollment of 190,000 students, over 98% of them part-time. By contrast (although they are not directly comparable), course registration four years later were 472,153, and six years later, 363,899. The 1,363 locations reported in 1972 had grown to 2,985 in 1976 and then dropped to 2,507 in 1978. Thus it is apparent that something caused a dramatic growth in enrollment between 1972 and 1976, and that something else caused a decline between 1976 and 1978. (This decline will be discussed further below.)

Recurrent education occurs primarily in the off-campus setting. In order to obtain information on off-campus programs offered by community colleges, CPEC sent a questionnaire to 20 colleges of varying size, geographic location, and commitment to off-campus operations. Of these, 14 responded.

Table 4 shows the number and types of courses, and types of faculty. The faculty are categorized as "full-time, on-load," "full-time, off-load," or "part-time." The first of these refers to regular, full-time faculty who are teaching an off-campus course as part of their normal assignment. "Full-time, off-load" refers to regular, full-time faculty who are teaching an off-campus course in addition to their normal assignments. "Part-time" refers to individuals who are not regular faculty members with full-time teaching contracts but are hired on a course-by-course basis.

As shown in Table 9.4, there is no consistency among the 14 colleges as to the distribution of credit and noncredit classes. College K offers all of its courses for credit, while 92% of College J's courses are in the noncredit category. Similarly, Colleges C and G have 75% and 85% of their courses in the noncredit area, respectively. Of the 14 colleges, 10 have a majority of credit offerings while 4 have most classes in the noncredit category. The fact that one of these institutions also maintain both the high school adult program and the regular community college program helps to explain the preponderence of noncredit offerings, but this is only a partial explanation.

Part-time faculty are currently teaching 84.4% of the off-campus courses in the 14 colleges, while the total number of part-time faculty is about two-thirds of all community college faculty on a headcount basis. Given the urgings of accrediting agencies for greater use of regular faculty in off-campus programming, the implications of such overwhelming reliance on part-time instructors are significant.

Table 9.5 shows course lengths and fee charges in the 3660 courses noted in Table 9.4. Community colleges use off-cammpus facilities to conduct classes very similar in format to those offered on campus, either during the day or in the evening. This format is the standard lecture/discussion system. The fact that 76.4% of all classes are quarter or semester length indicates the similarity with on-campus programming. The fact

TABLE 9.4 Courses and Types of Faculty Teaching at Selected Off-Campus Locations in the California Community Colleges, Fall 1979

	Courses			Faculty		
College	*Total*	*Credit*	*Noncredit*	*On-Load*	*Off-Load*	*Part-time*
A	254	228	228	71	11	172
B	110	110	71	6	11	93
C	767	194	573	149	10	608
D	231	210	21	71	5	155
E	119	100	19	15	2	102
F	453	277	176	9	5	439
G	226	33	193	26	11	189
H	72	34	38	1	2	69
I	445	435	10	96	9	340
J	480	39	441	22	9	449
K	226	226	0	39	8	179
L	113	109	4	0	2	111
M	56	34	22	1	4	51
N	108	100	8	13	0	95
Totals	3,660	2,090	1,570	519	89	3,052
Percentage	100	57.1	42.9	14.2	2.4	83.4

SOURCE: CPEC (1980).

that about 16% of the classes are not of a traditional length indicates flexibility in meeting special needs. Of the 583 courses reported to be under 10 weeks long, 312 of them are offered for credit and 271 are noncredit.

FISCAL PRIORITIES IN AN ERA OF RESOURCE RESTRAINT

With the foregoing discussion of California's postsecondary education structure in mind, I now address:

- the so-called California taxpayers' revolt;
- the impact of Proposition 13 of 1978 on recurrent education efforts in public institutions; and
- recurrent education's position in the political priority structure.

TABLE 9.5 Course Length and Fees Charged in Off-Campus Classes in 14 California Community Colleges, Fall 1979

	Number	*Percentage*
Course Length		
2 Weeks or Less	93	2.5
2-10 Weeks	490	13.4
Over 10 Weeks	2,795	76.4
Unknown	282	7.7
Totals	3,660	100.0
Course Type and Fee Status		
Credit		
Fee Charged	169	4.6
Fee Not Charged	1,850	50.6
Noncredit		
Fee Charged	311	8.5
Fee Not Charged	1,220	33.3
Unknown	110	3.0
Totals	3,660	100.0

THE TAXPAYERS' REVOLT

The decades of the 1960s and 1970s witnessed an extraordinary growth in the level and scope of government services. For example, during the past 10 years, the percentage increase in federal spending far outstripped the rate of inflation (170% versus 104%). The expansion was even more dramatic in California, where state spending increased nearly 2.5 times the percentage increase in prices.

The extraordinary growth did not just happen by accident. The citizens of California and the nation demanded that it happen. The rise of social consciousness in the late 1960s and early 1970s created public pressure for better schools, health care, air quality, and environment. Government action was viewed as the panacea for the creation of "the great society." Consequently, our elected representatives were just following orders.

It is important to understand the form that these demands took. The public did not demand that government grow and the private economy contract, nor did they demand that government take an increasingly large share of income. The public demands were focused on individual programs and services, rather than on the bottom line of total cost.

As we move into the 1980s, we are told that a taxpayers' revolt is in progress in California and perhaps nationally. There are many manifestations of this revolt, including:

- Propositions 9 and 13, as well as other measures aimed at reducing taxes;
- indexing of income tax and other measures aimed at reducing the growth in taxes;
- Proposition 4 and similar measures aimed at limiting the growth in spending; and
- efforts to balance the federal budget.

The concern, then, is not that elected representatives are failing to respond to the public's demands, but rather that they are doing too good a job of it, and the public does not like the fiscal consequences. While the public has become disenchanted with government spending in general, there is evidence that large segments of the public continue to believe that government can and should take on society's problems—the "there ought to be a law" attitude seems to be surviving despite the revolt. Evidence of this is widespread. In California, for instance:

- The number of bills introduced in the legislature last year was only slightly lower than the number introduced in the previous legislature.
- The testimony taken by legislative committees is indistinguishable from that taken prior to the enactment of recent initiatives—representatives of the public invariably plead for bigger budget appropriations and there has been no outpouring of public sentiment aimed at reducing individual items in the budget.
- The success of incumbents seeking reelection to the legislature has been very high. In November 1978—5 months after the voters expressed great dissatisfaction with government by approving Proposition 13—they reelected nearly 90% of those incumbents on the ballot.

What is new about the "taxpayers' revolt" is the feeling in many quarters that the public's appetite for government services is too healthy—that they demand more from government than they are willing to pay for. The expression "a million here, a million there, and pretty soon we are talking about real money" sums up the problem. Legislative bodies are caught up in the absurdity of trying to maintain spending for each of the individual items in the budget while concurrently being pressured to reduce the level of total spending.

It is this frustration—this recognition that representatives say "no" to individual progams—that has led many to advocate the kinds of broad limitations on government revenues and expenditures that are associated with the "taxpayers' revolt." The argument goes like this: If the amount of revenue that government receives, or the level of expenditures that it can make, is arbitrarily limited, willpower will of necessity be enhanced.

The point is simply this: It is not clear that the public has "sorted out" its priorities regarding government as yet, and until it does—until there is a balance between what is expected of government and what the public is prepared to spend on government—the public sector is going to be in a state of flux.

PROPOSITION 13's IMPACT ON RECURRENT EDUCATION

This brings us to the concern for recurrent education in the context of fiscal restraint. I am not referring to a moderate recession in financial support that all programs can survive with modest belt-tightening; I am talking about a time of deep academic recession caused by declining enrollments of up to 20% occurring in an era of limited resources. There will be the required analysis of the priorities of programs—some programs will expand, most will be fortunate to just retrench, while yet others will be reduced or eliminated. Based on my analysis of the impact of Proposition 13 of 1978, it is the last category into which recurrent education is likely to fall.

A brief orientation would be useful to those who are unfamiliar with the California voter initiative process. The California initiative process was established by special election on 10 October 1911. California became the tenth state in the nation to enact the initiative and referendum.

The initiative provides the people a mechanism to propose statutory revisions and constitutional amendments, and to adopt or reject those proposed by the legislature. The initiative allows the voters to bypass the legislature and have an issue of concern put directly on the ballot for voter approval or rejection.

In order to qualify a direct initiative for the ballot, a title and summary must be obtained from the attorney general, petitions circulated and signatures gathered, and the petitions must be filed with the county clerk of each county in which signatures were collected. Petitions supporting statute revisions must be signed by registered voters equal in number to 5% of the total number of votes cast for all candidates for governor in the last gubernatorial election; those for constitutional amendments require 8%.

An initiative that qualifies for the ballot goes before the voters at the next statewide election held at least 131 days after it qualifies. The governor may call a special statewide election for an initiative measure.

Any initiative measure approved by a majority of the votes cast at any election takes effect the day after the election unless the measure provides otherwise. An approved initiative is not subject to a governor's veto, nor may it be amended or repealed by the legislature without a vote of approval by the electors.

Proposition 13 on the 1978 June ballot was a constitutional revision initiative designed to limit the amount of revenue that could be derived from the taxation of property. The proceeds of such were used primarily to support local government and schools (including the community colleges).

Technically, Proposition 13 added Article XIIIA to the California Constitution, limiting property tax revenue to 1% of the market value of property plus an amount necessary to repay existing voter-approved debt. Article XIIIA also rolled back the assessed value of property to 1975 levels, limited increases in assessed values to 2% per year, and restricted the imposition of nonproperty taxes by state and local governments. The electorate approved the measure by a vote of 2 to 1.

Proposition 13 did not specify how the remaining property tax revenue would be distributed among taxing jurisdictions. Chapter 292 (SB 154) and Chapter 332 (SB 2212), Statutes of 1978, provided for this distribution of property tax revenue and provided $4.4 billion of state funds as fiscal relief to local governments in order to partially offset the loss in property tax revenue.

Proposition 13 reduced city, county, school district, and special district property tax revenue by about $6.9 billion, or about 55%, from the estimated property taxes that would have been levied in 1978-1979 if Proposition 13 had not been enacted. The property tax reduction was about $5.9 billion, or 51%, when compared to 1977-1978 collections.

TABLE 9.6 Comparison of the Property Tax Revenue Loss Resulting from Proposition 13 (in millions)

		1978-1979	
	1977-1978	*Without Proposition 13*	*Actual*
Property Tax Levies	$10,277	$11,258	$5,047
State Subvention for Homeowners' and Business Inventory Examptions	1,172	1,217	536
Total Property Tax Revenues	$11,449	$12,475	$5,583
Reduction from 1977-1978	–	n.a.	–$5,866
Reduction from 1978-1979 (Without Proposition 13)	n.a.	–	–$6,892

SOURCE: Office of Legislative Analyst (1980).

Table 9.6 provides information on property tax reveues in 1977-1978 and 1978-1979. The extent of the reduction in total revenue to each city, county, and special district varied according to: (a) the proportion of total revenue the city, county, or special district collected from property taxes; (b) the entity's legal authority to offset the property tax revenue losses with alternative revenue sources and the extent to which such authority was used, and (c) the amount of replacement revenue received from the state government.

Proposition 13, of course, is not an expenditure limitation, but merely a limitation on one source of revenue, the property tax. Proposition 13 does not say anything about whether total government expenditures can grow 20%, 30%, or 40%; it just says that you cannot fund government by more than "x" from the property tax. And because of this its primary impact in postsecondary education was on the community colleges. Prior to June 1978, community colleges in California were 60% to 70% funded from the local property tax, with the remainder from the state (20% to 30%) and federal (10%) governments. So it was clear that the community colleges had to adjust their planning to take account of fiscal constraints.

More interesting, however, is the fact that, as shown in Table 9.7, Proposition 13 has also had a direct impact on support for the University of California and the California State University and Colleges, which had no property tax support. In fact, the most bewildered people

TABLE 9.7 State General Fund Support to Postsecondary Education Pre- and Post-Proposition 13 (in million)

		1978-1979	
Segment	*1977-1978*	*Pre-13 Estimated*	*Post-13 Actual*
CCC[a]	$1,218	$1,303	$1,124
UC	737	819	767
CSU	666	734	683
Totals	$2,621	$2,856	$2,574
Reduction from 1977-1978	–	n.a.	–$47
Reduction from 1978-1979 (Without Proposition 13)	n.a.	–	–$282

SOURCE: Office of Legislative Analyst (internal office data).
a. State and local support.

in the capitol after the passage of Proposition 13 were from those segments of postsecondary education.

What developed, obviously, was a political environment involving the fiscal condition in general, and not just the property tax. The general climate of opinion was against government spending in all forms. Postsecondary education was not given any special high-priority protection (for reasons I will discuss), nor was recurrent education.

Details of Proposition 13's impact on recurrent education are sketchy, but some synthesis is possible. I will briefly discuss its impact on UC, CSUC, and CCC, recurrent education.

Of course there was no impact at the University of California, which had abandoned its External University program prior to 1978. In the CSUC system, as shown previously in Table 9.3. The development of recurrent education came to a halt. This is because the legislative fiscal committees began to question the very purpose of recurrent education activities. There was a general concern that much of the growth of recurrent education had occurred without adequate legislative involvement or oversight, especially with regard to enrollment levels, instructional quality, and equity of student charges. The postsecondary education commission was directed by the legislature to "define and study the various kinds of extended education. . . . Such study shall address questions of access, support, student needs, and quality." This study was conducted, however, as of this date, a final policy on the CSUC recurrent education activity remains unresolved by the legislature.

Community colleges reported that, within the operating budget, outlays for credit instruction were reported to be down by 1% while noncredit instructional expenditures were reduced by 27%.

Proposition 13 affected the colleges' ability to carry out the community college mission and functions. While few programs were cut, 6% of 60,000 courses and 13% of 125,000 course sections were eliminated statewide. The average size of remaining course sections increased by 4%, from 23 to 24 students. Courses qualifying for Vocational Education Act support (that is, with occupational objectives) were least affected. In fact, these courses increased slightly in number while all other courses were decreased in number by 16%. As shown in Table 9.8 noncredit courses were most affected. Of these courses, 20% were eliminated and another 10% were shifted to fee-supported community service status. Community service activities, in turn, were reduced overall by slightly more than one-third. All but four districts reduced overall by summer session offerings due to the uncertainty of funding and timing of Proposition 13-related decisions. Statewide, the number of summer courses declined by about 50%.

Community college staff were reduced by about 10,000 employees (14%) from 72,000 to 62,000 between spring 1978 and fall 1979. Of the 1,500 decline in full-time employees, two-thirds was attributed to normal attrition; but in most cases, the empty positions were not filled. Of the total decrease, most (7,000) took place among part-time faculty. In nearly all cases, part-time faculty were not rehired either due to classes that were not offered because of buget reductions or were offered then canceled due to inadequate enrollment. In many cases, noncredit classes experienced low enrollment due to the charging of fees. There was a 23% decrease in part-time staff, but just a 9% decrease in ADA. Consequently, many full-time staff took over part-time duties on an overload basis.

Prior to the passage of Proposition 13, the Department of Finance had projected increases of 3% in enrollment for community colleges during 1978-1979. The actual enrollment change between fall 1977 and fall 1978 was a decrease of 162,000 students, or 12.3%.

The fall 1978 enrollment loss was greater among part-time than among full-time students, greater among males than among females, greater among older than among younger students, and far greater among those enrolled only in noncredit courses. The enrollment of those taking only noncredit courses decreased by more than 50%, and the enrollment of full-time students attending only in the evening declined by one-fourth. There is little doubt that the bulk of the enrollment loss can be attributed to budget and programmatic cutbacks directly related to the significant reduction in fiscal resources caused by Proposition 13.

TABLE 9.8 Comparison of California Community College Enrollments for the Fall 1977 and Fall 1978 Terms, by Program of Studies[a]

	Total			Full-Time			Part-Time		
Category	*Fall 1977*	*Fall 1978*	*Change*	*Fall 1977*	*Fall 1978*	*Change*	*Fall 1977*	*Fall 1978*	*Change*
Head County Enrollment									
Credit Only	803,868	760,132	–5.4	233,362	206,918	–11.3	570,506	553,214	3.0
Credit and Noncredit	19,778	10,114	–48.7	7,481	4,309	–42.4	12,297	5,835	–52.5
Noncredit Only	45,227	19,668	–56.5	–	–	–	45,227	19,668	–56.5
Unknown	6,166	3,013	–51.1	306	43	–85.9	5,860	2,970	–49.3
Total	875,039	792,957	–9.3	241,149	211,270	–12.4	633,890	581,687	8.2
Percentage of Total									
Credit Only	91.9	95.9	4.0	96.8	98.0	1.2	90.0	95.1	5.1
Credit and Noncredit	2.2	1.2	–1.0	3.1	2.0	–1.1	2.0	1.0	–1.0
Noncredit Only	5.2	2.5	–2.7	–	–	–	7.1	3.4	3.7
Unknown	0.7	0.4	0.3	0.1	–	–0.1	0.9	0.5	–0.4
Total									

SOURCE: CPEC (1980).

a. Based on data from 81 of 106 colleges.

PRIORITIES

While it is difficult to make clear comparisons and conclusions, it appears that Proposition 13 had a major impact on postsecondary education in general and recurrent education in particular. There are a variety of reasons for the "softening" of the public priority for postsecondary education:

(1) The unprecedented increase in enrollment and expenditures for higher education. This not only makes it a highly visible segment of our public budget, but also causes a natural fiscal conflict between institutions of higher education seeking to maximize funding and elected officials seeking to minimize taxes.
(2) In addition, competition for money from new social programs, such as energy conservation and medical services, places pressure on decision makers to examine closely traditional programs and stress the reallocation of resources between and within agencies.
(3) The apparent vacuum of leadership in higher education. Right or wrong, academic leadership has the appearance of weakness. This vacuum is partially the result of the perception that leadership in higher education responds to internal special interest constituencies, particularly faculty, rather than to public needs. Also, the high turnover of academic leaders and their reluctance to be assertive contributes to this perception.
(4) The dissident students and faculty bringing higher education's dirty laundry to government's door.
(5) The push for access by women, ethnics, and disabled into the mainstream of society focuses attention on higher education as the gatekeeper.
(6) Reports of unemployment and underemployment of college graduates, particularly graduates of high-cost graduate programs, undermining some of the major rationales for support of higher education—economic development and social mobility.
(7) Finally, there is concern about competitive practices for student enrollments such as the lowering of entrance and retention standards and financial aid bidding. Elected officials see these actions as weakening the social fiber through lowering academic standards in order to assure institutional survival.

With these general concerns in mind, attention can be focused on recurrent education's position within the postsecondary education community. It is my thesis that, for a variety of reasons, recurrent education in California, and perhaps elsewhere, is in a politically vulnerable position given the politics within postsecondary education. While there are those like Daniel Perlman (1975), who see financial crisis as a stimulus for the expansion of recurrent education, I would argue that as it affects public institutions, just the opposite is true. The expansion in the 1970s was mostly due to the social pressure for increased access to higher education. Thus there was expansion in recurrent education despite leveling enrollments and financial difficulty—perhaps we can call this a state of "benign neglect." In a time of financial crisis, however, priority for recurrent education appears to be low due to a variety of factors, including:

- Its low visibility due to limited curriculum, limited staff, limited support services, and limited "alumni" hinders attempts to develop a broad-based constituency.
- Its organizational position, usually outside the academic institutional mainstream, exemplified by not being represented (a) in academic master plans, (b) in academic senates, or (c) in the line organization of the academic vicc president's office, weakens its position in academic "in-fighting."
- Its heavy reliance on part-time or low-ranking regular faculty raises questions of quality.
- Its service to a clientele that is often employed, white, and middle-class encourages the budget agencies to promote a self-support financing plan for recurrent education.

CONCLUSION

These factors lead to the conclusion that, within academic institutions that have been in existence for decades and within the society they serve, recurrent education is still the new kid on the block. It is constantly under the burden of proof—and it is our job to establish such proof. Perhaps this can be accomplished through a stronger alliance with the forces of vocationalism in business, industry, and organized labor. Perhaps through an expansion of the type of student served—a "more broadly casted net" if you will. Perhaps the answer lies in a better system of governance.

A few words on governance. As I see it, we need a governance system

- that reduces uncertainty and confusion by being easily understood by all parties;
- that provides an effective accountability mechanism without reducing institutional autonomy;
- that places governors and legislative bodies in their proper role of oversight, not detailed intrusion into administrative matters; and, finally,

- that provides that the tough reallocation questions be addressed systematically across the whole of the higher education community.

If there are negative decisions to be made (closings of departments, layoffs, and so on), they must be determined rationally. Decisions should not be based on who has more muscle in the state house, but on who delivers necessary quality teaching, research, and public service in a reasonably cost-effective mode.

REFERENCES

California Postsecondary Education Commission [CPEC] (1980) Degrees of Diversity: Off-Campus Education in California. Sacramento: Author.

——— (1979) CPEC Information Digest, 1979. Sacramento: Author.

California State Department of Finance (1980-1981) The Governor's Budget. Sacramento: Author.

California State University and Colleges [CSUC] (1977-1978) Statistical Digest, Continuing Eduction, 1977-78. Long Beach: Author.

——— (1975-1976) Statistical Digest, Continuing Education, 1975-76. Long Beach: Author.

McCABE, G. (1979) Discussion Draft: Should the State of California Finance Off-Campus Instruction by the California State University and Colleges? A Study of the Issues. Long Beach: California State University and Colleges.

MAYHEW, L. B. (1976) "The closing door: national tragedy or a shift in social values?" Presented at the National Forum of the College Board, New York, October.

Office of Legislative Analyst (1979) An Analysis of the Effects of Proposition 13 on Local Governments. Sacramento: Author.

PERLMAN, D. H. (1975) "External degree programs: alternative delivery systems for higher education." Liberal Education (October).

RICHARDS, L. (1979) Results of Lifelong Learning Priority Issues Study. Los Angeles: University of Southern California and the Association of Independent California Colleges and Universities.

SALNER, M. B. (1976) Continuing Education in the California State University and Colleges. Long Beach: California State University and Colleges.

TEMPLIN, R. G., Jr. (1977) "Lifelong learning and the politics of education," in Politics of Higher Education and Public Policy. Washington, DC: American Council on Education.

University of California Systemwide Administration (1978) Report of the Systemwide Committee on University Extension. Berkeley: Author.

University of California Systemwide Study Committee on Extension (1978) University Extension at the University of California. Berkeley: Author.

10

AN OPPORTUNITY DEFERRED
Lifelong Learning in the United States

PAMELA H. CHRISTOFFEL

On 3 October 1980, President Carter signed into United States law the Education Amendments of 1980, Public Law 96-374. The legislation, which extended and revised federal postsecondary education programs through 1985, took significant new steps toward expansion of educational opportunity for adults. The result of a two-year legislative development process, the new law amended the Higher Education Act of 1965, which provides the basic statutory authority for a variety of federal student aid and postsecondary educational institution assistance programs. Much of the existing legislation was extended unchanged. Portions of the law dealing with recurrent education were subjected to extensive debate in the Congress over the two-year period and received considerable support in both the House of Representatives and the Senate at that time.

The new law focused only on postsecondary (postcompulsory) education programs, including those serving adults.[1] Overall, it included a wide variety of programs and opportunities for adult learners. It provided more equitable treatment of adult students in financial aid programs and limited expansion of some financial aid programs to less-than-half-time students, many of whom are adults. The law authorized a refocused program of state and federal recurrent education grants directed toward adults who have not participated in such programs previously. New emphasis was placed on recurrent education in statewide postsecondary education planning activities. Adult learning studies were to be carried out by the National Institute for Education. The existing Educational Opportunity Center program was modified to include a sharpened focus on serving adults through community-oriented programs. And finally, colleges and universities with schools of education were to receive support for the retraining of elementary and secondary teachers and postsecondary faculty.

However, in November 1980 Ronald Reagan was elected president and Republicans took over political control of the Senate from the Democrats, and with these changes came resolve on the part of government leaders to cut back federal spending for social programs. The spring and summer of 1981 saw the Congress, encouraged by the Reagan administration, undo much of what was accomplished in the Education Amendments of 1980. This article reviews the development of the original recurrent education legislation enacted last year and outlines how the new administration and the Congress have used a complex budgetary process to revise and rescind much of the new law even before the bulk of the changes it authorized were put into effect.

BACKGROUND

Development of the new recurrent education legislation grew out of some fairly clearly defined policy objectives. First, Congress at that time was determined to find ways to improve educational opportunities for adult learners, especially those adults who were not then participating in recurrent education activities. The encouragement of equal education opportunity had long been a cornerstone for traditional federal involvement in postsecondary education. The new law extended this commitment to those adults outside the mainstream of postsecondary education in the United States. Legislators agreed that the primary focus of the federal government in adult continuing education should be on promoting access, particularly for older persons, the less educated, minorities, low-income persons, and those living in central cities or rural areas.

The Congress was also anxious to achieve several more pragmatic policy objectives, including program consolidation and improvement of the federal-state partnership in support of postsecondary education. Both of these objectives were included as themes in the recurrent education portions of the new law.

Finally, the legislators were concerned about predictions of sharply declining enrollments of postsecondary students in the more traditional 18-to-22-year-old age group and sought to rechannel existing postsecondary education resources into this emerging sector of recurrent education, where unmet educational needs still existed.

These policy objectives, as stated by the U.S. Congress, grew out of considerable research and data collection carried out in the past few years. Work by Peterson et al. (1979), and more recently Wagner (1980), Smith (1980), and others, has documented the extent of recurrent education undertaken currently. As an area of endeavor, continuing education has undergone dramatic growth in this decade: More and more adults are participating in formal education, and more and more institutions—among them colleges and universities with an eye on the diminishing pool of traditional college-age students—are seeking to serve them. The extent of this growth is substantial.

However, while current adult participation in education spans a wide range of backgrounds, previous educational experiences, and incomes, it tends to be greatest among one broad group: Today's adult learners are disproportionately young, white, well educated, and earning salaries above the national median family income. For example:

- 15.8% of those between 17 and 34 years of age take advantage of adult educational opportunities (excluding those enrolled full time in high school or postsecondary institutions), whereas only 4.4% of those over the age of 54 participate.
- 12.5% of white adults participate in adult education, whereas only 6.5% of blacks participate.
- 26.8% of those with four years of college or more participate, while 11.2% of those with only four years of high school (and only 3.4% of those with less than high school diplomas) participate.
- 17.7% of those with annual family incomes of $25,000 or more participate, while only 8.4% of those whose income is between $5,000 and $10,000, and only 5.4% of those with incomes below $5,000, participate.

Equally important, recent research (Aslanian and Brickell, 1980) indicates that the majority of adults enrolled in education have returned to formal learning because of specific job- or career-related factors—to obtain or keep employment or to avoid job or skill obsolescence—or because of dislocations in their personal lives such as divorce or death of a spouse. Women are returning to the work place in unprecedented numbers and many seek education to refresh skills or learn new ones. Older adults seek education for second careers or to help them adjust to retirement.

Yet the disparities remain, so as Congress began developmental work on the Education Amendments of 1980, it was faced with very real and well-documented needs. And it appeared unlikely that major improvements would be accomplished without some federal intervention. The next problem was to examine and choose among alternative methods for federal financing of recurrent education programs designed to meet these needs. Again, much research has been carried out in this area, both in the United States and abroad, including that of Levin, Kurland, and others (Windham et al., 1978). Support for individuals in the form of entitlements, loans, grants, and other methods has been debated widely, as have models that would provide funds to educational providers—colleges, universities, unions, local community centers, radio and television, and other nontraditional institutions and organizations. After reviewing the research, the Congress decided to write new legislation that would utilize a variety of financing schemes, some in current practice and others as yet untried. Financial aid was provided to individual adult learners in various ways. Modest grants were to be made available, through the states, to a wide assortment of educational providers. And a limited amount of federal funds was designated for state government agencies responsible for planning educational activities within the states.[2] In fact, the new legislation was viewed as a sort of test of alternative methodologies. More intensive use of one or another models was discussed by the Congress and rejected for the time being. The legislators decided that the variety of financing schemes included in the new law ought to be utilized and examined over the next five years, at which point new decisions based on observed demand for and success of the alternative strategies would be made.

DEVELOPMENT OF THE LEGISLATION

Work on the development of this legislation began in 1978. Representatives from a wide variety of Washington-based educational associations and other interested organizations began a series of meetings to frame the new legislation and sharpen the federal role in support of recurrent education. Among the more than 50 members of this working coalition were the American Library Association, the Adult Education Association, the American Association of Community and Junior Colleges, the American Association of Retired Persons, the United Auto Workers, and the College Board. This coalition representing education, unions, senior citizens' and womens' groups, and minority interests was a unique phenomenon, reflecting the breadth of interest in recurrent education across the country. Using as background a study defining the future federal role in this area (Hoffman, 1980),[3] coalition members testified repeatedly on the need for recurrent education programs at congressional hearings. Congressman William Ratchford (Democrat from Connecticut), a member of the subcommittee and former commissioner of aging for the State of Connecticut, took the congressional lead and introduced the major section of recurrent education legislation. The subcommittee reacted favorably to these various efforts, and the Education Amendments of 1980, containing new adult provisions, passed the full House of Representatives in November 1979.

Meanwhile, the Senate was moving at a more deliberate pace. But, after considerable delay caused by controversy over other portions of the draft legislation, the measure was finally approved by both houses of Congress and signed into law by President Carter on 3 October 1980.

The following is an outline of the various recurrent education provisions of the amendments intended to benefit adults.

Programs	**Relevant Provisions**
Financial Aid to Individuals	
Pell Grants	Grants provided directly to students. New law eliminated number of years students are eligible for these grants, and provided more equitable treatment of financially independent students (many of whom are adults). Home equity was eliminated in calculation of assets in determination of financial aid.
Supplemental Educational Opportunity Grants (SEOG)	Grants to students through the post-secondary institutions they attend. New law eliminated number of years students are eligible for these grants, and permitted (not required) up to 10% of these federal funds to be used for students studying less than half time (some of whom would be adults).
College Work-Study (CWS)	Part-time jobs for students with 80% of wages paid by federal funds. New law

	permitted (not required) up to 10% of these funds to be used for students studying less than half time (some of whom would be adults).
State Student Incentive Grants (SSIG)	Federal funds go to states, which then make grants to students. New law permitted students studying less than half time (many of whom would be adults) to participate in this program if the individual states chose to include them.
Guaranteed Student Loans (GSL)	Loans for students made by private lenders and supported in part by federal funds. New law increased the amount that financially independent students (many of whom are adults) may borrow.
Grants to Educational Providers and States	
Continuing Education Program and Planning	Grants to states, which then make grants to eligible organizations and institutions, with 10% of the funds reserved to the secretary of education for direct grants. New law focused grants on needs of disadvantaged adults, expanded eligible organizations to include unions, business and industry, local community centers, and others and required states to plan for recurrent education programs and provide educational information.
Grants for Other Recurrent Education Activities and Research	
Educational Opportunity Centers	Centers that provide education information, counseling, and tutoring to students. New law focused the efforts of these centers on adult students.
Teacher Training	New law established grants to train postsecondary education faculty and set up a new fellowship program to retrain elementary and secondary teachers of the handicapped.

National Institute for Education	New law established an additional research priority to focus on older, part-time, and "nontraditional" students.

In summary, what the Congress sought to do was to

- recognize again the importance of learning throughout a lifetime;
- focus the federal role on promotion of equal educational opportunity;
- sharpen the federal focus on unserved and disadvantaged adults;
- ensure a diversity of innovative programs;
- provide *some* flexibility by giving individuals some freedom of choice (particularly through the Pell Grant program); and
- meet the requirements of relative efficiency and, certainly, feasibility at that time.[4]

A final note about context must be made here. These new federal recurrent education provisions, had they all been implemented immediately, would have encouraged only a small part of the overall level of U.S. adult learning activity. Second, any funds appropriated would have remained only a small portion of the total level of federal dollars going to more traditional postsecondary educational programs and students. In addition, only a *very* small portion of these federal funds can be used to support recurrent education activities outside of schools (see Wagner, 1980, for an inventory demonstrating the extent of such activities).

THE REAGAN REVERSAL

January 1981 saw the inauguration of Ronald Reagan as president and the beginnings of a new mood of fiscal conservatism across the country. Hardly had the new president taken office when he sent to Congress a sharply reduced budget request, with the proposed cuts falling most heavily on federally supported social programs (especially education).

Prior to this move, it was expected that implementation of the new Education Amendments of 1980 would take place over the next 2 years. Some sections of the law became effective immediately, such as the 10% possible set-aside of CWS and SEOG funds for less-than-half-time students. Other changes in the student aid programs that affected adults were to be implemented in 1982. Planning to begin operations under the new Title I started in the fall of 1980 and was expected to continue, with new grants starting in the fall of 1981.

However, the sharply reduced Reagan budget proposals put an end to hopes of immediate implementation of these new adult provisions. The overall problem with the new legislation was discovered even before the new president took office. It was one of runaway costs within the basic programs contained in the amendments.[5] Many hours of congressional debate on the legislation had centered not on the merits of the individual programs but on the overall cost of the programs to the federal treasury. The two federal student loan programs, National Direct Student Loans (NDSL) and GSL, were identified in particular. While some changes were made in the two programs (and those few relating to adults were noted earlier), the balance of the GSL program especially was retained intact in the new law. Thus no control was placed on the soaring costs of the GSL program (up from less than $500 million three years before to a projected $2 billion in 1981).[6] At the same time, increased demand and the effects of inflation put additional pressure on funding levels for the other programs contained in the law.

The new administration moved quickly to stem this tide of rising costs. By manipulating the complex congressional budgeting and appropriations processes, the president, with the aid of the Republican-controlled Senate, succeeded in legislating changes designed to cut the rising costs of the GSL program, substantially reduced the funding levels of other programs, and eliminated appropriations for others altogether. The effect on the new recurrent education provisions of the programs is devastating:

- Pell Grants—authorization funding levels have been reduced.
- SEOG—federal funds can still be used for less-than-half-time students, but overall dollars available are not sufficient to meet demand, so institutions have not put this new provision into practice.
- CWS—same as SEOG, above.
- SSIG—same as SEOG, above.
- GSL—the increased amounts that independent students could borrow under new law has now been reduced back to the old limits ($2,500 annually and $12,500 total). In addition, GSLs are now limited to those

with family incomes of $30,000 or less and to those above $30,000 based only on defined need. These and other changes seek to cap the rising costs in this program.

- Continuing Education (Title I)—appropriations for Fiscal Year 1981 were cut to $2.2 million (only enough to keep the administration of the program operating), down from $15 million the previous year. Fiscal year 1982 levels, not yet decided, cannot exceed $8.0 million and could well be zero.
- Educational Opportunity Centers—these have survived unscathed so far.
- Teacher Training—no funds will be available.
- National Institute of Education—overall funding for research was cut substantially and little money for new grants will be available.

While much of the legislation aiding adult learners remains in effect (GSL changes being an exception), the lack of significant appropriations for the programs has significantly delayed the implementation of these new adult provisions. Just when the prospects for new funding can be expected to improve is, at this point, very uncertain. The extent of the reversal has been unprecedented. While there remains substantial support for the policies and premises of recurrent education around the country today, there is much less agreement about what the federal role, supported by public tax dollars, should be in this area of adult continuing education.

Over the next several years, it is expected that the Reagan administration will continue to sort out its priorities for spending on federal programs. Until the American citizens have a chance to analyze the effects of these new conservative spending policies, little change can be expected. For the time being, the federal policy supporting recurrent education in this country, particularly that aimed at disadvantaged adults, is enacted in legislation but remains an opportunity deferred.

NOTES

1. A comment on terminology is also necessary at the outset. Earlier federal legislation, which remained unfunded, used the term "lifelong learning." Members of Congress objected to that term, citing its vagueness. Recurrent education is not a term used widely in the United States. Therefore, the new law uses the phrase "continuing education," intending, however, that all three terms are essentially the same. I use the phrase "recurrent

education," finding that the definition used in the 1973 OECD report (Recurrent Education; Paris OECD/CERI, 1973) is applicable to this discussion.

2. State governments themselves are sources of major funding support for public (and to some extent private) postsecondary educational institutions within their borders.

3. This work grew out of a three-year $1.6 million grant from the Exxon Education Foundation to the College Board to examine "Future Directions for a Learning Society." The project sponsored research, demonstrations of innovative recurrent education techniques, dissemination of information, and promotion of public policy.

4. This list is matched against a similar list of criteria for financing systems for recurrent education found in a report by the Centre for Educational Research and Innovation (1980: 10).

5. This section draws heavily upon the "Report from Washington" (College Board, 1980).

6. Appropriations for GSL are nondiscretionary, and the federal government is obligated to pay these costs.

REFERENCES

ASLANIAN, C. B. and H. M. BRICKELL (1980) Americans in Transition: Life Changes as Reasons for Adult Learning. New York: College Board.

Centre for Educational Research, OECD (1980) "The costs and financing of recurrent education." CERI, Paris. (mimeo)

College Board (1980a) Paying for Your Education: An Aid Guide for Adult Learners. New York: Author.

——— (1980b) "Report from Washington." College Board, Washington, D.C., Office. (mimeo)

GLADIEUX, L. E. (1980) "What has Congress wrought?" Change (October): 25-31.

HOFFMAN, E. (1980) The Federal Role in Lifelong Learning. New York: College Board.

National Center for Educational Statistics (1980) Participation in Adult Education, 1978. Washington, DC: Author.

PETERSON, R. E. and Associates (1979) Lifelong Learning in America. San Francisco: Jossey-Bass.

PURGA, R. (1978) "Financial aid and the adult learner: federal and New York State financial aid programs." Adult Learning Services Office, New York State Education Department. (mimeo)

SMITH, G. B. (1980) "Employer-sponsored recurrent education in the United States: a report on recent inquiries into its structure." National Institute for Work and Learning, Washington, D.C. (mimeo)

U.S. Congress (1980) Education Amendments of 1980. 96th Congress, Second Session. P.L. 96-374.

WAGNER, A. P. (1980) An Inventory of Post-Compulsory Education and Training Programs in the U.S. and Sources of Support. Stanford, CA: Institute for Research on Educational Finance and Governance, School of Education, Stanford University.

WINDHAM, D. M., N. D. KURLAND, and F. H. LEVINSON (1978) "Financing the learning society." School Rev. 86 (May).

III

FINANCING PAID EDUCATIONAL LEAVE

11

THE SWEDISH MODEL

KJELL RUBENSON

During the 1970s, the eduational rights of adults came to occupy the focal point of Swedish educational policy. Higher education was opened to mature students, and other resources for adult education became the cornerstone of these activities, and the 1975 Higher Education Act stated that all subsequent planning of the education system was to be based on recurrent education as a regular model for the individual person's educational planning (OECD, 1980).

The Swedish reforms naturally reflect the prevailing political, economic, and cultural conditions. Before going into further detail concerning the changes in question, this chapter shall describe briefly the two aspects of Swedish society that have done the most to influence the direction and development of policy concerning recurrent and adult education: the trade unions' intervention in educational policy, and the educational explosion.

There are many conditions that must be met in order for a thoroughgoing transformation to take place in the direction indicated by Swedish policy on recurrent education. This chapter will analyze two of them: educational leave and finance, with the main emphasis being on finance. Finally, some concluding remarks regarding the strengths and weaknesses of the system will be made and directions for change will be suggested.

THE INCREASING POWER RESOURCES OF THE TRADE UNIONS

By the mid-1960s it was clear that the course of social development that generally had been presumed to be condusive to greater equality was tending to perpetuate inequality instead. The Swedish Survey of Living Standards revealed that, despite steady economic growth, a vast difference still existed between socioeconomic groups (Johansson, 1970). This contributed to a radicalization of the trade unions.

In the early 1970s, at the insistence of the Swedish Confederation of Trade Unions (LO), the Social Democratic Government appointed a number of official commissions to draft legislation designed to increase worker influence in working life. At the same time Social Democratic policy was reorganized, a process in which LO came to play a leading part. In this way the union movement broke with the established practice whereby developments in the labor market were governed by agreements between employers' associations and workers' unions, with the state remaining neutral (Korpi, 1978: 356). This process culminated in 1976 in the passing of the Co-determination Act, which formally abolished the sole right of employers to direct and allocate work and to hire and dismiss employees. The Co-determination Act was an important step toward increasing the power resources of workers and their unions.

Korpi's analysis of the Swedish working class and welfare capitalism leads him to propound that workers' demands can be expected to grow with their power resources. There is little likelihood, therefore, of workers being induced by rising living standards to accept their subordinate position as wage labor (Korpi, 1978: 356). Korpi's interpretation is that the collective power resources and social awareness of the Swedish workers have developed to such a degree that they will no longer acquiesce in the hegemony of capital in economic life (Korpi, 1978: 364).

Korpi's analysis and discussion are concerned mainly with the relationship between political and economic democracy in view of the fact that, despite 40 years in power, the labor movement has failed to achieve one of the essential goals of socialism—namely, economic democracy. Thus the radicalization of the unions included reforms in adult education as well as in the labor market.

But there is another dimension of vital importance, that of cultural democracy. The interest taken by workers' associations in educational questions is connected partly with the growing educational requirements entailed by the realization of reforms in working life. However, the increased activity in educational affairs may imply that the growing collective resources of workers have led them to generate renewed demands for "cultural democracy."

The growing interest taken by the labor movement in educational questions during the 1970s is also to be viewed in the light of the thorough school reforms introduced under the Social Democrats. Party ideologists regarded education as one of the most important instruments for achieving a more egalitarian society; education was to be the spearhead into the future. However, by the late 1960s scepticism and disillusionment concerning the role of schooling as the great leveler of social inequalities had become widespread. The labor movement therefore demanded not only changes in the system of youth education but also improvements in educational opportunities for adults, so as to influence the educational choices of young persons (LOVUX III, 1974).

Exaggerating somewhat, one might say that the labor movement is doing nothing less than challenging the traditional view that social changes are achieved through the compensatory influence of the school system. Instead of primarily transforming the situation of children, attention is drawn to the conditions of adults in society.

THE POSTWAR EDUCATIONAL EXPANSION

For a long time schooling in Sweden was dominated by a highly selective and hierarchical system of parallel schools in which those who were well situated financially received a very different education from those who were less fortunate. At the end of World War II, the Social Democratic Government embarked on a thoroughgoing reform of the education system. This resulted in a uniform school system in which all pupils receive nine years' elementary schooling, after which the majority go on to upper secondary school, most of them following study routes that qualify them for university entrance. The reform of the school system and a rising demand for higher education transformed the university and produced an explosive increase in the student population (OECD, 1980). According to OECD data, Sweden had the highest average growth rate in higher educational enrollments among the OECD counties between 1950 and 1965 (Premfors and Ostergren, 1978: 9).

By the mid-1960s it was clear that the great transformation and expansion of the education system had presented educational planners with a number of acute problems such as rising costs, and so ongoing expansion of the education sector had to be restrained. Educational planning and labor market planning required closer integration. The substantial prolongation of youth education had caused wide gaps between the generations, and these gaps would make themselves felt for the rest of the century. It was in this environment that the idea of recurrent education emerged from the 1968 Education Commission (U 68).

The interest taken in recurrent education as a planning strategy probably was not due solely to the expectation that such a system would confer economic and educational benefits and lead to a more egalitarian recruitment. One of the primary reasons for this interest was probably the question of total enrollment restrictions in higher education (OECD 1977: 50).

Another important factor was the effort to achieve the closest possible adjustment between the needs of the labor market and the output of the educational system. At the time of the U 68 commission, there was a general awareness of the difficulties involved in assessing society's future need of qualified workers and in predicting student flows. In the final report of the U 68 commission (SOU 1973: 2, 584), recurrent education was referred to as a means of partially offsetting the unpredictability of the future labor market (Stahl, 1968: 115).

It is arguable that adult education and recurrent education have been governed by different concepts of equality. The general policy on recurrent education appears to be based on the establishment of equal opportunities, while adult education policy is aimed at equality of results. Adult education policy could be regarded as an effort to maintain a minimum "equality threshold" beneath which it would be unjust to exclude people.

SWEDISH EDUCATIONAL LEAVE

In 1970 the Swedish Employers' Confederation (SAF) asked the LO and the Salaried Workers' Confederation (TCO) to collaborate in an investigation by a joint group of experts of educational leave. These discussions, however, failed to produce a consensus of opinion. Instead, a considerable disagreement between the parties was revealed. LO and TCO broke off the negotiations and turned to the Ministry of Education to get the principle of entitlement to educational leave established by the Swedish Educational Leave Act (OECD, 1976).

This law, which came into effect on 1 January 1975, guarantees the right of all public and private employees to take leave for educational purposes during working hours. To qualify, an employee must have worked for his company for six months or at least twelve months during the past two years. This minimum employment qualification, however, does not apply to trade union training. The right to educational leave covers all types of education—general, vocational, and that which is provided by trade unions. The act does not stipulate a maximum or minimum duration of leave, nor does it say how many employees from a company may be absent at the same time. Responsibility for these arrangements lies with employer representatives and those of the employees, and these points must be settled by negotiation. The act entitles an employer to postpone leave in individual cases, but he is required to inform the trade union in advance whereupon the union is entitled to discuss the matter with him. If educational leave is postponed for more than six months, the employer must obtain permission from the local union organization. The six-month postponement period is reduced to two weeks when trade union training and leave of absence are of one working week or less.

The act also assures the employee of the right to return to his job after a period of educational leave and to resume the status and income he had before. This applies even if the employee does not complete the course of education for which leave was granted. The local trade union has the last word in the event of a dispute. If either party wishes, the matter can be dealt with at a higher level; in that case, the central employee organization has to agree to the desired postponement

Lack of statistics makes it very hard to gauge the utilization of the act. According to a rough estimate by the Employers' Confederation, the total volume of educational leave corresponds to one week off for 1-2% of all employees.

The Employers' Confederation has objected to the act, calling for restrictions on entitlement to educational leave and a review of the statutory rules. The main grounds for this criticism are that the existing rules impede the planning of production. The employers also allege that overall the various leave of absence reforms in recent years have inflicted serious injury on Swedish enterprise. The objections raised by employers to the Educational Leave Act are primarily to be seen as a manifestation of their displeasure with the general increase in opportunities for leave of absence, not with the value of selective educational leave. Increased absences created by the act have led the Minister of Labor to appoint a commission to review the total effects of the legislation on leave of absence. Thus it is possible that the existing Educational Leave Act will be revised on a more restrictive basis.

It is sometimes said that the fundamental weakness of Swedish recurrent education policy is its lack of a suitable finance policy to support entitlement to educational leave. One of the basic principles of the Swedish legislation is the free choice of studies. A free choice combined with paid educational leave would produce an immense educational explosion. This, however, is precluded by the limitations of resources. Instead Sweden has chosen to separate educational leave and finance. Thus the adult education assistance introduced at the same time as the Educational Leave Act enabled a limited number of persons from a specified target group to study during paid leaves of absence. In this way finance during educational leave ties in with the general aims of present educational policy in such a way that the system of subsidies for students acts as a general steering instrument of adult and recurrent education policy.

FINANCE

There are three distinct systems of subsidies for students that are relevant to recurrent education (see Table 11.1). *AMS Grants* pertain to labor market trainees. The *loan-grant assistance* scheme applies generally to postsecondary students and to adults (persons who are 20-years-old and over) receiving elementary and secondary education. Finally, the *adult study assistance* scheme is primarily designed for undereducated adults intending to study at the elementary or secondary level. Adult study assistance also includes a special grant to facilitate short-term studies sponsored by an adult education association.

As has already been made clear, the structure of financial support for students is highly incoherent. Although the various types of benefits are planned for students in a particular sector, it is not uncommon for all three types to occur in the same case (e.g., in municipal adult education). The size and consruction of assistance (see Table 11.1) may be said to reflect the responsibility assumed by society for various groups according to their economic and social conditions. Those who are out of jobs and pursuing labor market training are given the most generous terms, while those who are attending higher education are given the least advantageous conditions. All types of education covered by any of the three systems of financing are entirely free of charge, although in practice there may be some expenses for study materials.

AMS GRANTS

Active labor market policy was developed towards the end of the 1940s by the LO economists Gösta Rehn and Rudolf Meidner. This

TABLE 11.1 Different Forms of Financing Recurrent Education

	Folk High School, Elementary, and Secondary Schooling for Adults	*Higher Education*	*Labor Market Training*	*Short-Term Folk High School Courses, and Adult Education Associations*	*Benefits as of 1 April 1980*		*Estimated State Expenditure 1981-1982 (Skr. millions)*
					Grant/Month (SKr.)	*Loan/Month (SKr.)*	
AMS grants	x		x		3,410–4,620 (taxable)	–	1,875
Loan-grant assistance scheme	x	x			242	2,263	2,672
Adult study assistance[1]	x			x	2,216-3,003 (taxable)	800-1,000	544

NOTE: The Swedish kronor is valued at $4.1503 using market rate figures for the second quarter of 1980.

1. Adult study assistance is not given for higher education with the exception of 700 persons at postsecondary vocational education (YTH). The adult study assistance also include a special hourly and daily assistance for short courses.

model was characterized above all by its assertion that an active labor market policy is a principal factor of economic stability. Full employment was to be aimed at, but not by generating a high level of demand in the economy which would lead to inflation. Since labor demand at any given moment inevitably varies from one economic sector to another, it was more effective to try to maintain moderately high demand in the economy and combine this with selective measures aimed at influencing the employment situations in sectors that were threatened with unemployment. These specific measures were to include public employment projects (known as relief work projects), sheltered employment, support for firms in regions of high unemployment, and efforts to stimulate the mobility of workers between different localities, sectors, and occupations.

In this connection, labor market training has come to be an important component in achieving mobility. The labor market training system arose out of the need to act swiftly against imbalances in the labor market. First, the system helped underemployed and unemployed workers to improve their employability in occupations with better opportunities. Second, it increased the supply of skills in industries where a shortage of suitably trained personnel tends to exacerbate inflationary pressures. The labor market training system now has a running capacity of more than 1% of the total labor force. With courses lasting for an average of four to five months, more than 3% of the labor force can be reached in the space of one year.

The main provisions of the scheme are as follows. Persons can attend training courses arranged by the labor market authorities in collaboration with school authorities or with employers under the following conditions: (1) if they are unemployed or their employment conditions are precarious (in the sense that they are threatened with unemployment either because they work in declining sectors or because of personal difficulties); and (2) if they are willing to leave their jobs (or take educational leave) in order to train for shorthanded occupations. Courses are free of charge and trainees receive taxable AMS grants of SKr. 3,410-4,620 ($852-$1,155) per month. These grants exceed daily unemployment benefits and amount to some 80% of ordinary wages after taxes.

The courses vary in duration and level of qualification. Some are short introductory courses designed to acclimate participants to working situations outside their experience. Others are two-year courses for skilled workers and technicians, some of which are at postsecondary levels. One of the important functions of this scheme is to pave the way for women to enter the labor market. In recent years, half the participants have been women.

Most training takes place at permanent or temporary centers. The training is administered jointly by the Labor Market Boad and the National Board of Education. These boards delegate responsibility to their county subsidiaries or make arrangements with vocational schools, (which are now integrated with the system of upper secondary education). There were 78,000 participants in this kind of training in 1978-1979.

The primary objective of labor market training is to provide unemployed persons with steady jobs. Regular follow-up studies have shown that some 85% of persons who have taken vocational courses and then entered the labor market have obtained jobs within three months of completing their courses. Approximately 85% of these successful job applicants obtained work in the occupational sectors for which they trained.

The AMS grants are not geared to the education sector but are related directly to labor market policy. In a system of recurrent education, however, the present boundary between education and labor market training loses its raison d'être. This applies not least to the present-day discussion of persistent labor shortages and the role of recurrent education as a means of securing a more equitable distribution of work, education, and leisure between different age groups and social groups. However, until now there has not been any closer coordination of recurrent education policy and other social sectors (e.g., labor policy and social policy).

LOAN-GRANT ASSISTANCE

The present system of loan-grant assistance was introduced in 1965 with two objectives: first, the expansion of higher education recruitment by means of social benefits for students so as to eliminate social and geographical bias; and second, general improvements to the economic terms offered to those who are pursuing or have pursued higher studies (SOU 1963: 74, p. 32).

Loan-grant assistance consisting of (repayable) loans and (non-repayable) grants can be awarded to upper secondary students of age 20 and to postsecondary students. The loan-grant assistance payable to a person studying full time for nine months during the academic year 1980-1981 was $5,636 or Skr. 22,546 (Skr. 2,500 per month). At present

90% of this amount is repayable. As a rough comparison, the average industrial worker gets about SKr. 3,500 ($875) after tax per month.

Repayable assistance does not carry interest in the normal way, but outstanding obligations are adjusted upward each year by means of an index. At present, debts on study assistance rise by 3.2% annually. The amortization period is usually over 20 years.

The main question or relevance for present purposes is whether the loan-grant system encourages or impedes recurrent education. As stated earlier, recurrent education was made part of the Higher Education Act. The primary aim was not to introduce recurrent education as a norm but to make it an equivalent educational alternative as far as possible (Govt. Bill Prop. 1976-1977: 59, p. 44). Turning to the system of finance, the goal as interpreted here implies that the system should be neutral with regard to the student's choice between the recurrent pattern and the traditional pattern of education. The neutrality of the system of finance should be viewed in relation to the transition in economic resources and material living standards of the student, both during and after studies.

The loan-grant system cannot be said to satisfy the requirement of neutrality by any stretch of the imagination. It creates special difficulties for those adults who have earned incomes because it does not cover even the loss of quite small earnings. Consequently, a person who wishes to study extensively and previously has been employed gainfully has to accept a reduced living standard. Calculations by the National Board of Statistics have indicated that a transition to full-time studies would result in a drastic increase in the number of households falling below the subsistence level (SCB, 1981).

Study assistance today consists mainly of benefits that are repayable after the completion of studies. The grant portion has remained almost stationary ever since the system was introduced in 1965. At that time the maximum grant payable was one-quarter of the total volume of loan-grant assistance, reducing the grant portion to 11%. Since the essential purpose of the student grant is to reduce the burden of indebtedness after the completion of studies, we may note that education policy has been developed in favor of recurrent education but the structure of study finance has tended to favor direct transitions.

Thus Blaug and Mace (1977) have argued that educational finance in Sweden is not supportive of a true effort to achieve a system of recurrent education. To be fair to the policymakers, the introduction of a separate financing system for adult education should be mentioned. However, this system was set up in order to help bridge the educational gap—not to favor recurrent education.

ADULT STUDY ASSISTANCE

The reform of adult education in the 1960s substantially augmented the opportunities for study and education open to adults. Municipal adult education was introduced in 1968 to give adults the chance to obtain formal education qualifications corresponding to those conferred by youth education. Improvements were made in the support given to independent and voluntary popular education, and radio and television were used more widely for educational purposes. One of the guidelines for the reform of adult education was that it should limit losses in production that result from removing workers from their enterprises during working hours. Accordingly, it was intended that studies be pursued in leisure hours and and combined with work in the home or outside it. The government, however, anticipated that full-time studies were destined to become increasingly important, and in 1968 a government commission on adult study assistance—the SVUX Committee—was appointed. This committee's proposals resulted in 1976 in the introduction of a separate system of study assistance for adults.

The overrriding goal of adult education is to bridge the gap between adults and youth. The question of resource requirements and priorities depends on the magnitude of the education gap in the Swedish society. Estimates of the gap and finance requirements are made in order to limit the effect of inadequate finances on enrollment. Total expenditures for meeting the calculated demand were estimated by the committee to be a resource increment of roughly SKr. 40-50 million ($10-12 million). It was recommended that plans be made to cater to the demand over a period of 20 years by means of gradual expansion. During this period, adult education would be given high priority in new education reforms. A phased expansion in itself would reduce the resource requirement to about SKr. 25 million ($6.25 million) due to the decline in educational predisposition with advancing age and the annual cohort's attainment of the age of 65. However, the committee did not believe that these were adequate to channel such heavy new resources into adult education, and a more modest and realistic build-up was suggested (SOU 1974: 62, 215).

The first five-year period was completed in 1980-1981, and it is possible to compare the actual allocation of resources with the proposed build-up. During the first two years there was a close correspondence between suggested and actual funding, but in the ensuing years a slow-down in economic growth and high levels of inflation contributed to a rising discrepancy which will probably continue to increase during the second five-year period. The discrepancy can also be expressed in number of grants. According to the committee's plan there should have been 50,000 one-year full-time grants in 1980-1981; instead there were only 15,800.

Adult study assistance is financed by means of a payroll tax surcharge equalling .25%. In 1980-1981 the revenues from this surcharge provided Skr. 588 million ($147 million) for purposes of adult study assistance. The following is a summary of the content and conditions of the various forms of adult study assistance.

Special adult study assistance

Special adult study assistance is available only for studies requiring prolonged and continuous periods of time. It is payable on either a full-time or part-time basis—that is, for a period of at least half a month's full-time studies (15 days) or for a full month's half-time studies (30 days). Special adult study assistance is awarded primarily for studies at the elementary and secondary school levels. At the postsecondary level it can only be awarded to students undergoing postsecondary vocational education (YTH).

The following factors have to be taken into consideration in the distribution of special adult study assistance:

- short-term previous education
- educational difficulties due to disability or for other reasons
- long-term vocational activity or its equivalent
- numerous dependents
- any previous receipt of special adult study assistance.

The assistance comprises a taxable grant and a tax-free loan and varies between Skr. 2,300 and Skr. 3,000 ($575 and $750) depending on income. The money allocated for the special adult study assistance 1981-1982 covers 15,500 grants of a nine-month duration.

Hourly study assistance

Hourly study assistance is payable to persons attending study circles and incurring losses of earnings as a result. Hourly study assistance in

1980-1981 stood at SKr. 33 ($8.25) per hour and was taxable. By way of comparison, the average hourly earnings of LO members on continuous triple-shift work in 1980 were SKr. 41.75 ($10.44). In the course of a fiscal year, assistance may be awarded for 70 hours. Hourly study assistance can be applied for by individual persons or collectively by a trade union organization. Most assistance awards are made in response to collective applications.

Hourly study assistance can only be awarded to a limited number of persons (25,000), and priority is given to those who have

- inconvenient working hours, especially as regards shift work;
- physically and mentally strenuous working conditions, whatever the arrangement concerning working hours;
- short-term previous education.

The resources available for hourly study assistance have not been fully utilized. The main reason for this is the problem of exercising entitlement to educational leave. Many people are unwilling to take time off out of loyalty towards their employers and fellow workers. The narrow range of subjects and the smaller amount of study assistance income in relation to average earnings have also had a negative effect (Stockfelt and Öberg, 1979; Naslund, 1980).

Daily study assistance

Daily study assistance can be regarded as a supplement to hourly study assistance. This type of assistance makes it possible for circle studies to be combined with short-term subject studies at folk high schools for additional depth. Daily study assistance in the course of a single fiscal year is subject to a maximum of 10 study days and 2 travel days per student. Daily study assistance can be applied for individually, or collectively by a trade union organization. There were 14,900 daily study assistanceships available in 1981-1982.

As the above description has shown, the reform of adult education financing (unlike the general study assistance) is geared to a particular clientele. The expansion of adult education in the 1960s and 1970s made policymakers aware that too much faith had been placed on the potential of a general augmentation of adult education resources. When one attempts to fulfill both allocation and the service-policy goals of individuals, the allocation effects turn out to be very limited and are accomplished at the price of great service-policy costs.

THE EFFECTS OF THE THREE SYSTEMS

Measuring the effects of changes in the field of adult education finance is highly complicated in terms of both the more theoretical considerations and empirical measurement. How can the effects of educational change be discerned in the complex process whereby present and future society is shaped in a permanent interaction of economic, political, and organizational forces at local, national, and international levels?

The reform of adult financing in Sweden has not been subjected yet to evaluation, so the only data available are annual study assistance statistics. By comparing these figures with the national educational statistics, which deal with adult education participation generally, one can, however, obtain some view of the recruitment effect of adult study assistance.

Available data indicate that the special adult study assistance has gone to the target group, at least insofar as that group is defined in terms of previous education (CSN, 1979; SCB, 1980: 5). The material does not say anything about how these individuals would have acted if no subsidy had been available. In other words, would these persons have participated in any case? However, there is research suggesting that a large proportion of the students would not have been able to participate without the special adult study assistance (see, e.g., Lövgren, 1978).

As an important part of the reform of adult education, outreach activities were given state grants and grouped together with adult study assistance. Grants towards outreach measures at work places are awarded in response to applications by trade unions. The passing of the Shop Stewards Act (1974) and the Educational Leave Act (1975) are important in this connection. The Shop Stewards Act entitles union representatives to engage in outreach activities at their own work places. The amount of time devoted to these activities has to be determined in consultation with employers.

The different reforms in Sweden have made it possible for outreach activities to be linked directly to the legislation concerning educational leave and study assistance in order to offer as favorable a study situation as possible. However, the existing statutory opportunities often are difficult to utilize. For example, in small work places workers have been reluctant to take leave because of the difficulties their absences create for their workmates (the Kronoberg Project, December 1977: 73).

The special adult study allowance in combination with eligibility for leave of absence has increased the proportion of daytime students. There are some indications that this might have led to a decline in dropout rates from the municipal adult schools. A 1973 study of evening courses showed that just over 30% of the participants completed the whole program (Borgström et al., 1979), and a follow-up study found that as many as 65% completed day courses (Rubenson, forthcoming). Thus with more people getting the chance to study full time, one might expect growing efficiency as reflected by a decreasing number of dropouts.

The existing evidence concerning hourly and daily study assistance does not testify to any substantial recruitment effect (CSN 1979; SCB, 1980: 5). However, hourly and daily study assistance benefits are not only aimed at recruiting the undereducated, they are also intended to facilitate educational activity on the part of workers with inconvenient work shifts or physically and mentally strenuous jobs. The available statistics tell us nothing about the effects achieved in these respects.

There has been criticism of the designation of hourly study assistance for participants in certain categories of study circles. When this special grant was introduced, its main purpose was to facilitate participation in study-circle activities aimed at eliminating the educational gaps. Surveys concerning the attitude of undereducated persons toward adult education have shown, however, that a freer choice of subjects geared to the working and everyday situation of the individual would be preferable to general education (Rubenson et al., 1977).

In order for allocation policy to be fulfilled, the following two conditions must be met. People with low resources (such as skills and income) have to be recruited, and by participating in this activity they should be able to obtain greater skills, income, and other resources. The crucial point with regard to a differentiated financing of adult education programs is which programs can be instrumental in redistributing resources. So far, owing to poor conceptualization, research in the field of adult education has little to offer regarding this question.

Parallel to the efforts made in recent years to reduce the social gaps in society, increasing attention has begun to be focused on the position of women and inequalities between the sexes. This has had repercussions on the structure of social benefits for students. When adult study assistance was introduced, it was resolved that no "needs test" would be imposed in relation to the spouse's income. As a result, homemakers are excessively compensated because they do not suffer any direct loss of income, so that the amount of assistance they receive exceeds any conceivable increase in expenditure entailed by a transition to education CSN, 1980a). There are two main reasons that this situation is harmful to the overall program: First, many applications are turned down because of the limited resources available; second, many gainfully employed persons are undercompensated because the maximum benefit rate does not cover their loss of earnings.

Where general study assistance is concerned, the rule before 1981 was that loan-grant entitlement was affected by the spouse's income—a rule that had been criticized ever since the introduction of the loan-grant system in 1965. The fundamental objection to a spouse's income being included in the assessment procedure was that in this way adults were not treated as independent individuals. Inclusion of the spouse's income has therefore been considered unacceptable for reasons of sexual equality. The problem with this approach is that it entails a conflict of goals between sexual equality and social equality. In considering social equality, the family's combined liberty of economic choice is most significant; in other words, how is the family's economic situation affected by choosing educational activities?

The elimination of spouse's income as a criterion for obtaining loan-grant assistance has tended to provide financial help for many women from advantaged backgrounds. The resources that are now going to these women could be used for specific measures designed to influence the educational interests of other hard-to-recruit groups. Exaggerating somewhat, one might say that social equality is being sacrificed on the altar of sexual equality.

CONCLUDING REMARKS

In the review of educational finance, it was pointed out that despite everything that has been done, the fundamental weakness of Swedish efforts to establish recurrent education was the lack of a scheme of student finance combined with entitlement to educational leave. The demands of the U 68 commission for special measures concerning social benefits for students have not been implemented. These measures were judged necessary if recurrent education was to become a realistic alternative to the traditional study route.

The critique should be analyzed with respect to the far reaching changes that were anticipated. When the idea of recurrent education was propounded in connection with the reform of higher education, the minister of education at that time stated the following:

> I anticipate that recurrent education—as a pattern for the utilization of the educational machinery—will gradually become a realistic alternative to the present order of things which is primarily based on continuous education during childhood and adolescence [Govt. Bill 1975: 9, 431].

Underlying the present debate is the conviction (evidently entertained by the planners) that recurrent education could evolve as a "harmonious model" without the need for a more distinct definition of priorities. Developments have shown that it was a mistake to suppose that in a situation characterized by limited resources, recurrent education could be developed without sacrificing harmony. New discord has come into being now that the issue at stake is not only the distribution of educational resources between different socioeconomic groups but also their distribution between young and mature students. This conflict is accentuated by the present economic crisis and approaching "hump" in the younger generation.

Another critical problem is the imbalance that has developed between the education sector and the labor market as a result of the economic crisis. One of the fundamental aims of Swedish economic policy today is to stimulate a structural transformation of enterprise and at the same time limit the growth of the public sector. This involves heavy pressure for a transformation of the education sector. The demand for the relatively cheap higher education designed for the public sector may conceivably diminish and be shifted to more expensive technical education, meaning that within a given financial constraint the number of places will be reduced.

We may note that the current situation has certain points in common with that which existed when the idea of recurrent education was first raised. Thus the demand for higher education among the younger generations is once more rising steeply and exceeding resources. The great difference today is that there is a powerful body of opinion against measures that would impair the ability of young persons to go straight on to higher education from upper secondary school. It is not surprising, therefore, that the Riksdag resolved to alter the rules of higher education entrance from 1981-1982. These alterations will tone down the importance of job experience and reinforce direct transitions. Thus in the present economic situation development of the more far-reaching approach to recurrent education whereby direct transitions are counteracted has come to a halt. Recurrent education in the form of in-service and further training, however, can be expected to gain strength in connection with the structural transformation of enterprise.

One possible alternative is to start charging fees for certain courses at universities and colleges. Enterprises and individual adults would then be able to purchase education. This policy would probably mean that Sweden would move in the direction of the French arrangement where paid leave of absence is closely bound up with a limited repertoire of mainly vocational courses.

Anything more radical that may happen in the area of financing is likely to be linked to developments in working life; for example, the trade unions might seek and get greater control of the education sector in enterprise. If this is the case, Sweden would be heading towards a situation in which the education provided by the community is geared more closely to employment. For example, collective agreements could be struck concerning entitlement to paid educational leave and a greater element of general education could be provided within the framework of in-service training.

REFERENCES

ARONOWTIZ, S. (1973). False Promises. New York: McGraw-Hill.

BLAUG, M. and J. MACE (1977) "Recurrent education—the New Jerusalem." Higher Education 6, 3: 277-300.

BORGSTRÖM, L. et al. (1979). Elementary School Studies for Adults. Summary report from the GRUV-project, 27. Stockholm: Pedagogiskt centrum, Stockholms skolförvaltning.

BROSTRÖM, A. and G. EKEROTH (1977). Vuxenutbildning och fördelningspolitik. Uppsala: Sociologiska institutionen, Uppsala universitet.

CERI (1973). Recurrent Education: A Strategy for Lifelong Learning. Paris: CERI/OECD.

CSN Studiestödsstatistik 1978-1979. Sundsvall: CSN June, 1979.

CSN October 29 (1980a) Det Särskilda vuxenstudiestödet—ATP villkoret och stödets storlek.

———August 27 (1980b) Anslagsframställning för budgetaret 1981-1982.

EKSTEDT, E. (1976). Utbildningsexpansion. En studie över den högre utbildningens expansion och ekonomins strukturella omvandling i Sverige under efterkrigstiden. Stockholm: Almqvist & Wiksell International, Uppsala studies in economic history 14.

Govt. Bill Proposition 1975: 9.

Govt. Bill Proposition 1976-1977: 59.

Govt. Bill Proposition 1980-1981: 20.

HOLMES, B. (1965). Problems in Education. A Comparative Approach. London: Routledge and Kegan Paul.

IPF, 1980: 4. Trender och prognoser, 1980.

JOHANSSON, S. (1970). Om levnadsnivåundersökningen. Utkast till kap. 1 och 2 i betänkande om svenska folkets levnadsförhallånden. Stockholm: Allmanna Förlaget.

KIM, L. (1979). Två års erfarenhet av de nya tillträdesreglerna till högskoleutbildning. Stockholm: UHÄ, 1979: 13.

KORPI, W. (1978). Arbetarklassen i välfärdskapitalismen. Stockholm: Prisma.

LOVUX I (1969). Fackföreningsrörelsen och vuxenutbildningen. Rapport från LO: s arbetsgrupp for vuxenutbildningsfrågor. Stockholm: Prisma.

LOVUX III (1974). Ny vuxenutbildning—ny skola. Stockholm: Prisma.

LÖVGREN, J. (1978). Yrkesteknisk högskoleutbildning 1975-1978. Erfarenheter från de två första försöksomgångarna. Stockholm: UHÄ 1978: 21.

NÄSLUND, N-E. (1980) LO och vuxenstudiestödet. Stockholm: LO.

OLOFSSON, L. E. (1980). Recruitment in the context of allocation policy," in R. Höghielm and K. Rubenson (eds.) Adult Education for Social Change. Lund: CWK Gleerup.

PREMFORS, R. and B. ÖSTERGREN (1978). Systems of Higher Education: Sweden. NY: International Council for Educational Development.

RUBENSON, K., (forthcoming). Till frågan om studieavbrott i vuxenutbildning. Stockholm Department of Educational Research, Stockholm Institute of Education.

——— U. BERGSTEN and B. BROMSJÖ (1977). Korttidsutbildades inställning till vuxenutbildning. Utbildningsforskning nr 26. Stockholm: Liber Läromedel/ Utbildningsförlaget.

SANDLER, R. (1937). Mångfald eller enfald. Stockholm: Tidens forlag.

SCB (National Central Bureau of Statistics) 1980: 5. Deltagare i allmänna studiecirklar läsåret 1976-1977.

SOU (Governmental Commission) 1977: 31. Studiestöd. Alternativa utvecklingslinjer.

——— 1974: 62. Studiestöd åt vuxna.

——— 1973: 2. Högskolan (1968 års utbildningsutredning).

——— 1971: 80. Vuxna-utbildning-studiefinansiering.

——— 1963: 74. Rätt till studiemedel.

STAHL, I. (1968). Utbildningsprogram och arbetsmarknadspolitik. Särtryck ur Tio Ekonomer om Arbetsmarknaden.

STOCKFELT, T. and S. ÖBERG (1979). Vem blev uppsökt och vad hande sedan? Sundsvall: CSN 5/1979.

TCO (1973). Vuxenutbildning, återkommande utbildning. Stockholm: Prisma.

12

FRENCH LAW ON CONTINUING VOCATIONAL TRAINING

PIERRE CASPAR

Over the past decade, there has been a great deal of international interest in the French system of continuing vocational training, particularly since the act of 16 July 1971 which called for the reorganization of vocational training under the more general heading of continuing education. Continuing vocational training in France has become both a right and a prominent aspect of economic and social life. In 1979, 2,900,000 members of the national labor force took part in training activities.[1] Total expenditures for these workers were some 15.8 billion francs (or $2.9 billion) of which 9.5 billion ($1.7 billion) were covered by firms and 6.3 billion ($1.15 billion) funded by various forms of state aid. (These figures do not include apprenticeships—that is, initial vocational training.)[2]

The 1971 act made it mandatory for firms employing more than 10 persons to devote at least 0.8% of their wage bill to educational spending. This was no more than a recognition by parliament of the prevailing practices of many enterprises; in fact, average expenditure by enterprises at the time amounted to about double the figure requested by law. The act encompassed and extended a number of arrangements made under a national interindustrial agreement signed a year earlier, on 9 July 1970, by most of the organizations representing labor and management. On the employer's side, these included the *Conseil National du Patronat Francais* (CNPF) and the *Federation des Petites et Moyennes Entreprises* (CGPME). For labor, the trade unions included the *Confederation Francaise Democratique du Travail* (CFDT), the *Confederation Generale du Travail* (CGT), the *Confederation Generale du Travail Force Ouvriere* (CGT-FO). Therefore, the 1971 act introduced a number of innovations into the French continuing training system based on a broad national consensus.

Continuing training in France, although slow to develop, has a long history. As long ago as the French Revolution, the creation of the *Conservatoire National des Arts et Metiers* (CNAM) in 1794 may be said to have marked the first stage of a national system for the training of adults—one that is open to all, multidisciplinary, and able to bridge the various sciences, crafts, and trades. Towards the end of the nineteenth and the beginning of the twentieth centuries came the creation of the *Universites Populaires* and the *Associations de Culture Populaire* and, alongside them, the vocational training courses given official status by the Astier Act (25 July 1919). Together they laid the foundation of the present-day state-provided, free, technical education, leading to the *Certificat d'Aptitude Professionnelle* (Certificate of Vocational Proficiency). In 1934, the first adult vocational training centers were established, which later culminated in the *Association pour la Formation Professionnelle des Adultes* (Association for Vocational Training for Adults; AFPA) which in 1979 was responsible for training more than 90,000 people.

Various other provisions and opportunities were developed during the twentieth century, but the system of vocational training was to take on a different and more coherent form after 1959 and even more so after 1968. It is this system which is described in the present Chapter, together with the rules and principles governing its financing and the special question of training leave.

THE LEGAL FRAMEWORK

The present statutory and regulatory framework took shape and became organized between 1968 and 1971. During this period, the government's approach was to get labor and management to study and integrate the main aspects of the organization and regulation of continuing vocational education in France before they coordinated and endorsed any resultant contractual system. Furthermore, the broad guidelines of current practice became clear during this time: compulsory contributions by employers to the financing of continuing training, wage-earners' entitlements to training leave, the remuneration of trainees, and the division of responsibilities between firms, unions, and government. The development of vocational training was explicitly linked to enterprise and national requirements for growth and technological progress, and to the need to improve employment throughout France.

Two milestones in continuing education resulted from this process. First is the national agreement already referred to between employers and unions of 9 July 1970. Among its agreements, two major rights of wage earners were defined as follows:

- the employees' right to absence from and continued remuneration during working hours to attend training courses of their own choice provided such training is approved by the employer/union commission of the appropriate industrial sector in which they work; and
- the employees' right to training paid for by the employer in the case of unemployment for economic reasons.

Second is the act of 16 July 1971, which was the response of the French government to this agreement. While most of the agreement was incorporated into the act, some new provisions were added, including the following four:

- All employees are entitled to training leave for training of their choice arising from their own initiative. Under the act, training proposed or offered by the firm as part of its own training program must therefore be distinguished from training personally requested by employees to further their knowledge in an area that interests them.
- All firms employing more than ten people are obligated to earmark 0.8% of the total wage bill for the vocational training of the staff. It was originally planned to raise this contribution gradually to 2%, and the current mandatory contribution is 1.1%. This sum must be used to pay for training activities inside or outside the firm or to purchase certain types of teaching equipment. Any money not so spent must be paid into the French Treasury (a stipulation that has frequently been erroneously described as a vocational training "tax").
- Employees, through their representatives on the works committee,[3] are able to have some say on matters of training since the firm must consult with the works committee on its annual training program. Failure to do so entails a fine (see Table 12.2).
- The state participates in remunerating trainees (see the following section for further details). Special provisions were also made for training of the self-employed.

Further measures were taken between 1974 and 1980 in order to improve the remuneration of trainees and the financing of training leave courses. These measures were also necessary in order to adapt the system to changing work and employment conditions—particularly for young people—following the economic downturn that began in 1974. Therefore, between 1971 and 1981 a considerable number of directives, additional clauses, counter-cyclical measures, and statutory acts have amended, clarified, and broadened the system outlined above. Among the most representative provisions are the following:

- *The Employment-Training Contract* (contrat emploiformation), introduced by decree (4 June 1975), is a work contract open to young people between the ages of 17 and 26[4] in which it is mandatory to include between 120 and 1,200 hours training. The employer receives a state subsidy for each eligible trainee taken on under this scheme.
- *The National Employment Agreements* (pactes nationaux pour l'emploi)[5] which are to help young people and people of certain other social categories seeking to enter or reenter working life. Supplementing the employment-training contracts mentioned above, the agreements aim at promoting apprenticeships by exempting them from social security charges. In addition, they provide opportunities for training periods that are paid for by the employer who is partially reimbursed by the state. These agreements offer practical guidance and a basic knowledge of the actual working conditions in an enterprise over a six-month period.
- *The Act of 17 July 1978,* which defined the scope of training leave in broader terms by explicitly including a cultural and social dimension. In the words of the act, "Training activities should enable a worker to change his job or occupation and to acquire a wider cultural and social outlook. Part or all of the training shall take place during working hours." The act also improved the provision of remuneration of workers on training leave. (Details of this will be spelled out below.) Finally, the act gives all employees an opportunity to take unremunerated "teaching leave" to engage in teaching activities for a maximum of one year. The teaching can be either full- or part-time in a public or private educational or training establishment or in a state-approved training course. Employees retain the same status as if they took training leave; that is, they remain members of their enterprises or establishments and are entitled to seniority privileges and paid annual leave.

THE FINANCE OF VOCATIONAL TRAINING

Adult training has become an important aspect of community life in France. Nearly 3 million people in 1979[6] (or one worker in seven) undertook training with a total of 350 million hours during the year and a budget of almost 16 billion francs ($2.9 billion). The total expenditures for 1972-1979 are set forth in Table 12.1. The contribution of firms accounts for over three-fifths of the total budget. It deserves, therefore, more detailed examination. The general data are given in Table 12.2.

TABLE 12.1 Training by Source of Funding: 1972-1979

	1972	*1976*	*1977*	*1978*	*1979*
Number of Workers in Training[1]					
State	958,000	805,000	894,000	993,000	1,041,000
Firms	1,049,000	1,814,000	1,856,000	1,831,000	1,686,000
Training Insurance Funds[3]	–	190,000	164,000	195,000	2,900,000
Jointly[2]	1,760,000	2,770,000	2,880,000	3,000,000	2,900,000
Trainee Hours					
State	182,000,000	189,000,000	206,000,000	250,000,000	242,000,000
Firms	78,000,000	107,000,000	107,000,000	104,000,000	92,000,000
Training Insurance Funds[3]	–	15,000,000	12,000,000	18,000,000	15,000,000
Jointly[2]	241,000,000	309,000,000	317,000,000	370,000,000	350,000,000
Budget (billion francs)					
State	1.7	3.1	5.1	6.8	6.3
Firms	2.8	6.5	8.0	8.7	9.5

NOTE: The figures given in this chapter do not include apprenticeships (i.e., initial training governed by an entirely different scheme and financed by a separate apprenticeship levy).

1. These are trainees enrolled in a course or part of a course during the calendar year.
2. Some sources are financed jointly by government and industry; this explains why the combined figures of rows 1 and 2 do not tally exactly with those of row 3.
3. Training insurance funds are handled by agencies empowered to collect finances and use them for training required by firms taking part in the scheme as well as by employees.

The figures in Table 12.2 reveal that while the rate of financial participation fixed by law is 1.1% of the wage bill, in fact the average amount spent in 1979 was significantly higher—1.8%. Participation in training varies considerably according to the level of qualification of the employee. Only 15% of trainees were unskilled workers, 47% were skilled workers, 23% were technical and supervisory personnel, and 15% were executive staff. Women accounted for no more than 25% of the trainees.

As Table 12.3 shows, the size of the firm also has a considerable influence on the scale of contribution. Whereas big enterprises with a staff of 2,000 or more spend on the average 2.88% of their wage bill on training, those on the 500 to 1,999 range spend 1.63%. The proportion then drops to 1.29% in the 50 to 499 range, and only 1.05% for firms with a staff of less than 50 people. It stands lower still at 0.94% for the very small firms that employ between 10 and 19 people.

In summary, we can look at the ways in which firms that are covered by this law meet their obligations under the 1971 act. Of the 1.1% they are obliged to spend on adult training, 0.2% is to be paid to the state to finance activities for young people and women seeking employment. Concerning the remaining 0.9%, there are several possibilities open to the employer:

(1) direct financing of vocational training schemes initiated by the firm itself, which may take several forms:
- training programs, provided by the enterprise;
- training by training associations (ASFOs)—that is, interenterprise sponsored;
- training set up by a group of employers or an industrial sector;
- training provided by training centers run either by the government (GRETA) or privately (chambers of commerce, private centers, etc.);[7]

(2) payments to a training insurance fund (FAF);

(3) payments to approved research institutes (up to 10% of the total amount required by law);

(4) payment to the French Treasury of any sums not spent in the above ways. In 1978, such repayments amounted to 221 million francs ($40 million).

The government may monitor the way these sums are used, but only by verifying whether or not statutory provisions and regulations are respected. The overall financial contribution of the state was 6.3 billion francs ($1.15 billion) in 1979. Of this sum, 2.8 billion were spent on trainee remuneration, 0.3 billion on equipping centers, and 3.2 billion on course operating costs.

TABLE 12.2 Finance and Participation in Training Financed by Firms: 1972-1979

	1972	*1976*	*1977*	*1978*	*1979 Provisional*
Total number of firms	113,000	124,000	127,000	126,000	126,000
Total wages paid (billion francs)	207	398	451	497	555
Minimum stipulated contribution (million francs)	1,700	3,908	4,513	5,465	6,090
Proportion of wage bill required as contributions (in percentages)	0.8	1.0	1.0	1.1	1.1
Actual outlay on training (million francs)	2,800	6,470	7,950[1]	9,070[1]	10,210[1]
Actual proportion of wage bill paid on training (in percentages)	1.35	1.62	1.76	1.82	1.84
Payments into French Treasury (million francs)					
for inadequate funding of training activities	170	250	209	232	225
fine for failure to consult works committee	7.5	12	10	10	11
Total number of employees	9,760,000	10,433,000	10,500,000	10,382,000	10,342,000
Number of trainees	1,050,000	1,814,000	1,856,000	1,831,000	1,862,000
Percentage of employees participating in a training course	10.7	17.3	17.7	17.6	18.0
Total number of training hours (millions)	77.6	106.8	106.7	103.7	101.8

1. Including financing of training activities for young job-seekers.

TABLE 12.3 Finance and Participation in Training by Size of Firm: 1979

	10-19 Employees	*20-49 Employees*	*50-499 Employees*	*500-1,999 Employees*	*2,000 Employees or More*	*All Firms*
Number of firms	47,000	49,000	23,000	2,000	400	121,500
Amount of wages paid (million francs)	32,600	74,300	154,700	92,200	169,800	523,600
Actual outlay for (million francs)	296	781	1,998	1,505	4,892	9,472
Proportion of wage bill paid on training (in percentages)	0.94	1.05	1.29	1.63	2.98	1.81
Payments into French Treasury (million francs)	74	92	39	3	–	208
Number of employees	669,000	1,536,000	3,135,000	1,704,000	2,769,000	9,813,000
Number of trainees	21,000	80,000	389,000	340,000	856,000	1,685,000
Percentage of employees participating in a training course	3.1	5.2	12.4	20.0	30.9	17.2

The average length of training varies considerably according to its nature. While reorientation and refresher courses for a given job last 140 hours on average, the average number of hours for qualifying or upgrading courses is 400 hours. For pretraining courses (the great majority of which are intended for young job-seekers and are financed entirely by the state) the average is 720 hours.

Of the employment-training contracts for young people mentioned earlier, 57,000 were signed in 1979, while another 30,000 signed in 1978 were still being completed. Of the trainees 57% were boys and 47% were girls.

Looking at the age of these trainees, 29% were under 18 years of age, 41% were between 19 and 21, and 30% between 22 and 26. At the end of courses 50% of the jobs were provided for relatively unskilled staff, as compared to 43% for skilled personnel and 5% for executive or technical staff.

Nearly 90,0000 people undertook an AFPA (Association for Vocational Training for Adults) training course in 1979.[8] All AFPA activities together total 53,830,000 trainee-hours and represent a budget of 1,271 million francs.

The preceding sections have thus outlined broadly how vocational training is financed in France and the way funds are used. Next, some of the technical and psychological difficulties that may arise and cause discrepancies between legal principles and actual practice will be examined with respect to the specific question of training leave. This is one of the most novel features of the French system.

TRAINING LEAVE: THEORY AND PRACTICE

RIGHTS AND REGULATIONS

Apart from the training leave provided for in the 1971 act and subsequent legislation, various provisions for leave for educational purposes are contained in a number of laws. These provisions enable beneficiaries to do the following:

- to work as teachers (teaching leave) as has been mentioned earlier;
- to prepare for certain examinations (examination leave);
- to request special training leave for young people;
- to enroll in trade union courses (workers' educational leave);
- to train for responsibilities in youth projects (leave for youth leaders and organizers).

On what condition is training leave available? To be eligible for training leave under the 1971 act, an employee must have worked in a given occupation for at least 24 months (not necessarily consecutively) with at least 6 of them at the firm concerned. Those who have changed their job because they were laid off for economic reasons do not have to meet this requirement as long as they have not taken any training course between terminating the old job and finding a new one.

It should be noted that a minimum interval has to be observed between one period of training leave and the next depending on the legnth of the previous course. For example, this interval[9] is set at six months when the previous training course was 80 hours or less in length, or one year if it was between 81 and 160 hours.

How long can training leave be? The duration of training leave may not exceed one year in the case of continuous full-time training, or 1,200 hours if it consists of periodic or part-time courses. Exceptions, however, can be made for certain state-approved courses.

What training may the wage-earner choose? The purpose of training leave is "to acquire a higher qualification, to change one's type of work or occupation and to acquire a wider cultural and social outlook." The wage earner has a free choice among specific training courses, although they must be directed towards the acquisition of theoretical or practical qualifications and must have a set curriculum. In no case may training leave be used for the organization of leisure pursuits or for relaxation.

Can an employer refuse a request for training leave? An employer cannot refuse a request for training leave, and may only defer it for one of two reasons. First, it can be deferred if he or she considers that the absence of the employee concerned will hamper the efficient running of the firm. In such a case, the request may be deferred for not more than one year, and then only after the works committee has been consulted. Second, it may be deferred if that would mean that more than 2% of the firm's personnel are on training leave, paid or unpaid, at the same time. For firms with fewer than 200 employees, the limit is fixed at the equivalent to 2% of the hours worked annually by the staff as a whole (including executive staff).

Under what circumstances is the worker entitled to remuneration while on leave? If the worker is to be paid during leave, the course selected must be either state-approved or recognized by the competent joint labor-management committee. In order to alleviate the financial burden on enterprises, the law fixes a ceiling on the number of workers who are entitled to be paid while on leave. Thus, paid training leave is granted to employees up to a limit of 0.5% (0.75% in the case of executive personnel) of the staff. For firms employing fewer than 200 people this figure is equivalent to 0.5% (0.75% in the case of executive personnel) of hours worked annually. If such a contingent of "working hour credits" is not used or not fully used, it can be accumulated over four years.

Regulations vary, however, according to whether the training course is state-approved, is recognized by a joint labor-management committee, or is not recognized by either. In the first case, the employee on training leave who attends a state-approved course is entitled to pay and continues to receive his previous wage. This is paid during the first part of the course by the employer and during the latter part by the state. Table 12.4 shows the conditions of remuneration.

When the training course attended by the employee is recognized only by the joint labor-management committee in his employment sector and not by the state, only the employer is required to maintain the worker's pay. The upper limit is either the first 160 hours or 4 weeks when the course is less than 500 hours, or the first 500 hours or 13 weeks when it is greater than 500 hours.

When the course attended by the employee is recognized neither by the state nor by the joint labor-management committee on employment for the sector concerned, the training leave is simply a leave of absence and neither the employer nor the state is obliged to pay the employee's wage. Employees may, however, request their employers to maintain their wages, since it is open to the employer to include the requests of individuals in the firm's own training program. If the firm subscribes to a training insurance fund, the fund may cover the employee's wage and training expenses either partially or in total.

Who pays the training costs? Training costs generally include registration fees, teaching materials, and in some cases the cost of travel and/or board. By law, employees on training leave are given preference in admission to state-aided courses which are usually free. Travel expenses are partly paid by the state if the worker is remunerated by the state. If the employee attends a course recognized by the appropriate joint labor-management committee, the employer is responsible for the training costs only if the course lasts more than 500 hours, in which case the firm reimburses actual costs up to a ceiling of 31.10 francs ($5.65) per hour. Above this ceiling, the employer pays an allowance equivalent to two-thirds of the training costs, but this allowance may not exceed 70.69 francs ($12.85) per hour. When the course attended by the employee is

TABLE 12.4 Conditions of Remuneration of Paid Training Leave for State-Approved Courses

Length of Course	*Trainees' Occupational Category*	*Remuneration Paid by the Employer*	*Remuneration Paid by the State*
Less than 14 weeks or 500 hours	All employees (executive and nonexecutive	For the first 4 weeks or the first 160 hours: previous wage	With effect from the 5th week or 161st hour: previous wage up to a ceiling equivalent to three times the SMIC,[1] calculated on the basis of legally established weekly working hours
From 13 weeks or 500 hours minimum to one year or 1,200 hours maximum	Nonexecutive staff	Previous wage from the start of the course for 13 weeks or 500 hours	Previous wage up to a ceiling equivalent to three times the SMIC,[1] calculated on the basis of legally established weekly working hours with effect from the 14th week or the 501st hour
	Executive staff	Previous wage from the start of the course for 16 weeks or 600 hours	Previous wage up to a ceiling equivalent to three times the SMIC,[1] calculated on the basis of legally established weekly working hours with effect from the 17th week or the 601st hour
Over one year or over 1,200 hours	Nonexecutive staff	Previous wage from the start of the course for 13 weeks or 500 hours	120 percent of SMIC[1] with effect from the 14th week or the 501st hour
	Executive staff	Previous wage from the start of the course for 16 weeks or 600 hours	120 percent of SMIC[1] with effect from the 17th week or the 601st hour

NOTE: In 1980, the minimum wage was 13.66 F per hour ($2.48), which is 2,367 F per month ($430.50) based on a work week of 40 hours.
1. SMIC: The guaranteed minimum wage (Salaire minimum inter-professionel de croissance).

not a recognized one, the employer is not required to reimburse the training costs but may agree to do so in the same way as applied to the case of the employee's wage.

TRAINING LEAVE IN PRACTICE

From the rules and regulations, the right to training leave appears to offer workers comprehensive opportunity to meet their vocational training needs. In practice, however, the use of this right is not as simple as was intended originally. In spite of the legislation, it is still more difficult for the worker to exercise his right to training leave than for the employer to frame his own in-house training policy. In most cases, the employee has to choose between the training provided by the firm (which is organized during normal hours and therefore remunerated) and the training of his or her choice. For the latter, finance may not necessarily be secured because of the type of training sought (i.e., if it does not meet recognized criteria).

For reasons of clarity, it should be stressed that under the 1971 act there was no obligation on the part of the employer to remunerate an employee for training while on training leave. Such an obligation was only introduced by the act of 17 July 1978 which established a new system providing for combined remuneration by employer and state subject to the conditions discussed in this section. Firms that signed the July 1970 agreement as well as those that subscribe to a training insurance fund are obligated to maintain an employee's wage during training leave. However, an employee who has a choice between training available outside the firm and in-house training (which may enhance his or her image in the employer's eyes) will be tempted to choose the second alternative rather than run the risks of the first unless the outside training seems to be particularly advantageous. This is confirmed by a 1972 survey showing that 93% of hours spent on training were provided by the employer.

Another restrictive difficulty is that the law provides financial assistance only for previously approved training courses. This may, in some cases, limit access to cultural activities that have no direct vocational content and have no chance of obtaining official recognition. For instance, while a decree of 11 July 1972 expressly aimed to increase recognition of educational cultural activities, firms in fact have received only a few requests for training leave for such purposes—in most firms, only a handful each year. While the 1972 decree may be considered a sophisticated legal instrument that offers workers a wide variety of choice, the decree is difficult to use for both financial and psychological reasons. This explains the rather limited utilization of this provision.

POSSIBLE FUTURE DEVELOPMENTS

The right to training leave can be considered an innovation of great value, but it has suffered from the tendency in France to create endless legal texts in order to cover every conceivable situation. This has reduced much of its creative potential significantly. In 1974 it was calculated (light-heartedly) that more than 487 pages of official texts on the subject had appeared already and that in the whole of the country there were not more than three or four specialists capable of saying exactly what the position was when a particular question was raised. While this may be somewhat overstated, the picture is not that far removed from the actual situation.

It is also true that there is a contradiction between the definitions laid down and the opinions voiced since 1971 concerning continuing training and the system of values and down-to-earth realities of industrial life. This may indicate that some of those who are trying to promote a system of continuing education and training in France act as though it is possible to find technical solutions to political problems. There is a tendency to believe that decisions on economic and social questions can be taken regardless of the relationships between social forces—as if they concerned personal choice alone.

Many of the efforts made during the 1960s to promote training for the individual failed because they overestimated the value of knowledge in power relationships. Today this illusion has faded, but at the same time the tendency to confine training within purely technical bounds deprives the concept of training leave of its full meaning. It can be said safely that as long as the remuneration question has not been settled satisfactorily and while there is still wide-spread unemployment, very few people will be prepared to assert their right to training leave in view of the financial risk involved and the danger of later jeopardizing their employment. Although training leave is a right, it is understandable that many will think, "What will become of me if I leave my job for six months or a year to train in something that interests me personally, only to find that when I come back my employer has learned to do without me?"

The trade unions clearly have an important role to play by putting forward demands that are more precise, backed by better information, and based on a consensus of their membership. But it would appear that adult education and training must, for the time being, recognize the far-reaching implications of unemployment and the economic crisis.

Any debate on future developments of training leave therefore is bound to reflect the question of regulations and legislation less and concentrate more on the concept and status of training itself as perceived by both policymakers and workers. It must consider the very structure of employment in the world today. As part of this problem, one must consider the question of the mobility of workers which depends on a number of factors beside education. Further developments must consider the ability of workers to make plans for themselves, to conceive these plans realistically, and to realize them as a normal expression of individual choice that is still in keeping with the society around them. The individual's ability to act as a responsible partner in an industrial democracy in the midst of economic and political constraints is of paramount importance.

SUMMARY AND CONCLUSION

In summary, continuing vocational training is characterized by two central features. First, enterprises are obliged by law to provide their employees with the opportunity for continuing training and to devote 1.1% of their payroll to that end. Second, all employees have the right to leave for training purposes during normal working time.

Both features, although based on the same law of 1971, are not linked directly to each other; while the former provision has resulted in massive training efforts by the enterprises, only a relatively small (and declining) number of employees has made use of individual training leave. In 1978 more than 1.8 million workers participated in training provided by enterprises, but only 49,000 took leave for a training course outside the firm (as compared to 58,000 in 1976 and 68,000 in 1975).

There are three basic factors responsible for this poor result. First, more often than not the employee exercising his right and asking for training leave does not receive any remuneration while on leave; moreover, he or she is left with the instruction costs as well. Only where the state or the joint labor-management committee have accredited the training activity does the employer or state pay remuneration. Therefore the employee often cannot afford to take training leave.

Second, employees are only entitled to training leave, if the enterprise does not offer a similar course as part of its training program. Since enterprises, especially bigger ones, offer a variety of training activities under their 1.1% payroll obligation, the justification for the demand for a leave to participate in an outside training activity is often difficult to establish. Third, as is the case in other countries with educational leave provisions, there are particular problems concerning the exercise of the right to training leave in small and medium-size firms.

The 1978 law has clarified and ameliorated the problem of wage maintenance and extended the scope of eligible educational activities by including courses with social and cultural components rather than just the purely professional. However worthwhile the intentions of this law and the improvements it actually introduced, there remain considerable problems in the complete and effective utilization of the employee's right to training leave.

NOTES

1. Not including civil servants, who are not covered by the same scheme.
2. Calculated on a basis of $1 U.S. = 5.50 French francs.
3. According to the law, there must be a works committee (comite d'entreprise) where more than 50 people are employed.
4. In certain circumstances women of all ages who wish to resume gainful employment may also benefit under this contract.
5. These were first enacted on 5 July 1977 and have been renewed annually since then. To give some idea of the scope of these agreements, the third (dated 10 July 1979) provided opportunities for 280,000 young people.
6. The figures that follow are those currently available, namely the 1979 figures as given in the 1981 draft budget.
7. These are known as the groupement d'etablissements scolaires—that is, training provided by high schools or colleges, established to provide continuing training for the firms' staff.
8. AFPA offers 297 types of instruction in 32 subjects at 125 vocational training centers for adults. Skilled workers usually undergo six months of full-time training, and technicians are trained for nine to twelve months.
9. This is called a *"delai de franchise."*

REFERENCES

ADAMS, R. J., P. M. DRAPER, and C. DUCHAME (1979) Education and Working Canadians: Report of the Commission of Inquiry on Educational Leave and Productivity. Ottawa: Ministry of Supply and Services.

BESNARD, P. and B. LIETARD (1976) La Formation Continue (Continuing Training). Paris: Editions PUF Collection Que Sais-je, 1655.

DAVID, M. et al. (1976) L'Individuel et le Collectif dans la Formation des Travailleurs (The Individual and the Collectivity in the Training of Workers). Paris: Editions Economica.

DELORS, J. (1973) "French Policy on Continuing Education," in S. Mushkin (ed.) Recurrent Education. Washington, D.C.: U.S. Government Printing Office.

HERTZ-LEBRUN, C. (1979) La Formation Professionnelle Continue. Paris: Lamy.

SCHWARTZ, B. (1977) Une Autre Ecole (A Different School). Paris: Flammarion.

STRINER, H. E. (1972) Continuing Education as a National Investment. Washington, DC: W. E. Upjohn Institute for Employment Research.

VON MOLTKE, K. and N. SCHNEEVOIGT (1977) Educational Leaves for Employees-European Experience for American Consideration. San Francisco: Jossey-Bass.

13

THE FEDERAL REPUBLIC OF GERMANY

HANS G. SCHÜTZE

In 1976 the Federal Republic signed the resolutions of the 1974 ILO Convention Concerning Paid Educational Leave committed

> to formulate and apply a policy designed to promote, by methods appropriate to national conditions and practice and by stages as necessary, the granting of paid educational leave for the purpose of training at any level, general, social and civic education, [as well as] trade union education [art. 2].

Before adopting the convention, educational leave in certain forms had been an established practice in Germany. For example, over half of the West German youth undertake vocational training under the "dual system" in which apprentices spend part of the week in the firm and part of it in vocational school (College Entrance Examination Board, 1979). Employer-sponsored training programs are also provided for employees beyond the apprenticeship age through training programs on the employers' premises or through employers organizations such as the Chambers of Commerce. These are indeed the most important training programs in terms of enrollment and expenditures. The focus of this chapter, however, will be on a narrowed set of programs—those concerned with educational leave. Not all workers are entitled educational leave (*Bildungsurlaub*), yet all provisions conform to the basic characteristics of educational leave (i.e., the individual right to educational leave with the guaranteed right to return to the working place). Most of these provisions maintain the employee's full salaries or wages or a percentage of wages during the period of leave. however, what has emerged in recent years has gone far beyond these approaches by increasing the role of individual choice in electing to take educational leave.

THE SETTING

Western Germany is a federal republic consisting of 10 federal states (Länder) and West Berlin. The latter has most of the characteristics of a state but retains a unique status as a result of the division of that city and the German nation in the wake of World War II. As in the United States, the federal states have the power to regulate educational matters autonomously. In fact, this power is the only really important responsibility of the states—unlike the United States and Canada where the states (or provinces, respectively) have retained many other important powers which in Germany are the domain of the federal government. In order to maintain some degree of uniformity, there is a Standing Conference of the States' Ministers of Education which coordinates educational policies and ensures equivalence among the states of educational qualifications, diplomas, and so on. The federal government has limited jurisdiction in educational matters. It is responsible for establishing the general principles and the institutional framework of higher education, for the promotion of scientific research, student aid and, most importantly, for all non-school-based vocational training (College Entrance Examination Board, 1979).

Educational leave falls under the jurisdiction of the federal government because of a clause in the West German constitution that gives the federal government the power to legislate on economic and labor market matters. In the absence of such federal legislation, the states are free to regulate the provision of educational leave.

Although the federal government expressed its intention as early as 1969 to introduce a bill on paid educational leave, it has failed to do so due to resistance from employers who would have been obligated to bear most of the costs (Görs, 1978: 51; OECD/CERI, 1976: 157-158). However, laws on paid educational leave have been passed in five of the federal states, including Berlin. The other states have so far preferred not to pass similar laws, although some of them have paid-educational-leave bills under consideration.

Although there is no general federal law on paid educational leave, there are a number of provisions in federal laws that give certain groups the right to paid leave for specific educational purposes. For example, civil servants and judges are provided with recurrent opportunities for continuing education. More importantly, under the Enterprise Constitution Act *(Betriebsverfassungsgesetz),* members of enterprise councils *(Betriebsrat)* have the right to educational leave for courses that provide knowledge needed in exercising their functions as worker representatives. Earnings are continued during the period of leave as required by law.

Similar clauses exist for employee representatives in public administration, as well as salaried physicians and civil engineers charged with health and security matters within enterprises (von Moltke and Schneevoigt, 1977). Most important, however, both in terms of people affected **and expenditures, is the Federal Labor Promotion Act of 1969** *(Arbeitsförderungsgesetz)* which provides educational costs and maintenance allowances for the unemployed and those threatened by unemployment who participate in continuing training or retraining programs.

In addition to the provisions contained in various Länder and federal laws, there are a number of collective agreements that provide for educational leave, both paid and unpaid. This chapter will limit itself to a description of the main features of some important leave schemes, and a discussion of participation, finance, and costs of recurrent education under these leave schemes.

LAWS FOR PAID EDUCATIONAL LEAVE IN THE FEDERAL STATES *(LÄNDER)*

The Berlin diet (the regional legislature) passed the first law pertaining to educational leave in 1970. This law granted 10 working days leave per year to workers, employees, and apprentices up to age 21. The law was amended in 1975 to include young people up to the age of 25. Its stated purpose was to enable young people to participate in educational activities, enhance participation in public life, and promote vocational education beyond the dual training system.

Laws for the four other Länder sponsoring educational leave were passed in 1974. Despite the seemingly concerted timing, these laws are not uniform but have diverging features concerning the eligibility of participants, the contents of accreditable courses and activities, and the procedure for accreditation. The only basic provision that is identical in all four laws is that they give the beneficiaries the right to leave for one working week per year or two working weeks for two consecutive years. The leave entitlement in Berlin amounts to two working weeks per year. During this leave, the salary or wage is maintained by the employer.

There are some restrictions to this leave entitlement, however. In the cases of Berlin, Bremen, Hamburg, and Hesse, the worker or employee must be employed for a minimum of six months before becoming eligible. This does not apply to Lower Saxony. However, in this state a ceiling has been fixed whereby the employer can refuse a request for leave if the total number of days during the course of one year is 2.5 times the number of eligible staff. This formula implies that no more than 25% of the staff is entitled to leave during the same year. Moreover, all of the state laws specify that a request for educational leave can be denied temporarily, if the functioning of the enterprise might be imperiled, or if there are requests for leave by other members of the staff with higher social priority.

As Table 13.1 shows, the Berlin and Hesse laws limit eligibility to apprentices and young workers up to age 25 while the other three state laws do not have an age ceiling. As in Berlin and Hamburg, the Hesse law is confined to courses of civic education or continuing vocational training; general education cannot be accredited. The Bremen and Lower Saxony laws, however, include continuing general education in the range of accreditable activities.

According to the ILO Convention on Paid Educational Leave, one of the objectives of such leave is to promote "the competent and active participation of workers and their representatives in the life of the undertaking and of the community" (art. 3,b). Although the wording of the definition of civic education in the German Länder Laws is slightly different, they essentially state the same objective—namely, to help workers understand their function, role, obligations, and rights, and to enable them to participate actively in social and public life, exercise their rights, and fulfill their functions. Under this definition, trade union education is part of—not separate from—civic education. In fact, about 50% of the courses and programs offered for this type of education are sponsored by the trade unions and those voluntary organizations that have strong links with the unions. The bulk of programs and courses of continuing education and training, however, are offered by the local popular academies *(Volkshochschulen)* sponsored by local government, while other voluntary organizations (like the churches) account for the remainder.

TABLE 13.1 State Laws on Paid Education Leave

	Berlin *Law of 7/16/70* *amended 12/17/76*	*Hamburg* *Law of 1/21/74*	*Bremen* *Law of 12/18/74*	*Lower Saxony* *Law of 6/5/74* *amended 12/17/74*	*Hesse* *Law of 6/24/74*
Eligibility	Wage and salary earners, apprentices; Age limit: under 26 years	Wage and salary earners, apprentices; No age limit	Wage and salary earners, apprentices, home workers and other dependent workers; No age limit	Wage and salary earners, apprentices, home workers and other dependent workers; No age limit	Wage and salary earners, apprentices; Age limit: under 26 years
Entitlement	10 working days per year; beyond this period there is a right to unpaid leave	10 (12) working days in two years	10 (12) working days in two years	10 (12) working days in two years	5 (6) working days per year
Contents of Courses	Civic education and continuing vocational training	Civic education and continuing vocational training	Civic education, continuing vocational training and general education	Civic education, continuing vocational training and general education	Civic education and continuing vocational training
Restrictions of Entitlement	after six months employment with the same firm; exercise of right can temporarily be denied by employer if and as long as there are compelling reasons regarding the functioning of the enterprise or if there are demands for leave of other salaried workers with higher social priority	after six months employment with the same firm; exercise of right can temporarily be denied by employer if and as long as there are compelling reasons regarding the functioning of the enterprise or if there are demands for leave of other salaried workers with higher social priority	after six months employment with the same firm; exercise of right can temporarily be denied by employer if and as long as there are compelling reasons regarding the functioning of the enterprise or if there are demands for leave of other salaried workers with higher social priority	employer can refuse, if a ceiling is reached. The annual ceiling is defined as a total of **days per firm equivalent 2.5 times the number of employees** exercise of right can temporarily be denied by employer if and as long as there are compelling reasons regarding the functioning of the enterprise or if there are **demands for leave of other** salaried workers with higher social priority	after six months employment with the same firm; exercise of right can temporarily be denied by employer if and as long as there are compelling reasons regarding the functioning of the enterprise or if there are demands for leave of other salaried workers with higher social priority

While the objective of continuing vocational training is to maintain, improve, or expand vocational qualifications and occupational flexibility (Hamburg law: sec. 1, par. 3), there is no comparable legal definition of general education in the two state laws that include general education in their range of accreditable activities. This leads occasionally to difficulties when employers refuse to grant educational leave to their employees for general education courses not related to job requirements (such as full-time language programs) or for courses such as sailing or yoga. Some of the workers have carried their cause to the labor courts which have, in the first instances, ruled that such courses are indeed covered by the term "general education." While results of these cases are at present pending before the Supreme Labor Court, there is growing resistance among employers against what are viewed as leisure-time activities. This resistance may eventually lead to a revision of the law on this point.

The Länder laws also differ considerably regarding the procedure for course accreditation. In Hamburg, the agency charged with implementation of the law is required to check every education or training course in terms of its compatibility with the law. In Hesse, it is confined to the accreditation of institutions and other providers of education and training. The courses offered by these accredited sponsors are then automatically recognized as eligible for paid leave. While Bremen and Berlin have similar provisions, Lower Saxony has adopted a blend of these two principles, allowing employees to seek recognition for courses provided by some nonaccredited institutions.

PARTICIPATION AND CHARACTERISTICS OF PARTICIPANTS

As can be seen from Table 13.2, participation in paid educational leave under the Länder laws is generally low. Although the participation rate is slowly increasing, it varies between less than 2% and 6%, and of a total of 3.75 million eligible employees only 87,000 exercised their right in 1980 (2.3%). Even taking into account the upward trend over the years, participation has neither lived up to the hopes and aspirations of the trade unions which were the driving force behind the Lander legislation, nor has it warranted the fears of employers who resisted it because of concern for the costs and the possible loss of productivity.

It is difficult to analyze the underlying reasons for this low participation or to assess the relative weight of the factors that contribute to it.

TABLE 13.2 Paid Educational Leave According to State Laws: Participation, 1975-1980

	Berlin	*Hamburg*	*Bremen*	*Lower Saxony*	*Hesse*
1975					
(a) eligible	105,300	614,926	330,000	2,011,595	403,692
(b) participants	4,277	3,000	3,190	8,985	6,407
(c) rate	4.0%	0.5%	0.9%	0.45%	1.6%
1976					
(a) eligible	93,400	702,771	322,000	2,011,595	412,900
(b) participants	4,946	3,550	6,785	20,168	8,322
(c) rate	5.3%	0.5%	2.5%	1.0%	2.0%
1977					
(a) eligible	94,700	697,792	323,000	2,061,968	433,500
(b) participants	4,563	6,000*	8,257	24,625	10,119
(c) rate	4.8%	0.9%*	2.8%	1.2%	2.3%
1978					
(a) eligible	109,741	700,000*	315,000	2,061,968	430,200
(b) participants	5,723	8,400*	9,893	29,523	11,242
(c) rate	5.2%	1.2%*	3.8%	1.43%	2.6%
1979					
(a) eligible	114,465	700,000*	315,000*	2,137,521	435,300
(b) participants	7,154	9,800*	13,187	33,897	12,927
(c) rate	6.2%	1.4%*	4.4%	1.59%	3.0%
1980					
(a) eligible	119,456	700,000*	315,000*	2,180,990	433,800
(b) participants	7,366	11,200*	12,380	40,930	13,570
(c) rate	6.2%	1.6%*	4.3%	1.88%	3.1%

SOURCES: Länder reports; Görs, 1982.
*Own estimate.

The trade unions see continuing resistance from employers and workers' fears of negative sanctions as the most important obstacles to higher levels of participation (Görs, 1978: 184-211; 1982). Employers, of course, deny that any such sanctions exist. This would violate the spirit and intent of the laws which generally forbid pressures or sanctions against workers who want to exercise their right to educational leave. According to employers, paid educational leave increases fixed labor costs and therefore has a direct impact on employment and competitiveness. They emphasize that accredited courses and programs often do not respond to the real demand which, according to them, is the upgrading of occupational skills and knowledge. In particular, employers have strong reservations against what they see as trade union education in the guise of civic education, and leisure activities in the guise of general education.

Apart from this conflict of views—which underlines the polarized and highly political nature of the debate about educational leave in Germany—there are a number of more objective factors that play an important role. First, there is a widespread lack of suitable courses (i.e., programs that are tailored to the needs of both workers and employers and are of the appropriate duration) as the majority of the Länder laws exclude courses shorter than three or, in some instances, five working days. Second, despite the provision for salary maintenance, the instruction and travel costs are not borne by the employer and so must be met by the participants themselves or some other sponsor. In addition, there is often a marked lack of information about available courses and the procedure for requesting educational leave. This is particularly true in small enterprises where union influence and worker representation is low or nonexistent.

One of the main problems concerning participation is the impact of previous education on the demand for recurrent education. It is, therefore, one of the acknowledged objectives of a recurrent education strategy to enhance participation in further learning among those with a low level of educational attainment. According to Table 13.3, employees possessing only a high school diploma are heavily underrepresented. In contrast, those with a technical school or upper secondary school diploma (which are prerequisite for access to higher education) are significantly overrepresented. The data regarding the occupational status of participants show fewer differences as the official German distinction between blue collar *(Arbeiter)* and white collar *(Angestellter)* is no longer an accurate distinction in a modern, technological economy. They nevertheless give an idea of orders of magnitude. Apart from Berlin and Hesse (where eligibility is limited by an age ceiling, and hence the majority of participants are apprentices) the figures for Lower Saxony, which is at present the biggest and most representative state with educational leave legislation, reveal that workers are slightly overrepresented. While this seems somewhat at odds with the general dependence of participation on educational attainment, it shows that targeted outreach programs, in particular by the unions and the enterprise councils, have been successful in overcoming this barrier.

TABLE 13.3 **Paid Educational Leave According to Lander Law: Characteristics of Participants: 1977 (in percentages)**

	Berlin	*Hamburg*	*Bremen*	*Lower Saxony*	*Hesse*	*Educational Attainment and Occupational Status of Total German Working Population**
Educational Attainment						
Without diploma	n.a.	1.1	2.0	n.a.	n.a.	n.a.
With high school diploma	n.a.	35.2	33.3	n.a.	n.a.	72.4
With intermediate school diploma	n.a.	42.7	30.1	n.a.	n.a.	17.5
With technical school diploma	n.a.	6.0	22.6	n.a.	n.a.	n.a.
Abitur or equivalent	n.a.	13.1	5.0	n.a.	n.a.	9.3
Nonclassified	n.a.	1.9	6.9	n.a.	n.a.	n.a.
Occupational Status						
Blue-collar workers	n.a.	n.a.	36.0	52.9	10.8	43.0
Employees	42.3	n.a.	55.7	36.9	15.1	35.5**
Apprentices	57.0	n.a.	8.3	10.2	74.1	5.4**

SOURCES: Lander reports on paid educational leave, Hönigsberger.
*Federal Statistical Bureau (microcensus of April 1978).
**Own computations.

The composition of participants is also highly variable from year to year, as can be seen by comparing the 1977 figures in Table 13.3 with the 1980 figures for Lower Saxony of 44.3% workers, 46.5% employees, and 9.2% apprentices, as well as from course to course. A Lower Saxony study for the year 1977 showed that in courses offered by an educational institution sponsored by the trade unions, enrollments of workers amounted to 76% of participants as compared to 29% for courses offered by the local popular academies. Even this latter figure is significantly higher than worker participation in continuing education outside employers' premises, which is generally below 5%. It is thus evident that workers have indeed benefited from paid educational leave.

A third factor of significance regarding participation is the size of the firm. Large firms can cope more easily than smaller ones with the short-term absence of a small number of employees because they represent a low proportion of personnel and because the large firm has possibilities for internal substitution. In addition, those enterprises with strong worker representation and unionization tend to be far more active than others because they provide information and stimulate demand for eligible leave. Since these are characteristics of large and medium-size firms, the marked differences shown in Table 13.4 are not altogether surprising. This may be partly due to the fact that 40.3% of all Lower Saxony participants in 1978 were employed by Volkswagen (Görs, 1982)—an enterprise which is not heavily unionized, but one in which the president of the powerful metal workers union is a member of the Board of Directors.

In summary, the experience with paid educational leave laws suggests that a variety of factors are contributing to their underutilization. Although the trend is an upward one, participation in paid educational leave may not live up to the hopes of its protagonists (i.e., the trade unions and the Social Democrats), at least not in the immediate future. On the other hand, it must be acknowledged that, because of these laws, some 85,000 employees a year participate in some kind of further education. Most of them are ordinarily underrepresented in continuing education and probably would not have participated otherwise. In addition, plans are under way in Northrhine Westfalia (by far the most populous and industrialized of the federal states) to pass paid educational leave legislation. If these plans succeed, the number of employees eligible for paid educational leave under the Länder laws will more than double, bringing the total number of eligible persons to around 8 million (i.e., more than one-third of the entire work force in the Federal Republic). Such legislation would considerably enhance workers' opportuni-

TABLE 13.4 Participants in Paid Educational Leave in Lower Saxony According to Size of Firm (in percentages)

	Number of Workers Employed					
	1-9	*10-49*	*50-199*	*200-299*	*1000 and More*	*Public Sector*
1977	2.9	6.7	8.5	17.4	51.0	13.5
1978	2.7	3.3	8.8	14.1	56.0	13.1
1979	4.7	9.5	10.1	15.9	44.1	15.7
1980	3.8	6.0	8.3	14.3	53.9	13.8

SOURCE: Lower Saxony Report, 1981.

ties for continuing education and can be expected to make paid leave an important component of recurrent education in Germany.

THE ENTERPRISE CONSTITITUION ACT: PAID EDUCATIONAL LEAVE FOR WORKERS' REPRESENTATIVES

The federal Enterprise Constitution Act regulates worker participation in management decisions of the enterprise and the procedures to be followed, and accords special leave to members of the enterprise council. This leave is granted for participation in seminars and courses that provide the knowledge required to be a workers' representative. In principle, this right is not limited to a specific duration, and the enterprise council as a whole determines which of its members is to attend a specific course. The council also considers the timing of participation with respect to the proper functioning of the enterprise and its process of production. If there is a conflict between the council and the employer, a mediation board makes the final decision.

In addition to this collective right, the law provides an individual entitlement for each elected workers' representative to three weeks per elective term of three years, amounting to one week per year. Members of work councils who are fulfilling this function for the first time are granted an additional week. During these leave periods the salary is paid in full by the employer. This individual leave entitlement is in addition to any right to paid educational leave an employee might have under one of the state laws or under one of the collective bargaining agreements.

As might be expected, courses are mainly provided by the unions (84%), while employers and their associations and voluntary organizations such as chambers of labor or educational institutions sponsored by political parties and the confessions account for the rest—5.6% and 10.3%, respectively (Federal Ministry of Labor, figures from 1978).

Enterprise councils are not a branch of the union. Even if the majority of council members are union members, they have responsibilities only with respect to their own enterprise. These responsibilities are enumerated and defined in the Enterprise Constitution Act. Confidential information about the enterprise obtained by council members in the exercise of their function cannot be passed on to third parties, including the unions of which they may be members.

According to the law, enterprises between 5 and 20 salaried persons have the right to a single representative. Those of 21 salaried persons or more are guaranteed the right to a work council whose size is determined in proportions to the number of its personnel (e.g., three members for 21-50 salaried persons; 5 for firms of 51-150; 7 for firms of 151-300, and so forth). For the elective period 1975-1978, a total of 191,000 workers' representatives in the Federal Republic were eligible for special leave under the Enterprise Constitution Act (Federal Ministry of Labor).

A rough estimate of participation is derived from the fact that there were 9,592 courses during the 1975-1978 term which on average lasted one week and accommodated between 20 and 30 participants (Federal Ministry of Labor, 1979). This constitutes an approximate total of 239,000 participants during three years, or almost 80,000 per year. This suggests a participation rate of approximately 42% which is significant in comparison with the participation rate of educational leave generally.

The Enterprise Constitution Act extends the same right to leave for youth representatives—that is, the elected representatives of those under 19 years of age, most of whom are apprentices. Educational leave of a similar kind is also foreseen for the representatives of handicapped workers and employees who are responsible for the working conditions of handicapped personnel.

PAID TRAINING LEAVE UNDER THE LABOR PROMOTION ACT

While participation in educational activities under the Länder laws on paid educational leave is regulated largely by what is often called "social demand," the provision of training and retraining opportunities under the Federal Labor Promotion Act of 1969 is strictly based on a manpower requirement approach. The law is an instrument of what has come to be called an active labor market policy. It states as its purpose the achievement and maintenance of a high level of employment, the constant improvement of the employment structure and, thereby, the promotion of economic growth (for details regarding the law see Striner, 1972, and von Moltke and Schneevoigt, 1977). More particularly the measures under the law aim at the following:

- preventing the occurrence or continuance of unemployment or underemployent, on the one hand, and labor shortages, on the other;
- safeguarding and improving the occupational mobility of gainfully employed persons;
- preventing, offsetting, or eliminating the negative effects that technical developments or structural changes in the economy may have on gainfully employed persons;
- improving the employment structure in different geographical areas and economic sectors;
- and providing employment opportunities for the handicapped, women, the aging, and other hard to employ groups.

In addition to regulations concerning job counseling and placement, the act provides for the promotion of vocational training, continuing training and retraining through financial subsidies to individuals engaged in such training. With respect to continuing training, such subsidies are paid to participants who have completed an apprenticeship or possess appropriate work experience and wish to participate in programs designed to maintain or extend their professional skills and knowledge, adopt them to technical developments, or enhance promotion. Such subsidies are also available for the retraining of the unemployed or employees threatened by employment who "participate in programmes designed to enable them to transfer to some other form of suitable employment, with the particular objective of ensuring or improving their occupational mobility" (sec. 47). Such programs are no longer than two years when attended full-time, but part-time participation, including study by correspondence, is possible where part-time provision is available. Participants are paid a maintenance allowance calculated on the basis of the wage previously earned; until the end of 1981, this stood at 80 percent of the net wage or salary.

Under the impact of heavy resource restraints which required important budget cuts, the act was amended in 1981. This reduced the maintenance allowance to 68% of the previous net salary and narrowed certain of the eligibility criteria. Among these, the criterion of "threatened by redundancy," in particular, which previously had been interpreted very widely, was made more stringent by restricting it to salaried persons who had either received a notice of redundancy or whose enterprises had been declared bankrupt.

Eligibility for further training and retraining subsidies is dependent on membership of the compulsory unemployment insurance scheme, since it is from this fund that subsidies are paid and the scheme is administered. These measures are thus financed—as with unemployment benefits, vocational counseling, and placement services—by equal contributions of salaried workers and employees on the one hand, and employers on the other, with additional contributions from the federal government to meet the deficit in the budget of the scheme.

In 1980, 176,500 salaried persons received subsidies for continuing training courses, of which 65,300 (37%) were unemployed at the time they started the course, while the others were in gainful employment. An additional 38,000 persons were in retraining courses of which 60% were unemployed. The total of these two groups was 214,500 employees, or about 1% of the total workforce.

As can be seen from these statistics—in particular from the fact that some 50% of those in continuing training or retraining programs were unemployed—we are not dealing here with educational leave in the proper sense but with a labor market program designed to upgrade professional skills and thus to enhance employability and upward mobility. While this scheme resembles paid educational leave schemes in some of its features such as the maintenance of a proportion of the salary of an employee engaged mostly in training off the job, it lacks one important characteristic of educational leave—it fails to guarantee the right of return to one's job in the same enterprise upon completion of the training activity.

Nevertheless, this scheme has been included in this chapter for two reasons: First, because this kind of investment in human resources is of general interest when talking about lifelong learning in a recurrent pattern. It may also prove that such an investment is a sound one yielding concrete benefits that offset the costs incurred. Thus, according to a recent survey by the Federal Employment Institute, one in two participants in the retraining program had found employment within one month of completing retraining, and a total of 87% were in positions commensurate with their newly acquired qualifications within two years after completing their retraining (for a fuller discussion regarding costs and benefits, see Striner, 1972).

The second reason for mentioning the program in this chapter is its particular mode of financing. Whereas in the case of paid educational leave both under the Länder laws and the Enterprise Constitution Act the wages are maintained in full by the employer; in this case maintenance allowances are paid by a collective fund financed by equal shares from workers and employers. This emphasis on continuing training and retraining as an instrument of enhancing employability, and hence employment and its mode of financing, find their parallel in the French system of continuing training (see Chapter 12 in this volume) whose underlying concept of collective or parafiscal finance is also discussed elsewhere in this volume (see Chapter 4, and more concretely with respect to training, Chapter 14).

PROVISION IN OTHER LAWS

Besides the leave schemes discussed above, there are a number of other federal and state laws that accord a right to leave for educational purposes to particular groups. Some have already been mentioned in passing (e.g., the provisions for security engineers and employed physicians responsible for occupational health). Among these, the scheme of providing full-time continuing education and training for members of the armed forces serving beyond the compulsory conscription period is probably the most important in numerical terms (von Moltke and Schneevoigt, 1977: 106-107). However, these laws must be considered to be marginal in comparison with the ones described above.

PROVISION FOR EDUCATIONAL LEAVE IN COLLECTIVE BARGAINING AGREEMENTS

A sizeable number of collective bargaining agreements contain clauses providing for leave, both paid and unpaid, for various reasons. Based on a survey by the Federal Minister of Labor in 1967, it was found that only 57 out of 900 agreements included in the survey had clauses that entitled every worker to educational leave, while the majority of leave provisions in the agreements were limited to union members or workers' representatives. The agreements also differ considerably with respect to the duration of such leave, the contents of educational activities allowed under these clauses, and the maintenance of wages (which was covered in only a small number of cases—18 out of 900 agreements).

According to a survey sponsored by the unions in 1973, agreements with educational leave clauses affected 2.2 million salaried employees, representing some 10% of the workforce. A later survey counted a total of 204 agreements with such clauses affecting a total of 2.8 million workers (i.e., 14% of the workforce). Of these, only slightly more than one-third were entitled to full wage maintenance by the employer while on educational leave, and about one-half of those eligible did not receive any wage or allowance from their employer during such leave (for details, see Görs, 1982).

Although these figures seem important, the leave provisions in collective bargaining agreements probably have a marginal impact in comparison with the various legal entitlements to paid leave. This is due to several factors, not least of which is the bewildering variety in content of the leave clauses in the various contracts as well as a considerable overlap with similar legal entitlements. Thus, while workers' representatives might be entitled to leave for labor union education under the collective agreement for their sector of industry, they are also entitled to essentially the same right under the Enterprise Constitution Act. Although these entitlements do not necessarily preclude each other, it is obvious that in practice they are not accumulated, given the stipulation contained in both the law and most of the agreements that the exercise of this entitlement must not negatively affect the production of the enterprise.

Given this rather marginal nature of leave clauses in collective labor contracts, it is not astonishing that there are not even estimates available as to the extent that these contractual entitlements are being utilized. It can probably be safely assumed that current utilization is very low.

COSTS

We have already referred to the resistance on the part of the employers to the wide scale introduction of paid educational leave on the grounds that such entitlements would further increase labor costs and would therefore impair the economy as a whole in its competitiveness with other industrialized countries. Strangely enough, no concrete figures of any degree of accuracy were put forward in support of these arguments. Estimates given ranged from DM 600 million to 5 billions per year ($300 million to 2.5 billion), but these figures were rejected by the unions as unreliable and far too high (Görs, 1978: 196).

There are only scant data on the actual costs of existing leave schemes. Two of the states with paid educational leave laws have suggested concrete figures. Thus the authorities of Berlin have assessed the total annual burden for the employers at almost DM 3 million, including wages and contributions to the social security fund. Divided among the number of participants, this would amount to around DM 415 ($207) per participant (figures from 1979). The estimates given by the Hesse authorities are lower still—DM 3.9 millions for 13,570 participants (in 1980), thus around DM 290 ($145) per participant which is not more than 0.00048% of the total wage bill of that state.

However accurate these official estimates may be, they are not representative of the levels of outlays normally incurred. As has been pointed out, both Berlin and Hesse laws contain an age ceiling of 25 years which means that the majority of participants consist of apprentices and young workers whose allowances and salaries are considerably lower than that of the average employee. Based on an average salary, the figure for a one week entitlement per year (5 working days) would amount to approximately DM 1,000 ($500) per participant. Based on the 1980 participation rate and making allowance for less costly participation of apprentices, one can estimate the total cost at approximately DM 150 million ($75 million) which German employers had to bear for income maintenance of their employees while on paid educational leave—not counting empoloyers' contribution to paid training leave under the Labor Promotion Act. This figure does not take into account, however, instruction and indirect costs that must be borne either by the participants themselves, by the various sponsors of education and training courses, or by the states via subsidies to such sponsors. Because of the enormous variety of sponsors and programs and the lack of relevant data, not even a cautious estimate can be given regarding such costs.

This is not the case for the Continuing Training and Retraining Scheme under the Labor Promotion Act mentioned above. For the 214,500 participants (in 1980) in continuing and retraining courses, instruction cost, transportation, housing, and contributions to the social security fund amounted to DM 752 million. Together with almost DM 1.5 billion spent for maintenance payments, the Federal Employment Institute spent a total of DM 2.25 billion ($1.22 billion), thus around DM 10,500 ($5,250) per participant. In comparing these figures to the above estimates for paid educational leave schemes, account must be taken of the fact that the duration of more than 20% of these courses is between 18 months and 3 years, and that half of them last between 4 months and 1 year. Table 13.5 gives an idea of the total outlays for educational and training leave in the Federal Republic for the leave schemes mentioned above. It must be emphasized that this table is not only incomplete with respect to other costs besides maintenance, but is also based in part on estimates. It serves the purpose however of indicating the order of magnitudes involved.

MODES OF FINANCING

There are two principle modes of financing educational leave schemes. In one, the individual employer provides for the maintenance of wages and salaries. This is the case for the leave schemes provided in the Länder laws, the Enterprise Constitution Act, and those collective bargaining agreements that contain a paid leave provision. The second mode of financing is a collective approach: Outlays for continuing and retraining under the Labor Promotion Act come from the Unemployment Insurance Fund which is financed by compulsory contributions from both the employers and employees and is calculated as a percentage of the wage bill.

In addition to these two main sources of funding, paid educational leave schemes are publicly subsidized in several ways. First, as wage maintenance costs can be written off against profits for tax purposes, the state contributes in the form of tax revenues foregone. Second, in spite of the principle that the Unemployment Insurance Fund is collectively funded by contributions from employers and employees, the federal government has been obliged in recent years to provide massive subsidies in order to balance the deficit resulting from rising unemployment. Finally, instruction as well as indirect costs are being publicly subsidized in a variety of ways, mainly through grants to education and training institutions providing eligible courses or through payments to the sponsors of such courses (such as voluntary organizations, churches, and

TABLE 13.5 Educational Schemes and Leave for Continuing Training and Retraining: Participants and Costs, 1980

	*Participants (in 1000s)**	*Outlays for Income Maintenance (in Mio DM)*	*Outlays for Instruction and Direct Costs*
Lander Laws for paid educational leave	87**	79**	n.a.
Federal Law concerning paid educational leave for worker representatives (Enterprise Constitution Act)	80**	72**	n.a.
Provisions for Paid Educational Leave in other Laws	n.a.	n.a.	n.a.
Paid Education Leave according to Collective Bargaining Agreements	n.a.	n.a.	n.a.
Paid Leave for Continuing and Retraining (Federal Labor Promotion Act)		1,498	752,000

SOURCES: Federal Employment Office, Promotion of Training, Participants Statistics (December 1981).
*Numbers have been rounded.
**Own estimates.

unions). It is extremely difficult to quantify the amount of public funds contributed in this way to the financing of education and training leave, especially since such funds come from federal, state, and local budgets rather than from a single source. However, it can be assumed that these public subsidies are substantial.

Problems in this area of financing arise at two levels. First, small firms often find it difficult to release a worker and then to face the problem of maintaining his wage during his absence while it is easier for large enterprises to cope with replacements and the financial burden. This problem is reflected in the participation data which show that workers from larger firms are overrepresented and those from small firms are underrepresented. In order to remedy the financial burden on the small firm, it had been suggested in the discussion and debate on legislation on paid educational leave in Bremen and in Hesse that a hardship fund that would reimburse about half of the expenditure incurred by small firms on wages during such leave should be created. This idea was not adopted, but it is clear that the present mode of financing places small firms—and hence workers from such firms—at a disadvantage.

The second problem concerns the participants to the extent that they are left with part of the cost for instruction and other course-related costs. Although courses are often fully subsidized from either public sources or from the sponsors (e.g., union funds) still some costs are incurred that are not met by these subsidies. While a minor financial contribution on the part of the participant may not be a problem for the average employee, it might constitute a real barrier to those who are financially less well-off (Kiausch and Schenk, 1978).

LABOR MARKET EFFECTS

From the discussion of costs and who has to shoulder them, we now turn to the question of whether or not present paid educational leave schemes have concrete labor market effects, and how these effects can be quantified. Ironically, the main points of this discussion were formulated at a time when labor supply was a problem and the opposition to leave laws on the part of employers was partly based on the argument that the implementation of leave laws would create considerable supply problems.

Over the last few years, in Germany as in the rest of the Western industrialized countries characterized by excessive labor supply, this question has been taken up by the unions and widely used in favor of paid educational leave. Various model calculations have been put forward that suggest that paid educational leave could in fact be used as a labor market instrument in that it would reduce actual labor supply. While most of these calculations concerning the quantitative effects of educational leave schemes tend to equalize the amount of hours lost and the additional demand, it is fair to assume that the net demand is considerably lower. It is natural that enterprises will tend to keep additional hiring (and hence costs) to a minimum and will thus try to compensate by means of temporary changes in work organization and the mobilization and better utilization of existing human resources.

Thus the Institute of Labor Market Research (which is attached to the Federal Employment Institute) has estimated that the potential net employment effect of leave schemes is less than half of the calculated increase in demand (Reyer et al., 1979).

However, these calculations remain largely theoretical as long as participation is as low as it is at present and the full potential of paid educational leave for relieving the pressures of labor supply is not really put to a test. Nevertheless, it can probably be assumed that the employment effect would remain relatively small, even if the participation rate were higher, as long as the size of the leave entitlement remains at the present level (i.e., one week per year). But even with this level of entitlement, the necessity for an employer to hire additional labor might be greater than at present if entitlements could be accumulated over a number of years thus enabling the employee to take more sizeable periods of leave. The maximum leave time is currently two years.

A final word must be said concerning the order of magnitude of educational leave entitlements. When considering their employment effects, their relative importance should be assessed against the background of other kinds of leave entitlements. These have steadily grown in Germany over the last few years, and the total average annual leave entitlement for salaried employees was almost six weeks (30 working days) in 1981. In addition, there are 12 official holidays per year, and several special leave entitlements for certain groups such as handicapped employees who are entitled by law to another six working days of annual leave. Effective yearly working time has thus been reduced to 211.4 working days in 1978, compared to 248.3 in 1960 (Reyer et al., 1979). It is in this context that paid educational leave at present levels can be said to have comparatively marginal effects on labor supply.

CONCLUDING REMARKS

It has been argued in some quarters that given the relatively generous annual leave entitlement in Germany compared, for example, with the United States, there is no real need for additional leave for educational purposes, and hence the low level of utilization. Educational leave, however, cannot be treated as a holiday, any more than, for instance, an apprenticeship or studies for a college degree could be. And it is obvious that skilled automobile workers, even with six weeks of annual leave, cannot normally be expected to use their leave to enroll in a short-term education or training course, even if such a course were available and accessible. But reasoning that treats educational leave the same as other sorts of leave illustrates the current lack of understanding and acceptance of the need for educational leave.

This may be one reason that paid educational leave has not lived up to its potential or to the hopes of its proponents, but it is not the only reason. The low degree of utilization is also influenced by the lack of educational and training offerings that are suited to the needs and expectations of adults, particularly adults with little or no more than compulsory schooling. The lack of individual motivation and self-confidence with respect to organized learning is probably more of a barrier to participation than pressure from employers, although the fear of negative sanctions in times of high unemployment must not be underestimated. In order to overcome this barrier, the federal government has therefore sponsored some extensive model programs in which the needs, interest, and motivation of special target groups (e.g. young people, migrant workers, women, the unskilled or semiskilled, industrial workers) have been studied and evaluated in order to assess which kinds of outreach, counseling, and course content can best reach these groups.

Paid educational leave in Germany is at a beginning. Except for the important continuing and retraining program under the Labor Promotion Act and the special leave for members of the enterprise councils, educational leave is still marginal in quantitative terms. However, the level of participation, although still very low, has been steadily growing since the right to educational leave was first introduced. It can probably be expected that the introduction of a general legal right to educational leave in the populous industrial State of Northrhine Westfalia will provide new momentum and lead to greater recognition of learning as a lifelong process and of educational leave of absence as an important instrument for the widespread implementation of this general principle.

REFERENCES

ADAMS, R. J., P. M. DRAPER, and C. DUCHAME (1979) Educationa and Working Canadians: Report of the Commission of Inquiry on Educational Leave and Productivity. Ottawa: Ministry of Supply and Services.

College Entrance Examination Board (1979) The Educational System in the Federal Republic of Germany. New York: Secretariat of the Standing Conference of Ministers of Education.

DEGEN, G. R. (1980) Bildungsurlaub (Educational Leave of Absence). Dusseldorf: Landesinstitut fur Curriculumentrwicklung, Lehrerfortbildung und Weiterbildung.

GÖRS, D. (1982) "Erfahrungen und sozio-okonomische Probleme der Bildungsurlaubsregelungen in der Bundesrepublic Deutschland" ("Experience with Educational Leave in the Federal Republic and Related Socio-Economic Problems"), in D. Kuhlenkamp and H. G. Schütze (eds.) Kosten und Finanzierung der beruflichen und nicht-beruflichen Weiterbildung (The Costs and Financing of Continuing Education and Training). Frankfurt Main: Diesterweg.

——— (1978) Zur politischen Kontroverse um den Bildungsurlaub (The Political Controversy about Educational Leave). Cologne.

HÖNIGSBERGER, H. (1977) Bildungsurlaub nach Gesetz (Legal Provision for Educational Leave). Heidelberg: Arbeitsgruppe fur empirische Bildungsforschung.

KIAUSCH, U. and P. SCHENK (1978) Bildungsurlaub nach Tarifvertragen (Provision for Educational Leave in Collective Agreements). Weinheim: Beltz.

KUHLENKAMP, D. and H. G. SCHÜTZE [eds.] (1982) Kosten und Finanzierung der beruflichen und nicht-beruflichen Weiterbildung (The Costs and Financing of Continuing Education and Training). Frankfurt Main: Diesterweg.

MUSHKIN, S. [ed.] (1973) Recurrent Education. Washington, DC: U.S. Government Printing Office.

OECD/CERI (1978) Alternation Between Work and Education: A Study of Educational Leave of Absence at Enterprise Level. Paris: Author.

OECD/CERI (1976) Developments in Educational Leave of Absence. Paris: Author.

REYER, L., H. U. BACH, H. KOHLER, and B. TERIET (1979) "Arbeitszeit und Arbeitsmarkt-Volumenrechnung, Auslastungsgrad und Entlastungswirkung" ("Working Time and the Labour Market-Volume Calculations, Degree of Utilization and Net Employment Effects"). Mitteilungen aus der Arbeits und Berufsforschung 3/1979: 381-400.

SCHÜTZE, H. G. (1982) "Das OECD-Konzept 'Recurrent Education' und Kriterien fur die Finanzierung lebenslangen Lernens" ("The OECD Concept of Recurrent Education and Criteria for Financing Lifelong Learning"), in D. Kuhlenkamp and H. G. Schütze (eds.) Kosten und Finanzierung der beruflichen und nicht-beruflichen Weiterbildung (The Costs and Financing of Continuing Education and Training). Frankfurt Main: Diesterweg.

STRINER, H. E. (1972) Continuing Education as a National Investment. Washington, DC: W.E. Upjohn Institute for Employment Research.

TIMMERMANN, D. (1982) "Das Staatsfinanzierungsmodell als Finanzierungsalternative fur Recurrent Education (The State Financing Model as an Alternative to Financing Recurrent Education"), in D. Kuhlenkamp and H. G. Schütze (eds.) Kosten und Finanzierung der beruflichen und nicht-beruflichen Weiterbildung (The Costs and Financing of Continuing Education and Training). Frankfurt Main: Diesterweg.

VON MOLTKE, K. and N. SCHNEEVOIGT (1977) Educational Leave for Employees: European Experience for American Consideration. San Francisco: Jossey-Bass.

14

PAID EDUCATIONAL LEAVE
A Proposal Based on the Dutch Case

LOUIS EMMERIJ

Paid educational leave has the advantage of meeting a variety of societal objectives. Depending on the economic and social situation, some of those objectives should be given greater stress than others. For this reason, paid educational leave will be explored for its implications in addressing unemployment. It is my contention that the industrialized countries will be quite unable during the 1980s to return to full employment as it is defined today. This has much to do with the slowdown in the rate of economic growth in the industrialized countries relative to the number of people who enter the labor market in search of employment in the majority of Western industrialized countries.

The rate of economic growth will not be such that full employment can be maintained given present technologies and in particular the forthcoming microelectronic and information revolution. If it is impossible to create enough jobs, something different must be done to reduce unemployment. Constructive interventions on the supply side of the labor market must be flexible however; if, during the 1980s for example, a different labor market situation emerges—given demographic tendencies—it must be possible to adjust policy measures on the supply side of the labor market accordingly. This is an important constraint on any search to identify such measures for reducing unemployment. The debate has only just started in the countries of the OECD, and although much has been heard about measures such as shortening the working week and early retirement, no clear line of action has yet emerged.

PROPOSAL FOR A FLEXIBLE MIX OF WORK, RECURRENT EDUCATION, AND LEISURE TIME.

A different and more comprehensive approach is required to reduce the amount of time that individuals spend in the labor market during their life spans. Such an approach would not be limited to relatively unimportant measures of labor market policy, but would consist of a more global package including educational policies, labor market policies, and social policies, combined with economic restructuring and development cooperation policies.[1]

Consequently, a social and cultural policy package must be proposed in addition to purely economic proposals. The foremost characteristic of the new package is that its progressive policy would maximize the opportunity for an individual to increase his or her control over shaping careers and life patterns relative to the present. Such a global approach must also be able to deal with the allocation of labor, but as a byproduct rather than as its major—or even sole—objective. Therefore one must ask what the countours would be of such a global approach to the unemployment problem in industrialized countries.

The life of an individual is divided into three parts, separated in most countries by impermeable partitions:

(1) the period spent at school and, for the more fortunate, at a university;

(2) active life, whether spent on the labor market or not and whether remunerated or not;

(3) the retirement period.

These periods follow one another sequentially. We go to school at an early age and remain there until age 16 or 18 (depending on the country) or, in the case of university students, very often to the age of 25 or even older. Then we enter the period of so-called active life until the age of 60 to 65 when we are kindly but firmly asked to take retirement. It is very difficult—particularly in most European countries—to reverse the sequence of these three events. It is the essence of a system of recurrent education to transform this rigid sequential system into a more flexible recurrent system in which it will be possible to combine or alternate periods of education, work, and retirement throughout one's adult life.

The idea of recurrent education that spans the first two periods of life mentioned above was launched some 10 years ago and has been discussed ever since. The complementary idea of retirement "a là carte" (freely selected by each individual) has been discussed less frequently, but it is the logical extension and the mirror image of recurrent education because it encompasses the second and third periods. Individuals could even be given the opportunity to combine all three periods by, for example, taking a period at age 30 of six months of anticipated retirement in order to continue or resume further education. Although this sounds extremely straightforward and simple, in reality it amounts to a social and cultural change of the first order.

The advantages of such an approach for the various partners, social and individual, in OECD countries is important to stress. In the first place, this much more flexible approach would enable an equally flexible labor market policy to be introduced that would have advantages both for employers and for workers. The employers would obtain a labor force that could be more easily and more quickly retrained in response to technological changes; the workers would have easier and more frequent chances to reorient themselves.

The educational system as it exists at present is extremely rigid and has long time lags between policy changes and outcomes. These were some of the reasons why in the 1950s and 1960s forecasts of occupational and educational structures of the labor force became fashionable. These long-term forecasts reflected the long gestation periods inherent in the educational production process. Indeed, it takes approximately six years to complete each of the main levels of the educational system. Hence, the school will react very slowly to changes in technology, and this in turn has implications for the required skill structure of the labor force.

Experience has shown that it is almost impossible to make more or less reliable long-term forecasts of the occupational and educational structures of the labor force. It is therefore much more realistic and desirable to shorten the gestation periods because by doing so, the educational system will become more adaptable. In other words, the relationship between school and work will become closer, more effective, and more beneficial to all parties.

In the second place, there is a specific advantage to the individual in terms of self-fulfillment and of being able to better realize his or her full potential. We know that motivation occurs at very different moments in a person's life and not necessarily at those points in time required by the sequential educational system. Educational opportunities and achievements will definitely be enhanced if individuals can go back to school when they are motivated to do so instead of being pushed by parents or by other persons in authority to remain in school. In the present setup it is difficult to return to school after having dropped out.

What is true for educational opportunities is equally true for occupational and income opportunities. In the global approach favored here, one has more than one occasion to orient (or reorient) oneself in the labor market. Furthermore, individuals can be offered a period of anticipatory retirement earlier in life during which they do not necessarily have to return to school but can do other things that they are strongly motivated to do at that particular time.

In the third place, its flexibility also makes the suggested approach an effective anticyclical weapon. At times when a particularly strong but temporary economic storm flails our countries, more people could be encouraged to withdraw for a while from the labor force in order to benefit from recurrent education or from a sabbatical period.

In the fourth place (and this is also an antistructural weapon) fewer people on average will be in the labor market at each point in time than is presently the case because people will, on the average, spend more of this time in the first and third blocks of their life rather than the second. In this way, the total labor supply will be reduced.

Thus the approach advocated here is on the one hand a generalization of traditional trade union demands for shorter working hours, more holidays, and earlier retirement and, on the other hand, supportive of the more recent proposals with respect to part-time work, the sharing of jobs, and rationing of the labor supply in general.

This global approach thus kills several birds with one stone: Economic structural limits for once will be consistent with the sociocultural objectives of the individual. Instead of a diminishing majority that works harder and harder and an increasing minority that is expelled shamefully from the labor market, it is proposed here that available work be rationed more intelligently and more comprehensively than it has been so far.

POLICY REQUIREMENTS

Next, let us look at the various changes that will be required if we are to move toward these new policies. First, it is necessary to introduce a system of recurrent education following the compulsory schooling period. There are however many definitions of recurrent education. For many it is a second chance that is parallel to the full-time formal educational system. This is definitely not the case. Recurrent education, as it has been conceptualized, is a comprehensive and flexible post-compulsory educational system that combines the present formal educational branches and various types of adult education. Recurrent education, therefore, does not necessarily imply the creation of additional types of education and training, but rather the integration of the existing types into one harmonious whole.

In order to speak about recurrent education, four conditions must be met:

- it must be able to receive people from all age groups beyond compulsory school age;
- it must be one integrated education and training system;
- it must offer "educational units" of variable and flexible duration that can be used as building blocks for and stepping stones toward a diploma or degree; and
- it must have exit possibilities at different levels, all of which are to be awarded with a diploma or degree.

With respect to the first point, it is to be expected that most youngsters who decide at the age of 17 or 18 to postpone the continuation of their studies for a while, will resume their schooling between age 20 and 30. This makes sense from an individual and therefore private rate-of-return point of view. It also makes sense from the macroeconomic and therefore social rate-of-return viewpoint. Were people to decide to start their university education at for example 55, they could not expect to receive important material returns in terms of income during the rest of their lifetime—and neither could society. It is to be expected that as people grow older, they will prefer to use stretches of anticipatory retirement in order to do things other than return to school.

The second point is important because in the approach suggested here, individuals must be able to travel along alternative educational paths and still achieve the same educational goal. People must have the opportunity to obtain the same "credits" by spending, for example, 52 long weekends at school as by attending full-time education during a period of three to four months. This flexibility must be built into the recurrent system or it will not be able to cope with the increased variety of students and circumstances.

This is much more easily said than done—hence the third point: the need for educational units that in relatively short time periods can provide a well-rounded part of a given educational career. The student or participant can thus build up credits in a flexible manner. Since they contribute to the total credits necessary to obtain a particular diploma or degree, they can not be viewed as isolated experiences. The fourth and last point refers to the necessity for recurrent education to have exit possibilities at different levels so that we do not fall into the "all-or-nothing" trap of current educational systems.

In summary, the educational characteristics of the recurrent education system suggested here are as follows:

- to hold as many options open for as long a period as possible;
- to transfer to a later age the emphasis on pursuing higher levels of education in order to interrupt the current tendency to spend more and more years of education in the existing sequential system even when there is no real desire to do so;
- to integrate formal and nonformal types of education.

The next component is the labor market policy. The proposals advocated here will have positive effects on the structural, cyclical, and individual levels of labor market policy. These have been mentioned above, so a brief reference will suffice here.

On the structural plane, recurrent education will be instrumental in creating a better linkage between the changing skills that are required and the educational and training supply delivered by this recurrent educational system. There is no doubt that one of the more important structural problems faced in industrialized countries—namely, the growing disparity between skills required and qualifications supplied—will be effectively countered by this system of recurrent education.

On the cyclical plane, the government can use appropriate incentives to stimulate more people to leave the labor force temporarily during an ebb tide in the economy. Even more precise targets can be attained. For instance, the government could well direct such measures to a specific sector of the economy or to specific groups of workers in the labor force. This could be done by giving higher financial rewards to people working in that sector or in that specific group—higher rewards for withdrawing for a given period of time into education or training. In other words, paid educational leave need not necessarily be the same from one group to another, from one sector to another, or from one period of time to another.

On the individual plane the advantages for individuals to reenter the labor market or to change within it are obvious and reflect those mentioned under the structural and cyclical components. There is, however, one additional point which needs to be emphasized: the possibility of obtaining an orientation period on the labor market between the termination of one's compulsory schooling and the start of recurrent education and training. During this period youngsters who have not yet firmly decided on their professional career would be able to explore various job opportunities. This would replace the training periods of today—training periods which are very often neither education, nor training, nor work, but rather are an unsatisfactory combination of all three.

A third dimension of this package concerns income distribution. What would the implications of the system of recurrent education and leave be for the income distribution of OECD countries? The "perverse" effects on tertiary income distribution of additional educational and other facilities have frequently been noted. Indeed, in most cases education is provided at low cost to the student through government subsidies that come from taxes paid by all. On the other hand, those who attend higher levels of education frequently come from the higher social classes. Such a situation is a clear example of how the poor subsidize the rich. This is one illustration of the perverse effects of providing not only education but also health and other facilities at subsidized prices. Care must therefore be taken that paid educational leave is granted as a matter of priority to those who have not been able to benefit optimally from educational facilities when young. In other words, a positive discrimination must be introduced in order to offset the perverse effects.

With respect to income distribution, Jan Tinbergen has drawn on time series from the Netherlands to show that education has expanded faster than warranted on purely economic and technological grounds. This apparent educational oversupply has resulted in a narrowing of income disparities between people with different levels of educational attainment (Tinbergen, 1975). If his conclusions are correct and can be generalized to situations in other countries, it would follow that recurrent education could have further positive implications for income distribution while at the same time it could maintain a somewhat better balance between the demand for skills and the supply of qualified workers.

A fourth dimension of the proposed plan for recurrent education would be to create a better work climate. The genuine opportunity to withdraw occasionally from the labor force is likely to diminish the number of those who declare themselves sick or otherwise unfit for work. Absenteeism due to sickness is a growing problem in most countries. Very often it is due to the fact that people work for too long a period under great stress. The safety valve provided by voluntary withdrawal could make a big difference.

Moreover, people who withdraw voluntarily from the labor force are in a very different psychological situation relative to those who are forcefully expelled. Pressure on health facilities can therefore be expected to diminish, implying a considerable saving of money in the health and welfare sectors—money that can contribute to financing the proposed recurrent education scheme. Finally, this policy package will almost necessarily imply the harmonization of the entire social security system. This also means that the great variety of pension schemes now in existence must be integrated in such a way that people are no longer confronted with bureaucratic problems concerning the right to retirement benefits when moving from one firm to another or from one job to another.

THE FINANCING OF PAID EDUCATIONAL LEAVE

Many may be inclined to think that the approach proposed in this chapter is a positive way by which to alleviate unemployment by redefining the concept of full employment. On the other hand, the costs involved might be such as to render its realization unlikely, particularly if large numbers of people were to be involved during the initial stages of introducing paid educational leave, as probably would be the case. Part of the solution would be to use the money now invested in social security schemes of all kinds to finance the proposed recurrent education and leave schemes.

Two groups will benefit from the approach advocated here: first, youth who proceed immediately to the new forms of recurrent education after completing compulsory education; and second, those who, after having worked for a certain period of time, withdraw voluntarily into a period of paid leave.

The financing of these groups will come from different sources. The cost of the first is now carried by the Dutch Ministry of Education's budget, combined with tax and other facilities granted to the parents involved. In the approach advocated here, the financial resources, insofar as they come from different budgets, will need to be centralized. In practice, this will amount to granting a student salary and to replacing present taxes and other provisions.

During periods of paid leave, the incomes of those in the second category must come from the amounts that are now paid through social security arrangements to people who are involuntarily expelled from the labor market. These people include not only the registered unemployed but also a portion of those who are declared unfit for work or on prolonged "sick leave."

Calculations have been made for the Netherlands regarding people who receive unemployment benefits, unfit-for-work benefits, and sickness insurance, but who should in reality be classified as "structurally unemployed." In other words, these groups consist of people who are either openly unemployed or are unemployed in a more or less disguised manner, and who find themselves in those categories because of the structural unemployment problem in the industrialized world. The essence of such calculations is to estimate the number of people that can withdraw voluntarily into paid educational leave at any point in time without additional costs being incurred by society, as compared to the present expenses involved in unemployment and social security schemes of all kinds to ensure the incomes of those who comprise the unemployed.

In estimating the potential size of the group that could take advantage of paid educational leave in the Netherlands, one must start by examining the number of young people of age 17 or over who are at present in the educational system. (In the Netherlands the number is approximately 350,000.) Next, the total amount of structurally unemployed people must be estimated, most of whom are hidden in a variety of social insurance schemes. The situation in the Netherlands is illustrated in Table 14.1, which includes a breakdown of the 377,000 people at present in a position of structural unemployment.

The social insurance categories according to which these people are paid are indicated by numbers I-IV because the exact names would have little meaning to foreign readers. Categories I and II represent those social security programs that accommodate people who are declared unfit for work. Category I was introduced fairly recently and it includes most cases in which people who had working accidents or otherwise are unable to continue working for some period of time. Category II includes those who are in reality quite fit for work, but are often put under this umbrella for humanitarian reasons. (Approximately 50% of those so classified are in this group.) For example, about half of the labor force in the age bracket 55-64 are found in this category. It is unlikely that all these people are disabled, and the only realistic explanation is that doctors tend more easily to certify people in that age

TABLE 14.1 Estimated Possible Withdrawals from the Labor Market Without Additional Cost (in 1000s): 1976

Social Insurance Group	*Total Number*	*Number of Which Are Structurally Unemployed*
I	93	20
II	380	190
III	244	112
IV	222	55
Total	939	377
Pupils and students of age 17 and over		350+
People who could potentially make use of paid educational leave		727

SOURCE: Emmerij and Clobus (1978).

group as "unfit for work" when they are in any case about to lose their jobs. Since it is extremely difficult for such people to find new employment and since the amount of income received under Category II is favorable as compared to unemployment benefits, it stands to reason that this category hides large numbers of people who otherwise would be openly unemployed.

Category III is that of the openly unemployed. It is estimated that half of the people to be found here are structurally unemployed, and the other half are cyclically unemployed. In other words, it is concluded that in a country such as the Netherlands there will always be about 100,000 persons who are *frictionally* unemployed.

Category IV represents those who are "absent through sickness for longer than three days." Actual absenteeism through sickness in the Netherlands is double the amount given in Table 14.1, but most people report back to work within one to three days. A conservative estimate is that approximately 25% of these people are on "avoidable" sickness leave and thus fall under the category of structurally unemployed.

This leads to the astonishing outcome that close to 1 million members of the Dutch labor force are absent from work at any point in time—about 20% of the total labor force. Out of this large number, about

377,000 are absent because of structural unemployment. If 350,000 pupils and students aged 17 and over are added, the potential size of the group that could make use of paid educational leave without additional costs being incurred by society is 727,000 people. In other words, close to 730,000 people in the Netherlands could make use of recurrent education through paid educational leave and receive between 75 and 85% of their most recent income, or a student salary. This would not represent a greater financial outlay than is now found in the budgets of the Ministry of Education and Sciences and of Social Affairs respectively.

Instead of spending the billions of guilders involved for *negative* reasons—expelling people from their working environment or forcing young people to remain at school while the majority would prefer to do something else before eventually returning to the educational system—the same amount of money could be used for *positive* reasons. This approach creates a new form of income maintenance for periods of inactivity. The difference is that involuntary inactivity for some (normally the weaker groups in society) is replaced by voluntary periods of nonwork for all.

The reasoning so far has focused on the financing of people's income during periods of voluntary withdrawal from the labor force. It has been stated that there are no *additional* costs involved as long as one substitutes a positive use of social security funds for the present negative use. This does not mean that no *other* costs are involved.

For example, it is likely that more educational facilities in terms of buildings and teachers will need to be provided. But here again, one must first look at the existing capacity. The Netherlands is experiencing demographic changes that will result in smaller numbers of youth. This, in turn, will have consequences for the employment of primary and secondary school teachers and for the utilization of school buildings. The education industry, like many other industrial branches, no longer functions at full capacity. Buildings remain empty and many school teachers are unemployed.

In such circumstances, it would again be comparatively inexpensive to make use of existing idle capacity to enable more people to return to school through paid educational leave. This example is given to indicate that additional costs caused by introducing a scheme like the one presented need not be as disastrously high as opponents might suggest.

Returning to the utilization of social security funds for the financing of educational leave, there are clearly a certain number of problems, but also possibilities. First, one might wonder whether it is realistic and indeed responsible to use funds that are typically used to remedy cyclical difficulties for the solution of structural problems. In other words, the argument is that such funds are meant to help people in periods of difficulty that are normally of limited duration—for example, sickness or working accidents that make people unfit for work for a few weeks or a few months at the most, or unemployment of the frictional type.

In the present proposal, these funds are largely set aside for educational leave that is meant to be with us forever albeit for rotating groups of people. This argument is valid as far as it goes. However, social security monies are used more often to alleviate or to hide structural unemployment problems; this assertion has been quantified in Table 14.1. The statement that these funds are used mainly for cyclical purposes thus already seems questionable. In actuality, social security funds are increasingly used to face up to a structural unemployment situation which, as explained earlier in this chapter, will surely last throughout the 1980s. This being so, it would be more honest to recognize this fact and to separate out those funds that are to be used for cyclical purposes as opposed to the rest, as has been done in Table 14.1.

Some people, while agreeing with the reasoning so far, will continue to argue in favor of using the structural portion of the funds for the creation of employment, particularly in the public sector, rather than "throwing it away in favor of educational leave." Of course, the creation of employment opportunities must remain a top priority. But what is to be done when maximal effort in that respect is not sufficient to supply all those who present themselves on the labor market with productive work? *Productive work* is indeed the key phrase. We would presumably not be interested in simply creating jobs at any price, if they are jobs of the most unproductive and unnecessary kind. It may be much better and also more productive to use the structural money not only to give people the opportunity to return to the educational system but also time to do other things (voluntary activities in the public sector, for example).

The educational part of creative leave would make people more productive, more flexible, and in general more inclined to follow and anticipate changes in their work environment. The noneducational part of creative leave would enable individuals to channel themselves into activities that they themselves consider to be useful. The chances are high that such activities will at the same time be more useful, and therefore more productive, for society at large than the creation of hosts of additional jobs in the public sector which would then become top-heavy as well as increasingly bureaucratized and tainted by interest groups and other lobbies. This debate between those who favor expansion of the public sector through means imposed by the government on the one hand, and those who want to give opportunities and insights to individuals on the other, will become one of the principle controversies of the 1980s, amongst all of the existing political parties.

Legal constraints are a second problem in proposing to use social security funds for more positive purposes such as educational or creative leave. In some countries, for example, if an unemployed person types a letter to a sick relative and an inspector happens to look through the window while he is doing so, that person risks losing his unemployment insurance because he will be accused of working. In the case of the Netherlands, where stringent regulations also hold, there is a clear tendency to take a more positive view towards the flexible use of social security funds, including their use for educational purposes.

A third problem (or possibility) concerns the introduction of incentives and disincentives to stimulate certain groups in society to take educational leave or discourage others. Policy measures on the supply side of the labor market must be sufficiently flexible and even reversible since it is possible that as early as the 1990s we may face a totally different situation on the labor market. In other words, the concern is with the general problem of how to ensure that the "right" number of people with the "right" composition withdraw voluntarily from the labor market at any point in time.

Overall, the total number of people involved might be influenced by changing the percentage of income to be paid: Instead of proposing the payment during the leave period of, for example, 80% of the latest income, this could be increased to 85% and in certain cases even to 90% in order to make it more attractive for more people to take the opportunity. The economic particulars could be differentiated—for example, by proposing a higher percentage for people who want to enroll in educational courses that are in high demand on the labor market than for those who want to go elsewhere. Along the same lines, people working in certain economic sectors could be stimulated more than those working in other branches of economic activity. These steering mechanisms, which any government has at its disposal, should be used to the fullest extent; in fact, the possibility of doing so is one of the original features of this proposal.

Finally, there is the problem of how to implement the whole scheme, assuming that all other obstacles have been cleared. If the proposal is to be of any real benefit to the employment problem, it is essential that people who are not in productive employment decide at the outset to take up educational leave. But that is not all. Not only must there be many initial recruits, but their working places must be taken up by people who are now unemployed. Only in this way can structural unemployment be replaced in due course by educational or creative leave. Otherwise, we shall be faced with an accumulation of structural unemployment *and* educational leave. The whole proposal would then break down.

Therefore, a matching problem presents itself: How can we make sure that those who withdraw voluntarily into educational leave have more or less the same qualifications as those who are at present unemployed? In this connection, it is clear that one must begin by convincing those workers with the lowest educational and training backgrounds to remove themselves from the labor market. This will serve two purposes: First, these are the people for whom educational leave is relatively the most useful; second, it is in this category that we find the bulk of the unemployed. In other words, the matching problem in this situaton would be much easier than in any other, and also more productive. The question of how the initial recruits and all those who take advantage of educational leave thereafter can ever be reinserted into the labor market is very easy to answer. Once the operation has started, a group of people will be away from the labor market at any point in time. This will be an ever-changing, rotating group; by the time the initial recruits return from their educational leave, another group will have just gone into voluntary retirement. Their places will therefore be vacated and will be refilled by the initial recruits, and so on.

THE DEBATE IN THE NETHERLANDS

The question of paid educational leave and its sources of finance has been presented from my perspective. The point at which official discussions in the Netherlands have arrived shall now be considered.

The Dutch government ratified the ILO Convention on Paid Educational Leave 140 on 14 September 1976. One year later, in September of 1977, at the request of the Minister of Social Affairs and of several of his colleagues, the Committee on Paid Educational Leave within the framework of the tripartite Social-Economic Council was installed. In October 1978, this committee presented to the government a unanimous first report in which it set out the general guidelines for the introduction of paid educational leave into Dutch society.

From the outset, the Committee on Paid Educational Leave has given a broader interpretation to its mandate than can be found in the ILO Convention 140. Paid educational leave in the ILO convention 140 refers only to leave granted to a worker for absence from the working place during a given period of time in order to benefit from schooling and/or training. The committee considered that since the convention had been accepted in Geneva in 1974 quite a few things had changed in Dutch society in particular and in the industrialized countries in general that made it necessary to look at the target population in a broader manner. The following are some of the considerations that guided the committee to this conclusion:

- the fact that the unemployment problem has become more serious since 1974;
- the low participation in the labor force of women in the Netherlands as compared to surrounding countries;
- an increased demand for adult education suggesting that many groups in the Dutch population who missed educational opportunities earlier in their lives now want another chance;
- the discovery that a significant percentage of the Dutch population can neither read nor write, in spite of compulsory education;
- the fact that during the last few years the Netherlands has been confronted increasingly with the problem of minority groups in the population, while the phenomenon of migrant workers seems to have become a permanent feature.

In summary, one is unavoidably led to the conclusion that it would not be justifiable to distinguish between the working population on the one hand, and the rest of Dutch society on the other.

Hence, the committee's declaration that paid educational leave must, as a matter of principle, benefit all groups of the population *and* cover all educational programs. Moreover, the committee has stated that this broad approach must be obvious from the start. In other words, in the initial phase of the introduction of paid educational leave, the target groups should include not only workers, but also other categories who will be given first priority to benefit from such leave. The committee has explicitly stated that *the entire Dutch population* must eventually be able to benefit. It is understandable that this ultimate goal cannot be reached overnight. Therefore, the committee has had to indicate its initial priorities. As has already been implied, paid educational leave in the Netherlands will begin by identifying target groups and providing them with a significant period of leave and a wide choice of educational programs. In other words, the committee wants to start with a few groups of the population, but wants to give these groups periods of paid educational leave of a meaningful duration which can be spent in schools of their own unrestricted choice.

The first and main criterion established by the committee for selecting these target groups is that the educational gap between population categories should not be increased. This implies that positive discrimination is necessary. If such precautions are not taken, a well-known phenomenon is bound to occur; namely, those who recognize the benefits of the additional opportunities and are ready to take advantage of them are as a rule those groups who already have better education and better incomes. These people have "learned to learn." This aspect makes education a self-cumulating and reinforcing process for groups with better educational backgrounds. People with little education are more likely to regard anything new with apprehension and even distrust—not because they are not interested, but usually because they do not immediately recognize what it holds for them. This gives the impression that they are less interested than those with a better education.

The fact that the committee decided to use the levels of education and income as its main criteria (people with low education and income levels will thus be the first to be presented with the possibilities of paid educational leave) means that a campaign must be started to inform and stimulate the target groups.

The next significant criterion that was used in selecting the target groups for the first phase of paid educational leave is the necessity to select a broad sample of population groups and not only workers. The more detailed results of this selection process and the five target groups that were ultimately chosen are shown in Table 14.2.

Turning now to financing aspects of paid educational leave, the committee reached the conclusion that the main source of finance had to be government funds because of the broad and representative selection of societal groups. If only workers had been selected, it would have been natural to discuss at length whether employers should pay or at least make a significant contribution. In the Netherlands, however, as Table 14.2 shows, there are significant target groups who are not in the labor force. The only way to make a start with educational leave and to ensure

TABLE 14.2 Target Groups for Initial Phase of Paid Educational Leave

	Categories			
Target Groups	*Workers*	*Self-Employed*	*Social Security Beneficiaries*	*Other*
I. Lowest education (secondary modern or lower technical school at most) including women	Lowest educated, including migrant workers and elderly workers in prepen-sioning-off phase	Lowest educated self-employed, people in agricultural, horti-cultural, and middle-income classes (mostly small shopkeepers and tradespeople)		Lowest educated without wage-losses and nonsocial-security beneficiaries
II. Long term unem-ployed and unfit for work (including women)		Social Security cate-gory I*	Social Security categories I, II, and III*	
III. Women			Social Security category III*	In households, or helping in their own (or husbands') shops
IV. Threatened by unemployment	In enterprises confronted by merger, rationalization, or closing down	In enterprises confronted by merger, rationalization, or closing down		
V. Other				

*See Table 14.1.

that this will be the beginning of a continuous and sustained movement is to make the financing independent of sources that cannot be counted on as always available at the required levels.

Starting from this general point, the committee declared itself to be in favor of using social security funds in order to facilitate procedures in times of great pressure on the public budget. It is true that the committee has done so prudently by emphasizing the fact that target group II (see Table 14.2) should be allowed to use its income out of social security funds to take up educational leave. In this respect, the committee's proposal is more modest than the one proposed in this chapter. However, it is interesting to note the reaction of the Dutch Social Security Council to questions put before it by the Committee on Paid Educational Leave. The main observations of the Social Security Council regarding the use that may be made of its funds for purposes of educational leave are the following:

(1) If participation in educational leave is consistent with the compulsion that the unemployed have to get back to work as soon as possible, it can be maintained that educational leave contributes to shortening the period of their dependency on unemployment insurance payments in the long run. In such circumstances, educational leave would therefore be fully consistent with the goals of the council's funds. In other words, if reinsertion into the labor market is the prime motive for educational leave, there is no problem whatsoever in using social security funds.

(2) In general, educational leave could be financed through social security funds by stating that persons are entitled to such an income during the period of their educational leave, and by requiring that the social security funds grant them a subsidy.

Concerning the first of these positions, it should be borne in mind that when we are faced with educational leave *during regular employment,* present legal constraints are such that social security funds are not automatically available. The Social Security Council however, has made a point of stating that possibilities *do* exist in principle, even within the present legal framework, but that a special case must be made for each individual. With respect to the second position, a new piece of legislation must be introduced for this to become a realistic proposition.

This initial reaction by the Social Security Council is important in that it is evidently willing to take considerable steps toward a system of financing recurrent education and is in fact already going somewhat further than the recommendation made by the Committee on Paid Educational Leave.

CONCLUDING REMARKS

What has been proposed in this chapter amounts to profound changes in the social and cultural domains of society with a view to achieving a better balance between remumerative work and other aspects of human life. If these changes can be brought about, the employment problem could also largely be solved.

In the face of lower rates of economic growth and continuing upward trends in technology and labor productivity, we must move from a defensive to a constructive attitude. The proposed policy package combines a progressive policy with restoration of maximum initiatives to the individual.

It has been shown that the proposed changes can be financed from existing public funds by changing their purpose and destination. Only few, if any, additional funds will be required. The proposed changes will be *equitable,* partly because of the built-in positive-discriminatory component. Equal educational opportunites for everyone will be advanced and income distribution will consequently become less skewed. Weaker groups in society, who are now becoming more and more vulnerable, will become stronger as they are given additional opportunities to return to education and other forms of self-development.

The proposed measure will also be *efficient* because it will boost labor productivty and improve the working climate. It will also increase the flexibility of the labor market and facilitate adjustments to technological changes.

NOTE

1. This proposal is duscussed in more detail in Emmerij and Clobus (1978). Later in this chapter I shall compare my personal opinions on the matter with the ideas of the tripartite Committee on Paid Educational Leave of which I am the chairman.

REFERENCES

EMMERIJ, L. J. and J.A.E. CLOBUS (1978) Volledige werkgelegenheid door creatief verolf—Naar een maatschappij van de vrije keuz (Full employment through creative leave—towards a society of free choice). Holland: Kluwer, Deventer.

TINBERGEN, J. (1975) Income Distribution: Analysis and Policies. Amsterdam: North—Holland Publishing Company.

ABOUT THE AUTHORS

PIERRE CASPAR is Professor for Adult Education at the Conservatoire National des Arts et Metiers in Paris, France. He holds a degree in civil engineering, a Ph.D. in Sociology, and a Master of Science which he received from the University of California. His academic activities prior to his present position included part-time lectureships at the Sorbonne University and the Ecole Nationale d'Administration while he was serving as Director of a counseling firm servicing enterprises with respect to personnel management and employee training. Dr. Caspar has published a number of books in these fields and has served as a consultant to OECD for a number of years concerning questions such as training, adult learning, educational leave, and industrial democracy.

IVAN CHARNER is Director of Research at the National Institute for Work and Learning in Washington, D.C. His research and professional interests include worker education and training, adult learning, and youth school-to-work transitions. Recent publications include "Another Piece of the Financial Aid Puzzle: Tuition Aid Offered by Companies and Unions," and "Documenting Youth Experiences: The Concept of a Career Passport."

PAMELA H. CHRISTOFFEL, Research and Development Associate in the Washington Office of the College Board, has written numerous articles in the area of public policy and adult learning. Her current work includes an examination of the use of new technologies to assist the education of adults and research on federal student aid programs.

WERNER CLEMENT is a Full Professor of Economics, Institute for Economic Theory and Economic Policy, University of Economics, Vienna, Austria. He has served on many advisory committees and as a consultant to the Federal Institute of Labor, Germany, as well as to the Council of Europe, UNESCO, and OECD. His published works include papers on labor market policy and educational finance in Austria as well as youth unemployment and employment policy in France. His specializations include labor economics, economics of education, comparative economic systems, and theory of economic policy.

LOUIS EMMERIJ is Director of the Institute of Social Studies in The Hague. Previously he served as Director of the Employment Planning and Promotion Department of the World Employment Program of the International Labor Organization, and he worked with the OECD Directorate for Scientific Affairs. He is the author of *Can the School Build a New Social Order?* and other publications. He has been especially concerned with issues of education and employment.

HAROLD E. GEIOGUE is the Principal Program Analyst for Education with the California Office of the Legislative Analyst. He has been involved in state-level education policy decisions since 1968. His recent activities include service as Vice Chairman of the California Student Financial Aid Policy Study Group and as a member of the advisory council of the Western Interstate Commission on Higher Education's Project on Expanding Regional Cooperation in Graduate and Professional Education. Recent publications include "Statewide Coordination in Higher Education."

HENRY M. LEVIN is a Professor of Education and Affiliated Professor in the Department of Economics at Stanford University. He is also Director of the Institute for Research on Educational Finance and Governance. His specializations include the economics of education and educational finance, economics of evaluation, and economics analysis of workplace democracy. Previously he was the president of the Evaluation Research Society.

GÖSTA REHN is Emeritus Professor and former Head of the Swedish Institute for Social Research at the Stockholm University. He was Director for Manpower and Social Affairs in the Organization for Economic Cooperation and Development from 1962-1974. Earlier he was Economist for the Swedish Trade Union Confederation and the Swedish Ministry of Finance. He is a specialist in labor market policy and as such has served as a consultant to various international organizations.

KJELL RUBENSON is a Professor in the Department of Administrative, Adult and Higher Education, University of British Columbia. His current work includes research on the Swedish system of higher education.

He has written numerous articles in the area of adult and recurrent education. Recent publications include *Adult Education for Social Change: Research on the Swedish Allocation Policy Lundl,* "Adult Education Research: In Quest of a Map of the Territory," and *The Adults—Dreams and Realities in the Swedish System of Higher Education.*

HANS G. SCHÜTZE holds an LL.M. from the University of California, Berkeley, and a Ph.D. from the University of Gottingen, Germany. He is a senior research fellow at the Paris-based Center for Educational Research and Innovation (CERI) of the Organization for Economic Cooperation and Development (OECD). In this function, he has been involved in work on recurrent education, higher education, schemes for educational leave of absence, education and training for health care personnel, as well as the evaluation of training and special programs for unemployed young people. Currently, he is directing an international study on the development and utilization of human resources in the context of structural and technological change.

GREGORY B. SMITH has served as Assistant Director of the Department of Justice Services of Multnomah County, Portland, Oregon. He was Senior Associate and Director of the Worklife Education Program of the National Institute for Work and Learning, Washington, D.C. He is a graduate of the Fletcher School of Law and Diplomacy. His research work has ranged across policy issues involving both domestic and international affairs.

NEVZER STACEY is a Senior Associate at the National Institute of Education. She has designed and managed research and policy studies that address various aspects of education and training in the workplace. Her publications and professional interests include research on corporate and union investment in human resource development. Under her direction the National Commission on Working Women was created, bringing together representatives from unions, business, and higher education to examine the problems faced by women in nonprofessional occupations.

DIETER TIMMERMANN is a Professor of the Economics of Education and Educational Planning at the Department of Education, University of Bielefeld, Germany. He has published diverse articles about finance and governance of education. He is concerned with the issues of efficiency in education, allocation of resources in education, and the cost and financing of education.

ALAN P. WAGNER, Research Associate, Center for Educational Research and Policy Studies, State University of New York at Albany, is an economist continuing an extensive research program on the economics of postsecondary education and training. His published work includes papers on the role of student financial aid in institutional and student decision making and differences in the returns to a college degree among different types of institutions and among fields of study.